"What is the actual, observable impact of a seminary education? There are gems of seasoned insight here in a tapestry of narratives and reflections tracing the 30-year careers of eight seminary-students-become-ministers. Warford provides an unprecedented perspective on the real outcomes of theological curriculum."
—*Theodore Brelsford, Director of Assessment, Candler School of Theology; pastor, Orchard Park Community Church; and coeditor,* Contextualizing Theological Education

Eight ministers offer us a rare glimpse into the story of their lives from the outset of their seminary education, through early ministry experiences, and the deepening of their vocation into well-seasoned practitioners. Mac Warford persistently tracked their stories, recorded first-hand accounts, sets the cultural and religious stage, and deftly interprets 30 years of their experiences. Such stories, revealed honestly and with great integrity, are indispensable for those seeking to understand how ministers are shaped and formed over time.
—*Kathleen A. Cahalan, professor, Saint John's University School of Theology Seminary, Collegeville, Minnesota and author,* Introducing the Practice of Ministry

As a progressive seminary survivor, I was thrilled by *The Spirit's Tether.* Malcolm Warford has composed the first credible description of my life in ministry from seminary onward. No one before him has written of the refiner's fire that burned away my tranquil faith, or chronicled the death of cheap grace.
—*Hollis G. D. Dodge, pastor, St. Michael's United Church of Christ, Bridgewater, Virginia*

These remarkable stories provide the clarifying and challenging markers needed for those beginning or continuing the vocational journey of ordained ministry. The more we know about these eight, the more we discover about ourselves. We are reminded that a good theological education prepares people for the lifelong learning that occurs in the practice of ministry.
—*William B. Kincaid, Herald B. Monroe Professor in Practical Parish Ministry, Christian Theological Seminary, Indianapolis, Indiana*

Only a wise theological educator, himself a minister of the Word, could gather and shape such poignant, respectful profiles of seminarians who entered Union's crucible in the 1970's and three decades later continue to nourish life in the crucible of congregational ministry.

—*Christa R. Klein, president, In Trust, the Association of Boards in Theological Education*

As a parish pastor, I commend Warford's examination of the journeys of these eight pastors. He insightfully draws out the tensions in which all pastors live: theological and psychological, social and personal, spiritual and ordinary, and offers hope for faithful vocation, nourished by trust in the God who calls.

—*Mary Baber Reed, pastor, The Presbyterian Church, Dover, DE*

This window into the lives and experiences of eight Christian ministers over a period of thirty years is a masterful contribution to our understanding of the links between individuals, congregations, and theological institutions. Insights for revitalizing Christian ministry are rooted in actual lives. An indispensable resource.

—*Tite Tiénou, dean, Trinity Evangelical Divinity School, Deerfield, Illinois*

Warford gives us marvelous insights that can help guide theological education, the church, and ministerial formation in the years to come. This book models the gift of looking backward in order to look forward to help craft a better future for generations to come in ministry.

—*Emilie M. Townes, associate dean of academic affairs and Andrew W. Mellon Professor of African American Religion and Theology, Yale Divinity School*

Narratives weave a beautiful, rough tapestry of pastors' lives wafted across decades of turbulent landscapes of American Christianity. *The Spirit's Tether* is insightful, moving, even affirming for pastors, teachers, and others recollecting life, calling, and meaning.

—*Raymond Williams, LaFollette Distinguished Professor in the Humanities emeritus, Wabash College*

The
Spirit's
Tether

The Spirit's Tether

EIGHT LIVES IN MINISTRY

Malcolm L. Warford

with Kenneth Huggins

 ALBAN

Herndon, Virginia
www.alban.org

The Alban Institute
2121 Cooperative Way, Suite 100
Herndon, VA 20171

Unless otherwise noted, all Scripture quotations are from the New Revised Standard Version of the Bible, © 1989, Division of Christian Education of the National Council of Churches of Christ in the United States of America, and are used by permission.

Cover design by Signal Hill.

Library of Congress Cataloging-in-Publication Data

Warford, Malcolm L., 1942-
 The Spirit's tether : eight lives in ministry / Malcolm L. Warford with Kenneth Huggins ; foreword by Donald W. Shriver, Jr.
   p. cm.
 Includes bibliographical references (p. 223) and index.
 ISBN 978-1-56699-415-6 (alk. paper)
  1. Union Theological Seminary (New York, N.Y.)--Students--Longitudinal studies. 2. Union Theological Seminary (New York, N.Y.)--Alumni and alumnae--Longitudinal studies. I. Huggins, Kenneth. II. Title.
  BV4070.U66W37 2011
  230.071'17471--dc22

                        2011014436

11   12   13   14   15   VP   5   4   3   2   1

*To the seventeen men and women
who participated in this study
and especially
the eight whose stories are told here*

Contents

Foreword

OF NECESSITY I AM DEEPLY, INTIMATELY IMPLICATED IN THIS book. These are the stories of eight seminary-educated ministers— how they came to decide on that profession, how they responded to several years of seminary life, and how, thirty years later, they assessed that decision, that seminary, and those thirty years of service. This is my profession, too. These stories resonate with my own life story. Any minister who picks up this book will experience the same resonance. Warford predicts it in his concluding sentence, "We can be grateful not only for what we have learned about [these eight ministers] but for what they have taught us about ourselves."

My case, however, is yet more personal, intimate, and potentially intimidating. This group of students came, in the 1970s, to the seminary of which I had recently been elected president. The questions central to the study might intimidate any faculty or administrator: While you were doing your educative work, what were students experiencing? While you were sharing knowledge from your discipline, working on institutional finances, and seeking to appoint new colleagues, what results did all this have for the receiving end? Students are the real bottom line of education. Did your efforts as an educator add up to discernible benefit in their lives? What you hoped to happen to them—did it?

Leaders of graduate education tend not to ask these questions in systematic inquiries. At the top of our academic profession, we are supposed to know what and how to teach the young. We do receive evaluation from them at the end of some courses we teach, and colleagues judge whether we deserve promotions; but rare is systematic inquiry into the lives of our students during their time with us in school.

These chapters comprise such an inquiry. They record the pre-seminary lives of the eight, how they felt called to the profession of ministry, and how they fared in their years of seminary study. Periodically during those years in the late 1970s, Malcolm Warford interviewed these eight students, asking just such questions. In interviews and discussion with them thirty years later, we listen in on how they now assess their profession and its multiple pathways of learning how to practice it.

One of Warford's major conclusions is that for these folk "the practice of ministry itself has been a school of lifelong learning." In a way, this is a comfort to us educators. We can do only so much for our students. To them belongs the responsibility for continuing their education. But this reassurance can be too easy. To assess the importance of formal education, one has only to remember the influence of certain teachers on one's own life from kindergarten to graduate school. We know that they entered our lives for much good and some bad. Our classroom teachers were important. They remain so.

A little less certain is the importance of the educational work we call administration. Faculty and students around the world probably share a propensity for downgrading administration as busywork, not really intellectual, academic, or essential. I have often countered this prejudice by continuing to teach and write as parts of my calling as a seminary president. In a more acerbic mood, I have sometimes said to the critics of *mere* administration, "So long as faculty and students enjoy breakfast and a roof over their heads, even a president is indispensable to the work of education."

I say "even" because of one particular reaction in my reading of this unique book. Like other ethically responsible researchers, Warford's interviewees remain anonymous. I have only hypotheses about their identities. But I know that I knew them, that they knew me. We were a small institution of a hundred employees and three hundred students, so we had a lot of contact with each other. But presidential and faculty contacts can brush only the surface of a student's life. The details about the eight student's lives described in this book have taught me a lot about the goings-on of their Union Seminary experience.

One learning for me is the primary influence of students on each other. They too are educators. Another is the importance of congregational church experience outside of seminary for the validation and revision of what they learn in the classroom. Yet another is the respect that teachers and students should cultivate for the fact that human life itself—and all occasions worth calling educative—is the great comprehensive educator. We are all forever on journeys.

Often in reading these pages I have thought of T. S. Eliot's lines from "Little Gidding," that we are destined to explore until we "arrive where we started / And know the place for the first time." As a religious educator, Malcolm Warford came to Union Seminary at my invitation to set up an Office of Educational Research whose role would be to discern the results of our daily work for students, churches, and the world to which we theologians claim to have some responsibility. With a generous fund provided by our board of directors, Warford's five years in our midst—before he himself became a seminary president—yielded many illuminating, sobering, and encouraging reports. Having no doubt of my own role in facilitating the start of his work, I now have to testify that what he records here about eight students over time constitutes for me a capstone of that work and a gratifying sense of partnership with him in that work. In short, this book helps this seminary president to reaffirm his own calling to spend twenty-one years of his life connected to Union Seminary.

To this I want to add one disclaimer and one testimony. At first sight, one might conclude that Union is a narrow lens for generalizing on contemporary theological education: eight students, sampled from one decade of the 20th century, one seminary in one big city—unique, in short. The founders and promoters of every institution believe in its uniqueness. If Union is really unique, the relevance of this study for the rest of theological education might well be doubted. But I agree with Warford's view that readers with experience in other seminaries will find here a skein of promises, perplexities, controversies, joys, and sorrows present in most of the two hundred seminaries of the United States and Canada. Cultural pluralism, theological diversity, decline and growth of churches, relations between theory and practice, ambiguities afflicting the profession of ministry challenge all of us in this niche of graduate education. At Union, from time to time, I had to caution my peers against celebrating our uniqueness over against our kinship with the great enterprises of faith, hope, and love in the global community of theological education. Occasionally we needed to rejoice in the varying vocations of other schools in the seminary world, a variety that offered supplements and other resources for education that our school could not imitate. Paul's imagery of the church (1 Corinthians 12) as one body with many members, each with a God-given calling, fits seminaries, too. To rejoice in the gifts and promise of one's own institution is not to denigrate others.

But I have a testimony: These narratives greatly reinforce my admiration and gratitude for my partners in this profession. In commenting on the era of Western history sometimes called the Dark Ages—the 7th to the 11th centuries—one historian pointed out that not all was dark in that age. We may know little about those ages and may think of them as a time when Europe suffered drastic decline and fall. But during all those centuries, village priests faithfully administered the sacrament, performed weddings, baptized infants, and buried the dead, all actions that lent dignity and love to even the most obscure people of the lands. I think of this history when I note that few if any of the eight ministers so carefully described here qualify as famous, rich, or otherwise prestigious. Unlike during an early century of American history, the ministry is seldom accorded in our national culture a place of great public honor. Not for that honor did these eight people feel compelled to enter this profession. They entered it to bring themselves and others to a "place where your deep gladness and the world's deep hunger meet" (in Frederick Buechner's well-known definition of a vocation). They entered it as a way to serve the church's witness to a gospel and to serve the needs of other human beings. These years later they are content to call it a servant vocation.

The services expected of a parish minister are many, varied, and difficult to compose without experiences of struggle, ambiguity, and mixtures of failure and success. Especially in the Protestant theological tradition, other professions can equally be godly callings. But ministers have a faith and a set of responsibilities that are hard to cram into the notion of a "specialty." Medical doctors, lawyers, and governmental leaders have opportunities to serve people in need; but often these services touch only a segment of human life. In contrast, ministers who lead congregations are vulnerable by choice to a longitude of human occasions extending from birth to death. What other profession baptizes infants, marries lovers, comforts the sick, counsels the despairing, and conducts final rites on the edges of graves? What other profession so surely exercises responsibility, not only for individual "clients" but for their social relationships in the life of a congregation? And what other is so surely obligated to think beyond that congregation to the welfare, the justice, and the politics of a whole human community?

One of the eight here (Anna) put it passionately in 2004, when she remarked that her life in ministry had allowed her to

> be a part of persons' lives at key times, to see lives changed, blossom, and grow through encounters with Christ and his church, to see strangers arrive, connect, and become part of the family of faith and love and service, to witness the rippling effects that even a small church can have on the surrounding community, to see compassion and mercy and reconciliation and peace and justice and liberation at work here, there, and beyond, to be even a small part of the good news being declared and revealed through the living Christ.

That improbable, glorious list makes it all worthwhile!

But no wonder that few of the eight speak of their success in all of this. The faith on which this profession is founded requires the faithful to confess that they fall short of fulfilling its high urgencies. Of course this is a troubled profession! It presumes that the Lord of All Being takes care for all the troubles of the world, and if only in faulty token of the same, some human must make it her or his business to give witness to that faith—day in and day out. The minister is that someone.

So I am proud to be a member of this profession, faulty and finite as must be the performance of all of us in practicing it. I am proud to number myself alongside these eight fellow ministers who sojourned with me for a few years in a place called a seminary. To have had any part in lives exhibiting such faithfulness is a profound privilege. Reading this book impels me to echo words of the Apostle Paul to his favorite congregation: "I thank God for all these remembrances of you." And I thank Malcolm Warford for giving us access to these memories.

DONALD W. SHRIVER, JR.
President Emeritus, Union Theological Seminary, New York

Stories of Work and Calling

IN THE MID 1970S, I SERVED AS THE DIRECTOR OF EDUCATIONAL research and then as advisor to the president and board of trustees at Union Theological Seminary in New York City. Union was experiencing at the time one of its periodic crises, and the seminary's new president, Donald W. Shriver, Jr., felt it important to have some relatively independent center of research and evaluation established at the school as the institution took account of its recent history and charted some new directions. The office of research was created to support and inform this forward movement by conducting research and maintaining a continuing inquiry into the nature of the institution and, most importantly, obtain some sense of the relationship between what Union claimed for itself and what it was actually doing. Central to this aim was a concern for students and a desire to gather, in a sustained way, insights into students' experiences and their perceptions of their theological education.

To help me achieve these aims, I conferred with William G. Perry, Jr., about creating an appropriate study. Mr. Perry was the long-time director of Harvard's Bureau of Study Counsel, but he was much more than that. He was a classicist who had done his own translation of *The Iliad*, and he was a quiet provocateur who had created a study of Harvard undergraduates grounded in the belief that by listening to their students, faculties and administrators might learn something beyond what anecdote and individual experience could offer. For four years, Mr. Perry met with a selected group of students as they entered and graduated from the college. The results of his research were published eventually as *Forms of Intellectual and Ethical Development in the College Years: A Scheme.*[1] Mr. Perry kindly agreed to help me create a similar study at Union, and with his assistance that is what I set out to do. My interests were broader than his for the Harvard study, so I made no attempt to follow his developmental scheme. It was more the spirit and simplicity of Mr. Perry's research model that I found so compelling.

The methodology was clear: Select a group of first-year students who approximated the diversity of the entering class and then listen to and talk with them throughout their years at the seminary. After conferring with Sidney Skirvin, Union's dean of students, I identified seventeen students whose backgrounds, gender, race, and religious affiliations might provide a breadth of understanding for this inquiry. The approach was straightforward. I met individually with each student every semester, and at each meeting I turned on the recorder and usually asked an open-ended question like, "How have things been going?" Then I listened to what the students had to say and raised questions, made comments, and engaged in conversation when I thought it appropriate. Each of their interviews was transcribed and kept in files. The tapes were maintained as well.

The first interviews were conducted in 1976. Occasional reports on the study were developed in subsequent years, and a final report with pertinent recommendations was presented to the president, faculty, and trustees in 1981. My assumption was that the study was now complete, but when I left Union to become president of Eden Seminary, I took my research materials and held onto them during subsequent moves. I kept my eye on the study's participants and informally had a sense of what each was doing over the years, although except for a few instances I had little contact with them. Years later when I returned to full-time teaching, I decided to resume the study and update the material, looking again at the transcriptions with the help of some colleagues.

In 2004, I began contacting eight of the participants who had spent almost all of their ministry as parish clergy and were currently in full-time pastoral leadership. While there had been seventeen in the original study, four of them had left the seminary before graduating, and one person had died. Three participants had gone into other work, and one who had been in another form of ministry was retired. Although it would have been interesting to include them in the follow-up study, I decided to concentrate my attention on the stories of eight who had been concerned about congregational leadership and were at the time still active in full-time parish ministry. The only exception to this was the person who will be called Sarah. She was going through the aftermath of leaving her position at a church and considering what options were ahead for her.

When I spoke with each of the eight and arranged a time when I could visit and talk with them, I was gratified that after all these years there was a sense of connection and an unhesitating interest on their part in resuming the conversations begun so many years earlier. In every instance, the participants were generous in their willingness to speak of their lives lived out over time and in many different circumstances since I had last seen many of them in 1981. The interviews were held over the next several years in various locations around the country.

In 2008, I invited the participants to meet in a colloquium gathered around the essays each was asked to write in response to their reading of their own transcripts. I asked them to compare the person they found in the transcripts with the person they perceived themselves to be today—what had changed, what had persisted in their lives, and what had been the significant events along the way. Over several days each had a chance to present his or her essay and to discuss it with the whole group.

In conceiving this inquiry, I did not want to be limited by any particular lens, so I have avoided a set interpretive model. I wanted, in the words of Robert Frost, "to hang around until I caught on" to what might be happening in the lives of the students and the institution. I have concentrated, therefore, on letting the voices of the participants speak for themselves, so they can present eight parallel and intertwining stories that can help us understand somewhat the lives of men and women who feel called to the profession of ordained ministry. More than that, these stories help us apprehend what sustains ministers and keeps them in this work and how they perceive themselves as they look back on their lives and calling.[2]

While Union Theological Seminary is obviously a significant context for the formation of these eight men and women, Union is not my primary subject. In this regard, I have tried to describe the seminary as it was in the mid to late 1970s and not as it is today. Some readers might assume that the lives of ministers educated at Union would not be relevant to theological students educated at other seminaries; but my experience suggests otherwise. During my nearly 40-year career of working with many different theological schools and a wide array of theological students, I have found that the stories of these lives are ones that can be shared broadly. Although Union in the 1970s might have seemed like a unique place, that uniqueness has diminished as increasing numbers of seminaries and divinity schools have found themselves facing the same issues Union encountered before them. How these eight participants dealt with the challenges they faced in seminary and how those challenges played out in various guises throughout their lives are issues I have found especially significant.

My first colleague in developing the study was Virginia L. Brereton, who was immensely helpful in working with me on the initial reports. I am grateful for her contributions and the times we shared in reflecting on the content of the interviews. Her life and work as a scholar and teacher were tragically cut short by her death in 2004.

Because this inquiry is primarily about narratives, I invited my colleague Ken Huggins to join me in completing a book on the study. Ken is a writer and editor whose skill as an interpreter of stories brought a distinctive and valued perspective to the project. My own background as an ordained minister, theological educator, and institutional consultant constitutes a base of experience that is fundamental to how I approached the study to begin with and how I have been engaged with it ever since.

Among the significant benefits of my work at Union were the ongoing conversations that I had with Don Shriver, who lived up to his promise to take seriously what I was finding in my inquiries. He brought me into the heart of the seminary and the life of the Board of Trustees, and what we learned from listening deeply to students made its way into how the president and trustees thought about the life of the school and the policies they created in its behalf. I am grateful to him for writing the foreword to this book.

In recent years, Union has gone through major changes in its life as it has dealt with institutional issues. The seminary's current president, Serene Jones, is setting new directions and building on past achievements, and I am very pleased that she accepted the invitation to write the afterword.

Over the years, I have called upon many persons—writers, ministers, therapists, and theological teachers—to share their perspectives on these interviews and sometimes the manuscript in progress, and I thank them for their assistance: Madge Treeger, Janet Beaulieu, Judith Blanchard, Wade Stevenson, Kaye Pullen, Kristen Bentley, Lois Zachary, and especially Victor Klimoski. At a key point, conversations with Michael J. Nakkula, who was then on the faculty of Harvard's School of Education, assisted me in making some fundamental decisions about methodology. Throughout these various readings and discussions of the interviews, the identities of the study participants have always been protected. Further, in the book itself names and places have been disguised for the most part or generalized according to the preferences of the participants. However, two of the participants, David and Marvin, have requested that their names not be disguised and that the details of their lives be described without anonymity.

All along, I have seen this as a collaborative effort, not a remote study of subjects, but as something collegial and shared. In light of this understanding, I invited the participants themselves to read and respond to what has been written about them. Besides the 2008 colloquium centered on the participants' reading of their transcripts, a second colloquium was also held in 2009 where I asked them to comment on the manuscript draft in progress. For three days, we discussed each of the chapters and their responses and suggested revisions to the text. As always, Katherine Marden provided significant administrative support throughout work on the manuscript and colloquium arrangements.

The final interpretations and arrangements of materials have, of course, been my responsibility, although I have had a lot of help from the participants, Ken Huggins, and those I have consulted at various points. Originally, the study was created to help an institution think about its life, its practices, and its policies, but it has become much more as I and others have followed these stories and been led into that which has called the students, formed them, and helped them find their way.

The continuing support of Lilly Endowment Inc. and in particular the leadership of Craig Dykstra and John Wimmer have made this work possible and sustained the initial interest and support of Robert Lynn and Fred Hofheinz. Michael Gilligan of the Luce Foundation provided a planning grant to resume the study in its current form and gave renewed momentum for moving ahead with the book. At the Alban Institute, Richard Bass has been an encouraging and always helpful editor, Lauren Mathews has been of immense assistance, and James Wind, Alban's president, signaled his interest in the project at the very beginning of our discussion of the study.

My aim in this book is to provide a window in time through which we can see a few years in a school's life as experienced by a group of students and to look at the vocation of ordained ministry as lived out by these same men and women. My hope is that readers from many different backgrounds will find something in these narratives that will inform their own stories as well.

In this documentary account of eight Union graduates, the organization of the material generally follows a chronological line in order to sustain a narrative thread for each of the participants in the study. I have tried not to impose thematic patterns or suggest developmental stages for their experiences. Instead, my purpose has been to document their life in seminary and ordained ministry and let their stories speak as much as possible for themselves. To help identify the eight, the following are brief descriptions:

Anna: An African American woman ordained in the Baptist Church, raised in the Midwest, educated at Spelman College before coming to Union, and now leading a nondenominational church with her husband. Graduated in 1979.

Beth: A white woman ordained as an Episcopal priest, raised in a small town in Illinois, and currently a parish priest in upstate New York. Graduated in 1980.

Chris: A white man ordained as a Presbyterian minister, raised in the South, and now the pastor of a prominent suburban church. Graduated in 1980.

David: An Hispanic man raised in Puerto Rico and New York City and now serving as the pastor of a Christian Church (Disciples of Christ) congregation in Florida. Graduated in 1981.

Marvin: An African American man raised in New York City and currently serving as the pastor of a Baptist church in Queens where he has been for many years. Graduated in 1979.

Ruth: An African American woman raised in New York City and now the long-term copastor with her husband of an urban Lutheran church on the East Coast. Graduated in 1980.

Sarah: A white woman raised on a Pennsylvania farm in a Church of the Brethren family, serving for many years as a church pastor, and now a hospice chaplain. Graduated in 1980.

Tim: A white man ordained as a Unitarian Universalist minister, educated at a well-known East Coast prep school and a graduate of Harvard before coming to Union, now serving a city church as a United Church of Christ minister. Graduated in 1979.

The title of the book, *The Spirit's Tether*, is taken from the hymn, "Draw Us in the Spirit's Tether," which was written by Percy Dearmer and set to the tune "Union Seminary" composed by Harold Friedell, who was a member of Union's music faculty.

MAC WARFORD

chapter 1

Setting the Context

We all seem to have a unique connection with radical edges.
Union didn't cause this, but something in us that drew us to
Union did, and Union fostered it. — MARVIN

IT IS SEPTEMBER 1976. THE COUNTRY HAS JUST CELEBRATED ITS
200th anniversary, and Americans are hoping to shake off the bitter
feelings of Watergate and the general economic malaise of the early
1970s. They are trying also to come to terms with the continuing
aftershocks of the war in Vietnam, the civil rights movement, and all
of the disorienting changes that have followed the hopeful first years
of the Great Society. Some people consider such developments—the
assertions of feminism and gay rights and the introduction of affirmative action, for example—as encouraging signs of a better, more
just future; others see them as an indication of moral and spiritual
decay, a betrayal of the national character.

Yet the 1970s is a decade that sees diminishing involvement in
many of the social movements that so dominated the 1960s. The
liberalism that had fueled progressive hopes is met by growing conservative forces. On the economic front, the industrial growth long
taken for granted stalls, the country goes through a recession, and oil
embargoes in the Middle East cause a prolonged energy crisis. Infla-
tion and unemployment run side by side. Distrust in government and
institutions in general is evident as many turn from public concerns
to private worries about their individual emotional and financial

1

well-being. What is widely understood as self-actualization is expressed in various popular psychological guises, and a new sexual freedom is pursued on campuses and in suburban neighborhoods as well.
Writer Tom Wolfe characterizes the era as the "me decade," while historian Christopher Lasch describes it as "the culture of narcissism."[1]

In the theological world, liberation theology is a significant
movement that questions traditional theological perspectives and
urges essential rethinking of theological aims and methods. Origi-
nating in advocacy for the poor and oppressed, liberation theology
becomes a large umbrella in the United States that covers numerous
ancillary causes as well. At the same time, denominations experience a decrease in numbers and a declining significance in the lives
of local church members. Liberal protestant congregations struggle
to find their footing and address their increasingly marginal status
while trying to understand the growth of conservative evangelical
churches. In this regard, the churches and their various institutions
reflect much of what is occurring in the rest of society. The issue of
diversity in particular, which increasingly dominates public forums,
becomes a focus of ecclesial debates.

It is in the midst of this cultural upheaval that four women and
four men—the same who constitute the center of this narrative—arrive at the doors of Union Theological Seminary in New York City to
begin their preparation for pastoral ministry.

Union Theological Seminary has long been at the center of American theological life, and by the 1970s it was once again a lightning
rod for the issues and questions that would eventually define much
of the mainline religious landscape.[2] In many ways, Union's location
on the corner of Broadway and 120th Street (now known as Reinhold Niebuhr Place) expresses what was once the Protestant establishment:[3] Union occupies an entire block and stands side by side
with Riverside Church, the famed interdenominational church first
led by Harry Emerson Fosdick and built with the resources of John
D. Rockefeller, Jr., which faces onto Riverside Drive and the Hudson
River. Adjacent to these two institutions rises the Inter Church Center whose cornerstone was laid by President Dwight D. Eisenhower
in the 1950s. It was designed to be the headquarters for the National
Council of Churches and to provide offices for many of the liberal

Protestant denominations. While the National Council remains, more and more of the denominational offices have moved out and various nonprofit agencies have moved in.

The seminary is located on Broadway in the upper West Side neighborhood of Morningside Heights, which is defined largely by the campus of Columbia University with Teachers College and Barnard College close by. Bounding the north side of Union's quadrangle is the Manhattan School of Music, now occupying the buildings that once were the home of the Juilliard School of Music before its move to midtown Manhattan. On the other side of Broadway, across from the music school, is Jewish Theological Seminary. Several streets north of Union lies 125th Street, the Main Street of Harlem; it is close to the seminary, but a world a way—racially, economically, and culturally.

The seminary itself is a neo-Gothic building in the quasi-monastic style of Oxford and Cambridge that so captivated higher education in the early twentieth century. There are few overt religious signs or symbols on the outside of the building itself and not many within either. There are two chapels where Christian symbols are notably present; otherwise, there is little iconography that would identify it as a religious institution, although the architecture itself evokes a religious-like ambience. In contrast, the school's identification with the Ivy League is clearly expressed in the names of all the elite schools etched onto the stone walls high above the quadrangle.

While Union's buildings may not contain many explicit theological symbols, they do establish a religious-like atmosphere that conveys the sense of power and cultural location that the space is intended to serve. The monastic traditions of learning and community that the architecture expresses are obviously no longer present, but their forms still have the ability to impress entering students with the gravity of their matriculation in these "hallowed halls of academe." Union's halls and quadrangle suggest the long lineage of scholarship, education, and lingering status conferred upon those who graduate from such institutions.

Walking into this carefully stylized space ushers one into a distinctive ethos, a place where theology and ethics, church and culture, meet in a school that embodies a heritage of boldness and willingness to engage controversial issues. During the 1970s, Union was very much a part of the intellectual and social movements that stirred American culture. Civil rights, the antiwar movement, liberation theology, the women's movement, and the emerging gay rights movement all found expression at the school. At the same time, Union faced internal political controversy that involved conflict within the faculty and a change in presidential leadership. Since the 1960s, Union had experienced significant decreases in the size of the student body and the faculty. The school had been running budget deficits for a number of years, but these deficits had at last reached a point of critical concern. In fact, Union's buildings betrayed this economic slippage. Plaster was falling off the walls in some rooms, low wattage light bulbs lit dim corridors, and faculty salaries and perquisites were declining. In the wider world of theological education, some critics felt that Union itself was beyond repair. However, the arrival of a new president, Donald W. Shriver, Jr., in the fall of 1975 prompted hope of better days, and the school's appointment of a diverse group of new faculty members in 1976 and for several years afterward offered a sense of new beginnings.

It is into the Union of these years that Ruth, Chris, Sarah, Marvin, Tim, David, Beth, and Anna enter. Although their ambitions are similar, many of their perceptions and expectations are quite different, and none knows what lies ahead.

Chris and Tim arrive with perhaps the most certain of expectations. Both are young, middle-class, and white. Both attended private prep schools. Tim, raised in New England, had gone on to graduate from Harvard before entering Union. Chris had considered both Yale Divinity School and Princeton Seminary before settling on Union. Both Tim and Chris are well prepared by the social milieu of their upbringing to enter roles of leadership in settings that have traditionally been dominated by white men.

Throughout their childhood they have seen—in church, media, and culture generally—exemplars of what they can expect to become themselves. In fact, their personas seem not unlike the muscular Christianity represented by Frank Scott, the Union-educated minister who leads a ragged band of survivors to safety in the novel and film *The Poseidon Adventure*.[4]

Although he is a Unitarian and intends to enter ministry in that denomination, Tim can trace his family back several generations to its German Baptist roots. While his parents are academics with little connection with the church, his grandfather and his great grandfather had both been religious leaders. As a theological student, he is hoping to find how best to express the ways of knowing and believing that shape his life, but he has little doubt that the work of pastoral leadership is something that he can do. It is this calling that he feels has claimed him after spending the years right after college working in various business ventures. Tim is most of all on a spiritual journey, and though this language has become commonplace and a cliché, it is nevertheless an accurate description of his intent as he enters seminary.

Chris is expecting something similar but with a more traditional form and spirit greatly influenced by the Southern culture in which he was raised. He grew up in a large Southern city in a family involved in the Presbyterian church as elders, committee members, and Sunday school teachers. The church in the South remains—in his perception at least—a strong institution in which the minister is a respected and influential figure in the community. Chris has come to Union because of the school's reputation as an institution where piety and politics join hands in ways that engage church and culture around significant public issues. Here, he knows, Reinhold Niebuhr taught and constructed the elements of his own thinking that made him a well-known public intellectual, and he appreciates as well that Union's new president, Donald W. Shriver, Jr., embodies a similar public presence. In particular, Shriver is a Presbyterian raised in Virginia who is known throughout the Southern church as an ethicist and activist. Chris aspires to become this kind of pastoral and public leader. At the same time, though, that he claims these roles, he realizes that all of this can be a bit of an "ego trip," a condition that he feels he must guard against.

Ruth and Marvin arrive at Union with somewhat different expectations. They did not go to prep schools. Ruth was raised in the projects of the Bronx, Marvin in Bedford-Stuyvesant and Brooklyn. Marvin never knew his father; Ruth's father was an alcoholic and died of pneumonia when she was fifteen. Both have been raised by mothers they greatly admire. Like many gifted African Americans growing up with financial hardships, Marvin and Ruth have had to overcome numerous challenges, but they each have earned bachelor degrees from respected institutions. When they applied to Union, they chose it not only because it was well known and was actively recruiting African Americans and other minority groups but also because it was in New York. It was home ground, and that provided some modicum of comfort and accessibility.

Despite the similarities in their backgrounds, Ruth and Marvin enter Union with differences, too. Marvin, like Tim and Chris, grew up in a religious milieu dominated by powerful men as pastoral leaders. He has had numerous and compelling role models for the ecclesiastical life he hopes to enter. His home church is a significant Black Baptist church, and he is quite comfortable with the thought of becoming a pastor in this tradition. In fact, Marvin has, throughout college, been chosen to take on various leadership positions in church and community groups.

Ruth's situation is far less traditional. First, she is a woman hoping to enter a vocation that has only recently considered the possibility that women can legitimately answer a call to be ordained ministers. Second, she is a black woman hoping to enter ministry in the Lutheran church, a denomination that is largely white. Although she has been encouraged by several male pastors to follow her calling, she is moving into uncharted territory, and her steps are tentative in many ways. Ruth taught elementary school immediately after college, but more and more she felt called to ministry, and with her pastor's encouragement she turned in that direction.

Anna is on a similar course. Like Ruth and Marvin, she is African American. But she grew up far from New York in a large Midwestern city where her father was the minister of a prominent black church. She went to public schools that were predominantly white and was never in a majority black academic environment until she entered Spelman College in Atlanta, one of the leading black colleges in the United States and, incidentally, another institution supported by the Rockefeller family. There Anna eventually became president of the student government. Yale Divinity School recruited her vigorously, but she seems to have chosen Union with little hesitation.

"Union," she says, "was the dream choice. My father had always wanted me to go to Union. When he was in seminary, it was the school to go to."

Like Ruth, Anna is on the verge of answering a call that a generation before few, if any, women like her were supposed to receive. Unlike Ruth, however, who has attached herself to a denomination that is more or less open to women in ministry, Anna intends to remain with her father's Baptist denomination even though it discourages female participation in anything more than secondary and subservient roles. She conveys both a sense of tenacity and some uncertainty about what she faces. She believes in her abilities as a leader and a promising preacher. Her experience as a student leader in college has reinforced her confidence in herself, but she is never quite far from uncertainty about what is going on around her or what may lie ahead. Anna can imagine herself as a pastor and preacher, yet she is not naïve about what this calling may cost her in terms of dealing with ecclesial politics and prejudice.

Beth and Sarah also face the challenge of being women who are attempting to embark upon a traditionally male vocation. As white, middle-class women, however, the road ahead is likely to be at least somewhat smoother—though not all that smooth—than it is for Ruth or Anna. The challenges they face are shaped by the differences between them, especially in the cultures in which they were raised.

Sarah grew up on a farm in rural Pennsylvania. She was raised in a devout Church of the Brethren household, a denomination related to the Mennonite and Amish traditions. She was encouraged in her calling by her church but arrives at Union in some doubt about where her next steps will take her. She feels a strong attraction to the denomination of her childhood and the ideal of a peaceful and loving community it encourages, yet she is growing uncomfortable with the constraints that such a community can create, and she wants the broadening experience of Union and New York. Further, she recognizes that women make up a large portion of the incoming class, and she finds that reassuring.

Beth comes from northern Illinois in the flat Midwestern farming country west of Chicago. She grew up Episcopalian and says, "it was a real centerpiece in my life as an elementary, middle-school,

and high-school student." By the time she arrives at Union, however, she professes probably more doubt about her faith than any of
the other students. Certainly she has had a variety of experiences
through which she has been able to expand her view of the world.
During her junior year in college, she took a semester off and spent a
month in England. She then traveled to Israel and spent two months
on a kibbutz. Following graduation from college, she worked with
Cesar Chavez and the United Farm Workers Union in California and
participated in California politics during the 1972 election campaign.
She then married and lived at Union while her husband was studying
for his Master of Divinity (M.Div.) degree. For several years, she took
on the role of a pastor's wife, first in the South and then in western
New York. She had not particularly enjoyed the experience of being
a student's wife at Union nor that of being a pastor's wife. Therefore,
she enters Union with the idea of giving herself one year to work out
once and for all her uncertainties about what she calls "this church
business."

David is Hispanic (a term he claims rather than Latino) and a decade older than the others. He was born in Puerto Rico in 1941 and
moved to New York with his mother and two older brothers when
he was six. He grew up fatherless in Brooklyn and left the Catholic
church at age twelve when a friend of his mother invited him to visit
a Presbyterian church. By age sixteen he sensed a call to ministry, but
he did not act on it until he was about thirty years old. At that point
in his life, he had spent time in the Navy Reserve and was beginning
what he hoped would be a career with the Bank of New York. He had
also switched from the Presbyterian Church to the Christian Church
(Disciples of Christ). While attending Sinai Christian Church, David
received what he believes to be his definitive call to ministry. Shortly
afterward, he enrolled at Bethany College, an institution related to
the Disciples, which is located in West Virginia not far from Pittsburgh. Upon graduation, he considered several seminaries but decided to return to New York City and applied to Union. Although
bilingual in Spanish and English, he struggles with writing in both
languages. What pulled him through college and will assist him at
Union as well is an indomitable spirit that refuses to give up in the
face of any obstacle.

Entering Union's space is a moment of unexpected drama, for the seminary's buildings envelop one in an environment resonant with formal traditions. But in 1976, the seminary seemed to be trying to break free of or at least transform its inherited space. In the chapel itself the pews had been rearranged to encourage a stronger sense of community, yet all of this rearranging had in it the air of a make-shift effort. Later, when the chapel was renovated and little was left of the older traditional form, there was some consternation as to how this new space might be used. It was a room that invited experimentation, and for those accustomed to screwed down pews facing forward, the shifting arrangement of movable chairs and the portable pulpit and communion table required a difficult adjustment. But all of this expressed the basic transitions that were occurring at the school. Instead of a stable setting, the eight students entered an institution in search of itself, moving from one definition of being a theological seminary to something else. For some of the eight, this institutional transitioning was exactly what they wanted as a context for their own searching. Others, however, spent much of their time at the school trying to come to terms with it.

Before turning to the students' experiences of their first semester at the seminary, we will take a closer look in the next chapter at the origins of each student's faith and sense of calling. What brought them to their decision to pursue a vocation in ministry? What made them think that God had called them in particular to be prophets and priests, preachers and pastors? To answer these questions, the students will describe the people, events, and conditions that helped form them into the individuals who first arrived at the seminary.

chapter 2

Childhood and Formative Events

It was planted and nurtured in me at a very early age and throughout my childhood that real living on this earth has something to do with hospitality and welcome. — RUTH

CHILDHOOD IS A NOTORIOUSLY RISKY BUSINESS. IT ENCOMPASSES what may turn out to be both the best and the worst of times. Youth face similar issues as they try out different ways of being and test the water with their own developing lives. For some the hurts of childhood and adolescence never go away. They may recede in immediacy, but they are always there to be dealt with in some way or another. When the origins of these scars are confronted and worked through, they no longer have as much power to hurt or wound again. Even those who had what might be considered happy childhoods have to deal with the usual challenges of growing up, and these, as we all know, are not insignificant.

The eight participants in this study reflect a relatively broad spectrum of childhood and adolescent experiences. Some have been able to recognize the issues they have needed to address. Others, however, have deferred the problems they have carried until they could no longer bear such burdens by themselves. They have also demonstrated in our conversations a variable inclination to recount childhood memories and connect their early years with the sense of vocation that brought them to a theological seminary.

My purpose in this aspect of our conversations was to ask them to recount the experiences among family and friends, in church and school, that were formative in their lives, especially those incidents that first raised for them the image of ministry and their sense of calling to this work. Most of the eight demonstrated a willingness to examine their lives honestly and in depth. Such examination revealed, for the most part, the presence of parents who loved them and took care of them, but it also revealed parents who were absent or burdened by their own difficulties. The eight remembered words and phrases that gave them encouragement and offered a way of being in the world. They recognized events and persons who hurt them, but others as well who offered models of the kind of person they wanted to be. For all of them, the church became a primary place not only for instructing them in the substance of faith and the nature of the Christian community but for introducing them to a wider world in which the struggle for justice and peace became a cause they wanted to join.

Ruth

"My mother, Emma, was from South Carolina and grew up poor and rural. Her mother died when she was two or three years old. Her stepmother favored her own children [and] was abusive to my mother and her blood siblings, and I believe that out of the flames of deep hurt and anger was forged Emma's wonderful spirit of an open heart, an open door, and open hands for others."

So begins Ruth's remembrances of her childhood in the 1950s and 1960s and the early experiences that influenced the arc of her life. Like Marvin and David, Ruth was raised in New York City. Money was scarce and life often unpredictable. Each of them was formed by this urban experience, and in one way or another it guided them in the type of ministry they chose to follow.

"I remember," continues Ruth, "the many that came and stayed with us in our fairly small and crowded apartment in the projects in the Bronx—her [Emma's] stepbrother and stepsister, each at separate times and each living with us for six months to a year until they saved enough money to get their own place in the transition from South to North. A second cousin on my father's side coming from Alabama and living with us for several months during his own migration. Two second cousins from South Carolina, ages three and six, staying with us after their mother died until the extended family could figure out the next solution for raising these small children. A first cousin from the South staying with us for the summer shortly after giving birth, so recently that she stood by the bed one morning with a pool of blood forming around her feet. At least six foster brothers and foster sisters living with us over the years. The many, many persons over the many years—house guests, relatives, church members, neighbors, friends, and strangers—who sat at our table, if there was a chair, sharing a meal.

"We never had a lot, but somehow my mother was always able to stretch it out to include someone else. It was planted and nurtured in me at a very early age and throughout my childhood that real living on this earth has something to do with hospitality and welcome, being open to receive others, taking the time and making the effort to care about the needs and burdens and interests of others. Almost as shy and quiet as my mother to this very day, I learned to listen to what was being said and shared by others, both spoken and unspoken, and to absorb and genuinely care about the people around me. And from her and from that diverse mix of the projects back then—black, Cuban, Puerto Rican, Irish Catholic, Italian, Jewish . . . all giving to and receiving from one another—I learned about true community with an ever widening circle. This inner heart of compassion connected to these extended hands of community certainly helped steer me into ordained ministry and helped shape the minister I have been."

Ruth then describes some of the lessons she learned from her mother in addition to the importance of hospitality, of taking people in:

"My mother had a third or fourth grade formal education . . . but was an avid reader as an adult. She always emphasized getting an education and reading as a way to a more fulfilled life. I never thought this emphasis had as much to do with getting rich or being superior as simply being empowered. My mother was always proud enough in the right way to work rather than beg or steal. When others were looking for handouts and shortcuts as the first and only option, she thought and taught that these were the very last options, if at all. Poor mouthing was not in her vocabulary. Cheating others and stealing from others were wrong, always. For instance, when my teenage brother proudly brought some frozen White Castle hamburgers that had found their way into his hands after a recent break-in nearby, she insisted he throw them in the incinerator, because, 'In this family we don't steal, and we don't ever eat stolen meat!'"

In the crucible of these early experiences, Ruth found the kind of knowledge that shaped her life and helped her understand what would matter most to her in the long run.

"When you have learned what is good and what is bad, what is right and what is wrong, and don't waver from these lessons—or even from the principle that there is a difference—you have some character that perhaps guides you toward and keeps you in ordained ministry. That's what I believe about my own life."

Ruth then describes some of the family secrets and traumas that provided her with insight into family members and family history and expressed as well some of the same dynamics that are played out in her later life and work.

"I was the oldest of five siblings in our family, but I was not the first child. My mother, who came to New York City when she was eighteen or nineteen, gave birth to a son one or two years later. She was young, unwed, and not able to take on that responsibility at the time. So my brother was raised by someone else in the family, and I believe my mother carried much guilt and regret throughout the years about this. It was many years before I knew this truth, and it was initially difficult for me to work through my shock and uncertainty.

"My father, Travist—nicknamed Buddy—was a hardworking man, a kind and friendly and caring man who also drank, and sometimes that much needed paycheck never made it home. He was a good and loving father, not abusive toward my mother or us, not absent from the family, trying to be a good husband, trying to do his best, but oh so troubled by alcohol. He died unexpectedly of pneumonia when I was fifteen years old. I remember that I felt so alone, so lonely at the

cemetery, missing him so much, feeling conflicted about how alcohol had destroyed his life and taken it too soon.

"I link these two memories—a mother's guilt and a father's turmoil—as an expression of a core belief that has affected my life and
my ordained ministry. It is this sense that each and every one of
us, as we live on this earth, has both good and bad, light and shadow, high and low, or, as Martin Luther would say, saint and sinner,
within us. Life isn't always easy, for any of us. We aren't always right,
none of us. And we all need help from beyond ourselves, all of us.
Help from each other . . . and from somewhere, someone, greater. I
have learned and not forgotten humility and our basic humanity."

To these early memories Ruth adds one particular example of
how being black in white American society made her the target of
prejudice. But the episode also illuminates an aspect of her own
character—the rock solid sense of integrity that so defines her. This
experience occurred during seventh grade while she was standing
in line.

"I turned to whisper something to the girl behind me, and a
white boy standing close by said, 'Shut your little black mouth!' I
was shocked. But I was more shocked when the teacher, who clearly
heard what the boy had said, looked at my face, saw my hurt, and
then simply turned away. I felt angry and embarrassed, but I didn't
know what to do or say. So I went home and told my mother. She
listened, but she didn't say that she would go up to the school and
complain. She said, 'You go back to that school tomorrow, put your
finger in his face, and tell him, first, he'd better never speak to you
like that ever again, and second, you are proud of who you are, and
he'd better never use the word black in a derogatory way when he
speaks to you.'

"I was nervous, but I needed to do it to calm the anger and heal
the hurt. During the homeroom period, I did it. He looked, listened,
didn't say a word, and didn't apologize. But it didn't matter, for at
that point it was for me. I felt proud and strong. In those words
my mother had given me a precious gift. I had received strength to
speak, strength to stand, and a pride in my black skin and heritage
even before the Black Power movement and the use of the term black
in identifying ourselves."

Unlike many black families, Ruth's did not belong to a church and rarely if ever attended one—an experience probably more common among black families than the stereotypes of African American life would suggest. From an early age, though, Ruth sought out this connection by herself.

"When I was ten years old," she says, "I began attending Sunday school at the local Roman Catholic church by myself." She goes on to describe the "mystery and ceremony" of Catholic services—"bells, incense, bowing, robed priests processing in and leading worship and then disappearing out the side door, lofty Latin phrases that probably meant something." She was both captivated and confused. She didn't feel personally involved with such services, but she did appreciate the Danishes, buns, and cold milk provided by the Sunday school. "And sometimes I was given a bag of leftovers to take home and share with my family."

After a few months of Catholic experience, however, she was invited—by "a friend from the neighboring building (now long dead from drugs)"—to attend a Lutheran Sunday school. "It was a smaller building and community of faith, classrooms divided by curtains, six to nine students crowded around a table reading and talking about Bible stories with a teacher, more African American than white, busy and noisy with distractions. . . . But I felt excited by the Bible and uplifted by the care, interest, and passion of my teacher."

This turned out to be the Church of the Abiding Presence, an American Lutheran church led by the Rev. Harry Fullilove, a white Englishman who sometimes spoke "movingly" in tongues and "who encouraged us to make a personal commitment to Jesus Christ. . . . Our Lutheran congregation sang songs from the African American tradition and was expressive in its worship, nurtured warm fellowship and genuine caring within the body, and reached out in bold invitation and in active ministry to the least, the lost, and the lonely."

Not until she grew to be a young woman did she learn that the "spirited worship and culturally relevant music" offered at the Church of the Abiding Presence were not normal Lutheran practices. She even began to feel that they were "something to be apologized for." Yet it is obvious from the enthusiasm of her description that she found great solace in this form of worship and must have resisted disavowing it, if that is what her later training in the Lutheran church called for.

The sense of belonging to the Lutheran tradition that Ruth felt at the Church of the Abiding Presence seems further demonstrated by her decision to attend a Lutheran college in the Midwest. However, given the predominantly white constituency of the school, Ruth often attended black Baptist churches while in the Midwest. Ruth majored in education and after graduation returned to New York to teach for three years in a Lutheran elementary school operated by a struggling congregation in the South Bronx.

"I loved the children. I loved the thrill of helping first-graders become readers, of sharing their excitement as they could do it better and better. I still have that memory of a little girl joyfully reading something out of her Bible to me, showing me she could do it." Yet she remembers, "There was a restlessness within me after those three years of teaching. Or maybe it was small voices of God spoken through persons placed around me." She remembers Rev. Fullilove's wife once asking her "if I had ever considered becoming a missionary, because she saw some potential in me. I hadn't. I remember thinking at that time of the mid-1960s that Africa probably did not need us to send over any more missionaries, that maybe there was a real need for people to work in our own urban neighborhoods. But a seed must have been planted. Some years later a successor to Pastor Fullilove, the Rev. Stanley Ellison, sat in the church office leaning back in his desk chair with feet propped up on the desk and asked me in the midst of a conversation I no longer remember, 'Have you ever thought about becoming a pastor in the Lutheran Church?' I hadn't. But another seed was planted. . . . I started thinking about it, I started praying about it, and I began to wonder that God would even have it in mind to lead me and use me as a pastor.

"I remember attending Bronx church coalition meetings and conferences back in those days of teaching and hearing over and over again that there were few black pastors in the Lutheran Church and how some of the participating congregations wanted black pastors. I remember thinking that Jesus had already captured my heart, thinking that I wanted to serve among persons pushed to the fringes of our society and forgotten about. I remember my own awareness of the injustices and the inequalities, the civil rights and Black Power movements, how faith in Jesus Christ linked with the power of God could build people up enough to live lovingly with self and one another and work together for a more just society and world. But I continued to wonder if God was calling me, if God could use me as a pastor.

"Still thinking and praying and wondering about it all, I investigated Lutheran seminaries, thought 'no,' then decided to apply to Union Theological Seminary and thought 'maybe.' I would go to seminary for one year, and if I felt God was leading, pulling me on, then I would continue to pursue ordination in the American Lutheran Church. If 'maybe' turned to 'no' again, I would work on a masters in education. So I entered Union with a maybe.

"Somehow the teaching experience in the South Bronx, listening to the burdens and seeing the strengths and gifts of poor African American and Latino peoples, the pastoral leadership I received, my own family background, receiving encouragement from lay people, and not doing or feeling so poorly in those first months at Union all seemed to be a cloudy word from God that I should continue the journey. So I did."

As with so many participants in this study (and many theological students generally, for that matter), Ruth's call to ministry was a "cloudy" one, fraught with uncertainty. In this regard, a sense of calling rarely follows a clear path. What is a sure conviction one day is uncertain the next, as doubts arise and personal and practical questions enter the picture. Seldom does a sense of calling begin with some kind of heavenly voice speaking in unequivocal terms; instead, calling tends to be a quieter voice, a growth in commitment over time in many different circumstances and experiences that together seem to point the way forward.

David

In contrast to Ruth and most of the other participants, David believes that he did indeed receive a direct call from God. From the age of sixteen on, he felt a growing sense of being called to ministry, but it was around the age of thirty, while attending a prayer service at Sinai Christian Church, that he heard a direct and what he felt to be a miraculous call. He had been well-received into that congregation, having been made "a deacon, a youth leader, the manager of the singing group of the church—Voices of Sinai—and Boy Scout master." The church often did revivals on Friday evenings, and when they did not hold Friday revivals, they held prayer services.

"It was customary," he says. "for the congregation to stand around the sanctuary and hold hands. During one of these Fridays we did just that. My pastor, Rev. Dr. Miguel A. Morales"—whom David refers to as his spiritual guide—"was standing by the altar and I by the exit doors. That particular Friday the prayer was fervent and spiritual. Without any warning, a voice came out of nowhere and said, 'David, I have called you many times. This is the last time. If you do not answer, attend to the consequences.' I thought it was one of the youth playing a trick on me. I began to look around to see who, but all of them were in the attitude of prayer, which was unusual, because they loved to make fun and bother each other. . . . After the last prayer and before we dropped our hands, Rev. Morales approached me and asked if I had heard the voice. To which I replied, 'What voice?' He proceeded to recite the words with no deviation. I said to him, 'If this is of God, I need confirmation.' . . . Then the missionary of the church walked over and told me the same thing."

Not long afterwards, David contacted the pastor and the missionary and began doing something that sounds not unlike the behavior of a character from the Bible. He began to bargain with God. Although he had taken some college-level courses, David did not have a college degree, and he knew that would be a prerequisite for entering a seminary. Further, he had recently become a supervisor in the Fiduciary and Servicing Department at Bank of New York, a job that seemed to hold great possibilities for him. If he were going to give up such a good job and commit himself to years of educational preparation, he wanted God to do a few things for him. So he told Rev. Morales and the church missionary, "If this is God calling, he needs to do three things to prove to me that it is him. First, I have no intention of applying to any college or university, so he will have to get it [college acceptance] for me. Second, I have no money. Third, once I am in the college he has chosen for me, I need to be preaching in a church."

By May of that year, 1972, Bethany College in West Virginia had recruited and accepted him. When he arrived on campus, he was told that he owed a balance of more than $2,000. On further investigation, though, school administrators' found that he did not, in fact, owe $2,000. Instead, an anonymous donor had paid for all four years of his tuition, which eventually came to $38,000. He was advised, however, that he would probably not to be placed with a local church, because West Virginia congregations were unlikely to call a Hispanic to be their pastor. Nonetheless, not long after beginning classes, he was offered a small church in West Virginia where he was invited to preach on Sundays. In David's view, God had answered and fulfilled the divine side of the bargain that had been made with him.

All of these elements—the voice, the admonitions of his counselors, his demands, his offerings in return—which have the air of the miraculous and the preordained, heightened David's sense of a special calling. He felt that he was singled out among many and given this vocation to ministry by a God he perceived as a father in heaven—a father more dependable and supportive than David's actual father whoever he might have been.

"My mother and father were separated when I was two years old," he once shared. "My father used to hang around the house, but he never had any direct contact with us. My mother was the one who raised us. She didn't speak English at all. She only spoke Spanish, so we had to deal with both languages at the same time.

"My mother was not a religious person; she had a bad experience with a priest at the Roman Catholic church the family attended back in Puerto Rico. . . . But she made sure we, my brothers and I, attended at least the high holy days of the Christian religion. She made sure that on Easter we were dressed in new clothing and went to church.

"When the elder of us three turned sixteen, he wanted to better our life and asked Mom if he could come to the mainland. Once in Brooklyn and living with an aunt, who had converted to Pentecostalism, my brother began feeling homesick. Every letter he wrote home, he [was] crying about how much he missed us and want[ed] to be with us. Mom convinced Grandpa, . . . the person that bought the house in Puerto Rico for us to live in, to sell the house and pay for our trip to the mainland. I was just a child [six years old] when we made the move. Living in our aunt's home, [everyone] had to attend church service. These were held nightly. My aunt helped us find an apartment. We moved to 191 Boerum Street, Brooklyn, New York.

"I have two older brothers. I'm the youngest in the family. Both of them, at that time, had not even finished high school, because they decided to go to work so they could help support the family. They considered that I was the one who was supposed to study.

"I think they seemed to sense that I was more like a bookworm since I went to school. You know, I kept on reading and writing and all that other stuff. They came up to the solution that the one that was going to study in the family was me. They were going to support me in every respect and every way possible. I'm indebted to them.

"I was lucky enough to be raised in a completely multicultural community. There were Jewish, Italians, Polish, Irish. There were very few Hispanics in that community when we started. My elementary school and my middle school primarily were composed of English speaking people."

At the age of twelve, while living on Boerum Street in Brooklyn, David met a boy named Tony, who became a close friend. Tony was attending catechism classes at a Roman Catholic church nearby, and David decided to join him and begin preparing to make his first holy communion.

"What happened next," says David, "is nothing short of a miracle. These classes were held on Wednesday after school. I felt sick, on this particular day, but did not want to miss [class] and went with Tony. During the class my stomach began to feel lousy. I asked the head nun to let me go to the restroom. She refused to let me go and demanded for me to sit. I requested permission to go to the bathroom [again]. Each time the nun's response was the same. Finally, I was not able to hold on and began vomiting on the floor. Immediately, the nun called the helper [and] had me rushed out of the classroom and cleaned and sent home. As I was leaving the church, what passed through my mind was never to return ever again to church."

David's resolve never to attend church again was apparently short-lived, because the next Saturday his mother was visited by "an old friend that had just arrived from the island. The lady was a member of *Primera Iglesia Presbiteriana de Nueva York* [First Presbyterian Church of New York]. During their conversation, the topic of religion came up, and Mom told her of my interest in church. Mom called me, introduced me to her. She then proceeded to write down the name and place of the church. The next Sunday I visited the church. It was a long distance to go, so one needed to take a bus. Once you got off the bus, one needed to walk several blocks."

David continued in this Hispanic Presbyterian church until he was sixteen years old. Then one Sunday after church, his minister, Rev. Colon, "asked me to wait on the side while he shook hands with the attendees. Once the last one came through, Rev. Colon introduced me to Rev. Isaac de Lugo and his wife Alicia, who were going to open a mission close to where I lived. They asked me if I would mind joining them in opening three missions—two in Brooklyn and one in Queens.

"We began the arduous task of visiting and inviting people to the missions. The one I worked on the hardest was on Pulaski Street. This one became my home church. Every Sunday we held service at Pulaski (*La Trinidad*) then went to Graham Avenue to call on homes and invite people to the mission, and in the afternoon we moved to Corona, Queens, doing the same. Pulaski in less than a year had over one hundred members and was able to be declared a church by all rights. Corona also became a church. It took longer. The one on Graham was much slower.

"During the work with the three missions, I felt a call to ministry but had made up my mind to study and become a doctor. [Pastoral] ministry was not part of my dreams at the time. After Pulaski was established as a church, Rev. Isaac de Lugo moved to open missions in other parts of the country. The church was without a minister. The synod in New York had no prospect, and the congregation needed to learn the process in search and call for a minister. Since the work of the Presbyterians with the Hispanics was fairly new, there were no internships provided. The synod asked me to take over the preaching on Sunday morning and teaching the adult class."

However, by this time David had joined the Navy Reserve, and, in June 1960, he reported for active duty. It was a full ten years later, therefore, that he felt that the voice of God called to him during the

Friday evening prayer service at Sinai Christian Church, and a full five years after that that he entered Union Theological Seminary to begin his preparation for entry into ministry.

Few of the other participants go into as much detail about their early years as do Ruth and David, but most give some hints about the events and circumstances that formed them.

Marvin

Like David and Ruth, Marvin did not have an easy childhood. He never knew his father and was raised by a single mother in Bedford-Stuyvesant, East New York, Brooklyn, and Bushwick. He had a brother, only fourteen months older, with whom he was very close.

"He ran track; I played football. And when we were in high school, in college, we would find time to stay up to the wee hours of the morning—go running. Then we'd just go sit in the park, because no one else was there at two or three in the morning. And then there was a reservoir not too far from us, and I would get up at six o'clock in the morning, the crack of dawn, you would see pheasant. Here you are in Brooklyn, and there are wild geese. . . . The pollution of the inner city had not yet woken up, so you could just go there and find a whole, serene, back-to-nature kind of experience and that was just a good time for me."

In the middle of an urban landscape, a geography not tended like more affluent parts of New York City, Marvin found a quiet place, a holy place for him that provided some sense of centering that brought his life into focus and gave him peace. Marvin was not aware of the fact that his wonder at the wild geese followed a long standing symbol in the Celtic tradition in which the lone wild bird points toward God and to the Holy Spirit. Here in the city, he found what George Macleod of the Iona Community often called a "thin place"— a location where the sense of the eternal and the holy has a better chance of asserting itself in the ordinariness of our lives.

In reflecting on these experiences of his youth, Marvin says, "I've always had a strong kind of metaphysical side that has allowed me to be just comfortable in the middle of a field or a meadow, believing that it was just a special time with God."

In fact, Marvin speaks quite appreciatively of a program called Camp Friendly in which inner-city children were invited each summer to stay with rural families, thus offering them opportunities to experience a life lived closer to nature. From childhood to his college years, Marvin spent several summer weeks each year with a family in northern New Hampshire. It became a valued and endearing relationship.

When pressed for more information about his childhood and family, Marvin mentions his mother and his older brother "and a younger brother who was the product of my stepfather. I never knew my biological father. . . . That has been kind of a, I think, a burden my mother has carried around with her, because I do believe that I have . . . half brothers and sisters around. And it's just one of those . . . I won't say family secrets, because there's no secret for me. . . . My mother is going to be eighty-four years old in November. I think in her early years she was involved with an individual, and I believe he was married with children, and she had two children by him. It's just something we've never been able to really get her to overtly talk about."

Marvin seems to have learned from his mother's behavior not to dwell too long on family history. Through learned habit and perhaps by temperament, Marvin prefers to concentrate on the here and now as well as on the possibilities that the future might hold. When talking of the past, he tends to speak of his adult past. However, when asked whether he has ever tried to locate his biological father, he tries again to be forthcoming.

"Yeah, I've tried," he says. "I've gone online. I have a little folder at home. I believe he's deceased, but I'm trying to dig up stuff. My brother, when I spoke to him about it—he's down in Baltimore as a school teacher, my older brother. At first, many years ago, I think we could have launched a good investigation into this if we had kind of joined forces. He was like, 'I don't care. He doesn't want to know me now.' But he's got this gorgeous little baby girl who was just born this year. He's like, 'You know, she has a grandfather she doesn't know about.'"

Marvin resumed the search for some information about his father after one of his sons was examined by a doctor who found that he had some issues with high blood pressure. When the doctor asked about his family medical history, his son could not say anything about his grandfather. When Marvin heard about this, he realized that he needed to know more about his father, not just for closure but for other practical things as well.

"So that's the time I sat down with my mother and attempted to have a heart-to-heart conversation with her. I got a name, some background, more than she ever wanted to share. I think it helped her a little bit, but she was very defensive. I'm like, 'Ma, you know you are eighty-something years old. I don't think child support is an issue. I don't think you have to worry about lawsuits. It's just a matter of knowing.'"

Marvin was not able to track down much more information about his father, and while this was not the outcome he sought, he decided that he could have turned up information he might have regretted. Marvin comments, "You gotta' know what to go after and what to leave alone."

While his father was not a presence in his life, Marvin had numerous relationships that did count and helped provide him with a sense of himself and what was possible for him. When Marvin speaks of relationships that were important in his childhood, he refers especially to his mother and brother and to his home church, Cornerstone Baptist Church in Brooklyn, all of which seem to have encouraged the best of his own natural inclinations to be outgoing, optimistic, and ethically grounded.

Anna and Tim

Anna and Tim are less revealing about the childhood influences that may have led them into ministry, aside from the fact that both had relatives involved in church work. Anna was raised in the church as a pastor's child and grew up with both the direct and indirect influences of that calling. As will emerge later, Anna has reasons not to dwell on childhood memories, but Tim seems at first too caught up in the present to reminisce much about childhood. Later on it becomes clear that his participation in church as a child and young person was somewhat itinerant, and it was not until he graduated from college and decided to seek conscientious objector status in opposition to the war in Vietnam that his spiritual quest began in earnest. He says he kept asking, "God, are you there?" But it was not until he asked, "God, do you love me?" that he received a response that encouraged him to continue further on his religious journey. While working in Pasadena, California, Tim became involved in and influenced by the local Unitarian–Universalist church. In fact, it was the minister of this Pasadena church, Brandy Lovely, who mentored him and influenced his decision to attend Union. As he says, "I found a home, and the UUs were good enough to let me figure out my theological education from there."

Somewhat more open to sharing episodes from their youth are Sarah, Chris, and Beth.

Sarah

Much of Sarah's discussion of her childhood and youth occurs when she is asked what she believed might be the origin of her call to ministry. She says, "I usually trace my call back to when I was a child, 'playing church' with my sister and our dolls on the narrow stairs of our farmhouse located on a dairy farm in Pennsylvania. I remember doing the preaching. Some years later when school guidance counselors started asking us to think about what we would like to do, I remember thinking I would be a preacher if I were a boy. I was not a boy, so I talked about other occupations, including being a math teacher. I was always good in math.

"I had no role models for women in ministry, so as a child, I set aside the idea of ministry without any questions."

She also talks about the effects on her call of "losing my left eye in an accident on the farm. Childhood experiences related to my eye, including the experience of having a friend call me 'ugly' when she saw me without my artificial eye in place, firmly placed me in the space of feeling different and somehow less than others. I believe that is why I fight for justice and inclusion and understanding of differences. That is also why I sometimes periodically question my own value and worth." Sarah also mentions that "I grew up in a culture that preached humility as the highest value. Fully claiming one's call with confidence runs contrary to this value. I have struggled again and again to reclaim my self-worth. The messages of childhood are hard to erase. I remember coming home with straight A's on my report card and my mother saying something like, 'Well, that's OK, but don't be too proud! Your older brothers could get straight A's too, if they studied as much as you do.' Without intending to do so, my mother passed along that culture of humility.

"On most days I feel confident and secure in who I am, but my confidence can be shaken, and I can fall into the depths of despair in circumstances where I do not feel anyone has my back. I am not an introvert, so I need other people (at least a few) to talk through the situation and help me to get out of the pit."

Interestingly, while her mother instilled certain traits of Brethren culture that Sarah feels may have reduced some of her reserves of emotional strength, she definitely appreciates other examples that her mother set. As she says, "I grew up in a family where we were honest with each other, especially my mother's side of the family—straightforward. You lay things on the line. You didn't fudge. And yet you loved each other. You loved each other incredibly, and you would never abandon one another or give up on one another. But you didn't pretend, pretend that you didn't disagree with one another if you did. If you disagreed with one another, you said so.

"Over time, I came to realize that the culture in my family of origin placed value on straightforwardness and forthright encounter over niceness. I clearly remember my mother and her sisters engaged in many lively debates and arguments. At one point the debates focused around religious beliefs when one of the sisters and her family left the Church of the Brethren to go to the Grace Brethren Church. One of the deepest concerns was that this sister would no longer be committed to the peace tradition of the Church of the Brethren. The arguments sometimes became heated, but they [the sisters] never left each other without hugs and expressions of love in spite of their differences. This way of dealing with differences was vastly different from the culture in the larger Church of the Brethren."

Certainly, therefore, Sarah feels that she has learned from her mother and the other women on her mother's side of the family that being forthright in her opinions and speaking openly about differences should not lead to irreparable breaches between friends, relations, and colleagues. Unfortunately, as she learns on occasion throughout her career, not everyone has the same high opinion of forthrightness and honest debate.

Whatever childhood feelings remained regarding a call to ministry, at the time she graduated from high school, she still foresaw no real possibility of such a vocation for herself. Therefore, "upon entering college, I chose a social work major but later changed that to anthropology/sociology, because the social work classes were boring to me. Also, the field of social work seemed too limiting in its scope. My faith deepened while I was in college, and I wanted to incorporate my faith with changing the world—especially the oppressive systems of this world. Through my sociology classes and personal experience, I became keenly aware of sexism in this world."

In this regard, she mentions in particular her sociology professor (and well-known evangelist) Tony Campolo. "His passionate faith, confidence, and courage released my own passion and courage and gave me the confidence to entertain the idea of ministry as an outlet for my own vision of a more just world."

Then in her junior year, a traumatic event occurred in her family. "My younger sister got pregnant and got married quickly. I remember being very upset about this and crying out to God with distress. In this experience, I had a clear sense of God's presence with me as a source of strength and peace. Within the next year, I talked with our district executive and began the process of entering the ministry. That district executive, Harold Z. Bomberger, was very encouraging to me in the beginning and throughout my career. My local congregation licensed me for ministry just after I graduated from college in May 1975 with very few, if any, dissenting votes.

"As I am reflecting on my call to ministry, I am wondering if my sister's 'fall from grace' by becoming pregnant before she was married (a shameful thing for my parents and the community in which we grew up) had something to do with my turn toward ministry. Likely it did, but I had not made that connection before."

Ultimately, though, as is the case with many people in ministry, Sarah asserts that her call came, not as a bolt of lightning or a voice direct from God. "My call to ministry was not a once-and-done event but an ongoing process of questioning and reaffirming my call throughout my life." In fact, she says, despite all of her subsequent years spent in ministry, "there is a part of me that is very insecure in my call." Yet she has found the strength to remain committed.

Chris

Although Chris has been through many personal and professional conflicts and challenges, he appears never to have doubted his own call to ministry. Something in him has always found a secure sense of belonging in the Presbyterian church, even when he has strongly disagreed with the leadership around him, both lay and clergy.

He was born in a large Southern city in 1955 and lived in and around that city until he left home for college. He has a younger brother, but according to Chris, "I was this star student, this star athlete. Never at home, always out doing church, doing sports, doing academic stuff."

Despite some evidence that one of his grandparents was an alcoholic, Chris's parents were stable and supportive, and according to Chris, the family's activities were founded on "three pillars of life"— sports, school, and the Presbyterian church.

"In the course of their lifetime, my parents both served as elder, treasurer, Sunday school teacher, and building committee member. They were quiet, nondemonstrative, sober Presbyterians. They were neither fundamentalist, evangelical, nor pietistic. Unlike so many people in the South, they bequeathed neither an overt racism nor an oppressive religious piety against which I needed to rebel to define myself. Church was simply a natural part of life."

As he grew older, however, he began to conclude that, while the family and church in which he was raised expressed the common values of their community, there were some ways in which they were not typical of Southern society in the 1950s and 1960s.

"Surrounding us was a Southern Baptist culture that eventually gave rise to the first president of that denomination who took it in the fundamentalist direction from which it has not yet emerged, and a culture, religious and not, that was mired in one of the least moderated forms of racism and Jim Crowism of any Southern city."

Although not openly racist, his parents were certainly conservative Southerners.

"They went through this period in the early sixties being truly
fearful of the communists. . . . I remember the '64 election when
Goldwater was [defeated], and they just thought it was the end of
the world. I can remember the John Birch literature, that book called
None Dare Call It Treason, I can remember it being on the coffee table.
But that really wasn't their personality. That just didn't seem to fit."

His father sold petroleum-based disposable products, such as sty-
rofoam cups and packaging materials. "My mother stayed at home
and kept his books and received his orders on a large, gray teletype
machine in his office in the spare bedroom." During the 1960s, Chris's
father became increasingly successful, and in 1965 the family moved
to a home in the suburbs, swimming pool and all.

By seventh and eighth grade, Chris was a basketball star, but when
he entered the local public high school in ninth grade, he found that
the school's basketball team was all black, so Chris asked his parents
to let him change schools, because he felt that the racial makeup
of the team wasn't going to give him much of a chance to play. He
transferred to a prestigious local prep school, and as he comments,
he "absolutely loved it, absolutely got caught up in the church work
and in the academics and didn't play sports for the last two years.
But it was a wonderful experience, because it was sort of this oasis of
thought and liberal faculty members, even though it was [in a privileged part of the city], which, at that time, was just awful. The city is
just such a neater place than it was when I was growing up."

In relating this history, Chris concludes that the elements of
church, school, and family shaped him in ways that made it "natural"
to go to a seminary like Union, because the school expressed so many
of the fundamental values that formed him as a young person.

Besides the three elements that so informed Chris's developing
character, a fourth important element was Chris's powerful moral
aversion to the racism he perceived around him. "I had," he says,
"deep within my silent, Southern soul, some sense that there had to
be a better way, a better way than both the [Baptist] piety and the
racism—and sometimes the poisonous mix of the two—that the majority of white [members of local society] both seemed to have and,

I later learned, did have." Then in the spring of his thirteenth year, "Martin Luther King was assassinated . . . following several weeks of heightened political and labor strife, which in my precocious interest in matters political and cultural I was following. The response of several white Presbyterian clergy, including the pastor of our church, to stand up and support Dr. King . . . met my sense that there had to be a better way.

"That summer I attended a Presbyterian youth conference at Montreat, North Carolina, at which I heard the then-Presbyterian but later to become successor to Daddy King, Joseph L. Roberts, preach, and at which I saw the documentary film *From Montgomery to Memphis*, both of which led me to have more or less a born again conversion to the Christian faith and the Democratic Party, the former a bit more intense than my parents appreciated, the latter a bit more to the left than their Goldwater heritage allowed. It was and is the most direct public rebellion in which I have ever participated, and the closest I have ever come to a religious experience that would have something in common with that sought by my Southern Baptist peers. . . ."

As he attempted to follow the model of Southern progressivism personified in liberal white Southerners, such as Hodding Carter and Ralph McGill, he found himself, like many others, struggling to live out his ethical choices in the face of contradictory pressures that sometimes brought him up short of his ideals. In particular, Chris still carries his conflicted memory of so wanting to play varsity basketball that he transferred to a private school where his chances were better than if he had remained in the public high school where the team was predominantly black. Such choices were day-to-day realities for him as he had to confront without much rationalization the cost of his commitments.

Beth

Like Chris, Beth is also propelled toward ministry by a commitment to social justice. Unlike Chris, whose concerns about social justice seem chiefly focused on the racism he witnessed first hand, Beth's commitments are more wide-ranging.

Beth grew up in northern Illinois, "a prosperous community due to factories that were unionized and rich farmland that mainly grew corn. People who worked hard could generally have a good life. Church was a central part of my life for as long as I can remember. My mother made sure that we attended the Episcopal church every week. Despite the fact that she had had only limited exposure to church in her own life, she felt strongly that her three children should have this experience.

"My mother perceived, correctly I think, that church was a place of elevated discourse, good music, aesthetically sophisticated surroundings, and liberal thinking. In the Episcopal Church, the small-mindedness of the local community opened up onto a larger world. . . . The clergy were more educated than anybody in the community. So we got exposed to someone at least with an education. . . . Then, of course, the Episcopal Church is highly symbolic. The whole ritual dimension of it really does speak to all the subconscious in a cognitive dimension. So I think, for me, it was formed really very early. . . . It was a real centerpiece in my life as an elementary, middle-school, and high-school student."

Beth's father "started out as a carpenter, as an apprenticed carpenter, and when I was about ten, he went into business for himself and became a very successful contractor, doing mainly commercial buildings. He figured out pretty early on that there wasn't money to be made in building houses, because the prefabs were coming in. . . . He built hospitals, factories, prisons, courthouses. . . . So he was very successful, and my mother . . . ran the financial part of the business."

Beth's mother was "a self-educated person who completed the entire twelve years of the Great Books program. She also took college courses in philosophy and creative writing. One of our Christmas presents one year was a typed copy of a piece by Plato which she had hand illustrated. Needless to say, this was not exactly an exciting gift for three high-school students."

"When I was about twelve, my mother stopped going to church. It was a crisis of faith for her that never got resolved. . . . She was fairly intellectual in terms of her approach to life, and she just couldn't reconcile it intellectually. But I think she really struggled with that."

By the time Beth was in middle school, neither of her parents were involved in the church—her mother for spiritual and intellectual reasons; her father through indifference. Then, during high school, social and political issues began to come to the forefront, and with the help of an Episcopal minister, "who later participated in the antiwar demonstration at the Democratic National Convention in Chicago in 1968," Beth was able to "sort through my thinking about the Vietnam war." While she was in college, however, her thinking about many issues continued to evolve. As she says, "I myself went through my own crisis of faith that was similar to that of my mother. The statements of belief as articulated in the Nicene Creed, which is recited every week in Sunday morning worship, were not ideas that I could grasp intellectually. I felt that I was compromising my integrity to continue being part of the church because of this. I stopped attending church while in college, though on an emotional level I really missed it.

"What I would call my religious commitment was expressed in college through social action. The spring that I turned eighteen, Martin Luther King was assassinated. Robert Kennedy was shot on the day of my graduation from high school. Two weeks before I was to begin college at the University of Illinois, I witnessed on television the Chicago police riot [at] the Democratic National Convention. All of these things were shocking to me and very disturbing.

"At the University of Illinois I was involved with the antiwar movement. Through that I came to know many campus radicals, several of whom were part of the SDS [Student Democratic Society]. I became disenchanted with them when their protests turned violent, especially when I recognized that the rampages were being led by people who were not part of the university community. I also was aware of how callous many of these people were in their personal relationships.

"When the campus protests evaporated in the fall of 1970, I was perplexed. Where was the depth of commitment, I wondered, that could be so easily shut off just over the summer vacation? I noticed that in the following spring, instead of antiwar protests, the quadrangle was hopping with what we then called Jesus freaks. It was disturbing to me that social action could so easily morph into a very personalized and superficial religious movement.

"I left college with the concern of how one lives a life that honors the personal nature of who we are with social activism. I volunteered in the summer of 1972 to work in Los Angeles with the lettuce boycott led by Caesar Chavez and the United Farm Workers Union. It was there that I met my husband. I was immediately interested in the fact that he was a seminary student at Union Theological Seminary in New York City.

"The farm worker movement was strongly supported by the local religious communities. Preceding major events, we would come together for a Eucharist celebrated by a Catholic priest. During the week that we were all gathered at the Farm Worker headquarters in Delano to get organized for this campaign, we came together for worship. Students, professional organizers, politicians, and hundreds of farm workers were excited but also nervous, because the stakes were so high. I remember observing an elderly farm worker during this service who seemed to be utterly confident and at peace despite the anxiety that most of us were feeling. It appeared to me that he manifested a faith that allowed him to work for what he strongly believed but to be sustained by God even when the outcome was not what he would choose. The image of that farm worker remains with me to this day as one who had integrated the struggle for social justice with an inner peace and trust in God. It seemed to be a faith that was not based on outcome."

Beth's struggle with her own call to ministry will continue throughout most of her years of study at Union, yet she seems always able to draw strength from the memory of that elderly farm worker and his seemingly untroubled trust in God. Despite her obvious penchant for self-analysis and her inclination toward intellectual scrutiny, she expresses a belief that religious faith and commitment have an emotional, nonrational dimension to which she tries to remain connected.

Since Beth, unlike the other seven students, has lived at Union previously when her husband completed theological study at the seminary, it is a familiar place, though different now that she comes to it in another role. As she has indicated, she did not enjoy being a student spouse, but now she is a student herself, trying to decide if she wants to stay in this new role.

These are the stories that the study's participants have been willing to explore in order to understand better their own motivations and formative experiences. These are the stories that have shaped them and provided them with narrative touchstones for interpreting their lives. Although such stories are often treated hesitantly, they are never static and are often revised and reinterpreted throughout life. Some participants have found such formative narratives readily accessible from their earliest days, while others have found that they could recount certain stories only later in their lives and ministries.

In the *Confessions*, Augustine thinks of memory as a great storehouse of images, events, smells, and feelings. He imagines it as well as a field in which he roams, a palace that he explores. Augustine recognizes that some memories come easily at his beckoning, others can only be dimly perceived, and still others seem lost to him in time. There is much he has forgotten and cannot recall; yet other memories seem to rush out without any effort at all.[1]

In this "vast hall of my memory," Augustine recounts, " . . . I meet myself and recall what I am, what I have done, and when and where and how I was affected when I did it."[2] He recognizes, however, that this work of memory is not like withdrawing something that is neatly wrapped up in the past, because in the recalling there is a kind of participation in the experience itself. What is recalled is from time past, but the boundaries are not all that distinct, because in the present moment they seem almost contemporary, inviting us once again to participate in what we thought was behind us but now appears before us.

We know that in our own work of memory we are selective. Often we can only remember that which we are ready to recall. Other things seem to lie in wait until their time has come, when there is some sense of readiness on our part to deal with them. We also know that there are emotions and events that come uninvited. They seem to pursue us, and we can neither shake them nor deal with them. They burden us in ways we cannot speak about, and we bury them from sight. We are fortunate if we learn ways to confront these memories that we think may overwhelm us. We figure out means to interpret them, live with them, and even transform their meaning for us.

Trying to remember when there was some first inkling of a call to ministry brings us to places we may have forgotten. We have probably created predictable and practiced stories that speak of moments when we feel God called us to ministry, but the more powerful and, probably, more truthful stories are those we have overlooked or deferred because they do not seem appropriate. We may think of biblical occasions of calling that seem straightforward, as in the calling of the disciples to leave their fishing and follow Jesus. But most stories of calling in the biblical tradition bring us to more ambiguous situations where the characters are not all that certain about what is going on, and it is only afterward that there is understanding. Hesitancy in answering the call and uncertainty about our ability to do the work are common reactions.

In the church, calling is both a call to discipleship and a call to the profession of ordained ministry. Frequently, however, we fall into language that fails to differentiate between them, and it is often the case that someone who has come to believe strongly in the gospel assumes that this call to discipleship means becoming an ordained minister. In an inverted way, of course, it is sometimes the case that men and women can perceive ordained ministry as a career choice that has little to do with any sense of discipleship until much later when the practice of ministry forces them to deal with this question.

For the eight, the sense of a calling to ministry has been central to their lives. While some have understood this call as a kind of direct command from God, most of them have seen their calling as something more gradual, more like a journey than a sudden moment of clarity. In this regard, a sense of vocation comes from within, yet it is not the usual self speaking; it is the awareness of a voice beyond the captivities of our ego that offers an emerging, persisting direction in our life. A sense of calling, then, gives some recognition of who we are and who we might yet become. In such moments, ironically, we perceive that we are alone in the universe, though not by ourselves.

We are accompanied by a presence that appears as Other but is revealed in personal terms. In fact, the voice of our calling bears the accents of the hill country in Nazareth embodied in Jesus whom we call the Christ. The shape of our calling is formed by the patterns of his life, and the men and women we are following understand that hearing this voice and feeling this sense of vocation leads them to cruciform places where they share Jesus's ministry.

None of this is clear-cut, and we have seen how the eight have struggled to follow the vocation they have discerned. More often than not, a calling comes to them in the form of questions, seldom as answers. Sometimes this has meant questioning the beliefs they once held and the assumptions they have taken for granted. The vocational questions of who we are and what we are living for invite us to delve beneath the surface of the world and begin to deal with the primary meanings out of which we love and work. The stories of the eight make us aware that wrestling with such vocational questions may cause us to recognize our relationships with others. We begin to see what we have overlooked and not seen in our preoccupation with ourselves alone. Sometimes we pursue such questions because we feel we have no other choice. At the time we may not be conscious of how our needs have distorted the nature of vocation itself, but even these shaky beginnings can be redeemed in time and recognized as the places, maybe the only places, where we could first hear this voice within us.

Sarah, Chris, Marvin, and Anna came to seminary directly from college, while Tim, Beth, Ruth, and David are older and have tried out other forms of work. For them, a sense of call is something they have felt but then deferred and are now reclaiming. Of the eight, David is the one who can point to a specific time and place where he heard a call to ministry, even though, as he relates the story, he took his time making sure this call was confirmed.

As the eight move forward in seminary, it is their sense of calling to which they will return time and again as they wonder whether they are doing the right thing or are in the right place. The same I think is true for almost all clergy whose sense of calling is the center of their life, even though their understanding of this call changes over time. In fact, the deepest sense of vocation comes when they perceive that

this calling is most of all a call to the deepest purposes of their life in
service to the world's needs and not a call to any specific work they
might choose. With this understanding they can claim pastoral ministry as a choice and not an obligation.

chapter 3

Beginning Theological Education

While I've never really seen God, while I've never really heard the voice of Christ speaking, while I've never really had a born again experience, I do see in the scriptures and in literature black print on white page, and in whatever it is that happens in the transaction between that black print and my heart and mind is a life-giving experience that I have long since come to believe is the presence of Jesus Christ to me. — CHRIS

THE WORD "MATRICULATION" IS SOMEWHAT ARCANE IN USAGE now, but it was once the common way of indicating the actual beginning of a student's enrollment in a school. Its origins are the Latin *matricula*, meaning little list, which describes the actual way in which students signed their school's enrollment book, a book often containing the names of students over many generations. To matriculate, then, literally means adding your signature to the book and becoming part of the entering class. Some schools still retain this tradition, most do not, but whatever term is used or whatever ceremonies may acknowledge this threshold moment, it is a significant time in a student's life. It signals the liminal nature of beginnings, those moments when we have left one place or status and are entering another, not quite sure of what is ahead or how we will adjust to the situation. By the end of the first term, however, most students have some sense of the institution and some understanding of how they might become part of its life. This is where we pick up the stories of the eight.

Tim

In his first interview at the end of the first semester, Tim shows himself to be thoughtful and self-reflective, passionate about his beliefs and enthusiasms, and willing to examine his motives and behaviors for flaws of logic or honesty. He appreciates the challenge of Union because it is, he says, "making me articulate and define and hone down my own beliefs through the challenge of a lot of people that don't agree with me."

He is twenty-six when he comes to Union, and while he does not come from a wealthy family, his educational background and connections denote at least places of academic and social privilege—four years in prep school, four years at Harvard, a girlfriend at Swarthmore, time spent in Berkeley, California. Although he considers his years in prep school not to have been happy ones and his years at Harvard ill-used, as demonstrated by his middling grades, he enjoys exploring ideas and pursuing intellectual issues.

His prep school, he says in a later interview, "was a very good school, and I learned a tremendous lot but it was not a happy experience. Harvard, '68 to '72, was a very torn time. And I spent a lot of time involved in what was going on on campus. . . . I did alright with my academics, but I didn't do outstandingly, because I think I was left with a feeling that I hadn't really served my potential there. Unless you go way out of your way to know faculty, you never see them, except in the distance. And because I was involved in other things, I didn't get to meet them, and I thought I missed an opportunity there. I have very good friends there. And I have some very happy memories, but at the same time the combination of the way the school was torn up, the country was torn up, and I was going through an adolescent crisis of my own, I don't remember it as a very happy time."

He begins Union as someone still uncertain of his relationship with traditional understandings of Christianity. In fact, he even

questions the need for Union to define itself as a Christian community. "If we increasingly define ourselves on issue after issue as
a Christian community, we are increasingly describing an exclusive
system of belief rather than an inclusive system of belief. This is
an important question for me, because, while I draw my tradition
and roots from Christianity, I'm not, strictly speaking, a Christian."
When asked where he expects to see himself going with an M.Div.
degree, he states categorically, "I want to be a minister. I spent a lot
of time during and after college trying to figure out what I wanted to
do, and I finally figured it out. I came in here sure of what I wanted
to do, and it's not particularly changed that."

His experience at Union, he says, "is perhaps strengthening my
own sense of personal theology and perhaps strengthening my ability to be a leader, be a minister in a congregation once I actually
get out in a parish. I think it's especially important in the Unitarian
Universalist Association, because so much depends on the personal
theology and confidence of the minister. It is defined by the minister
and the congregation and not by anyone else. Most congregations
live or die on the quality of the minister they get. That's true in all
churches, of course, but I think somewhat more true here, because
the emphasis on congregational quality is so strong. To give you a
good example, one of the most successful churches I've ever worked
with is this church in Brooklyn. . . . They're in their third minister
this century. That's a series of long ministries, as you can see. All significant people. Not necessarily terribly significant theologians but
with a very strong sense of values, which has seemed to hold the
congregation together extremely well through some hard times."

Tim knows where he wants to go; he is simply uncertain how he
will get there. He speaks little about his family or childhood or much
at all about his past; his conversation is filled with enthusiasm for the
here-and-now and his hopes for the future. He is pleased by the diversity among the faculty and the student body at Union, mentioning
in particular his experiences with black Pentecostals and participants
in the women's movement. Although he disagrees with almost every
student constituency on certain particularities, the diversity on campus and in New York City in general seems to reinforce his commitment to inclusivity.

He lives in a campus dorm. In fact, he remains in the same dorm room with the same roommate throughout his three years at Union. He seems to be an eager participant and even a leader in student activities. In his first semester, he speaks extensively of starting a group called "Worship for the Perplexed" that he has helped establish and for which he has expansive plans. He hopes it will help make a place for students like him who are uncertain of their Christianity, interested in other faith traditions, and intent on exploring their own spirituality. Although the group does not last long, it seems representative of his headlong commitment to his years at Union, perhaps a bit scattered but engaging nonetheless.

Beth

Like Tim, Beth is quite positive after her first semester at Union and is clear about her reasons for applying to Union:

"I was in college during the campus uprising and was much involved in that. College was important to me as a political experience, but academically I didn't learn. I wanted the academic, intellectual development. . . . Secondly, people here were very mixed. . . . I thought that would allow me to give expression to different dimensions of myself."

In fact, she was "not interested in going to a seminary other than Union. . . . I came to Union because of the questions that were being asked here. . . . I felt here I could get a broad education that integrated a lot of things that spoke to questions . . . that I had. I also saw Union as being an institution that explored the relationship of theology to the social situation, not only to poor people but also to the structures that keep people poor and our relationship to those structures. I must say after one semester, Union has lived up to my expectations. It's been a very exciting semester."

At one point during this initial interview, she contrasts Union with the Southern theological school near where her husband was briefly a minister and where she was unhappily required to play the role of the minister's wife. She describes the Southern school as "so self-contained that people forget the way the rest of the world lives. I could feel that happening to myself. . . . If I spent very much time on the seminary's campus, I found myself being a lot more conservative.

The issues that previously had been very live, somehow . . . weren't that crucial to me." At Union and being in New York, she says, students "cannot get away from the poverty and the destroyed lives" around them.

Beth wants very much to be engaged with the social and political issues of her time. She is committed to the concept of social justice, and she perceives a similar commitment at Union. Not surprisingly, she also expresses great satisfaction with the quality of the faculty and the students at Union as well as with the courses she has taken. "Not only have I learned a lot," she says, "but it just seems that what I'm learning in my courses are things that are very important to me. My early church history course, for example, . . . is very exciting because I grew up in the Episcopal Church and heard this jargon and it always sounded like jumbo. I thought it was just a way for all these church people to evade what to me were the crucial issues. I appreciate a lot more the tradition and the questions behind that tradition. Then I took the liberation theology course which filled in the gaps in my own thinking. In my own political interests, I'd never integrated the spiritual dimension very much."

Her response to her courses seems nuanced and thoughtful. She tells how her first four courses have helped her perceive a "relationship between contemplation and resistance. Resistance and activism have been very important to me, but it's been very exciting to me to see that . . . spirituality is not an escape from that but is a strong force in that." In speaking of the relationship between feminism and liberation theology, she says, "I'm very impatient with feminists who think they can ignore other liberation struggles." But she is also upset by self-styled revolutionaries who disparage the importance of feminism and often speaks critically of their attitudes.

Whenever she is referring to issues, whether personal, social, or theological, she examines her own motivations and internal conflicts in order to resolve troublesome issues to her own satisfaction. However, once she achieves resolution, she is prepared to act and expresses frustration with people who, in her mind, fail to act according to their conscience.

Referring to the student government's apparent inability to take a position on a moral question concerning the United Farm Workers Union, she says, "If we haven't gotten past the point here of realizing that neutrality is the support of the status quo, then that's pretty pathetic."

Nevertheless, when asked what she would say to someone considering coming to Union, she says, "I would strongly encourage it. I'll say one other thing I've enjoyed this year and that is the Catholic [presence]. I think the Catholic influence is strong this year. I've really enjoyed that. My tutor in psychology of religion is Catholic, and the course [in liberation theology] is Catholic, and that's a very different tradition. Being Episcopalian, it's not completely foreign to me, but it's still very different. There's a richness there that I think Protestantism loses a lot. I would say to people that the professors are very good, that you get into the courses and you're really learning. You have to work hard. I think you have to be ready to study when you come here. I think some people aren't necessarily, that's not their priority at the moment. It wouldn't have been my priority four years ago. I would say that there's a relatedness to the theology and to the issues that we confront."

Marvin

While Beth and Tim perceive their first semester at Union as the sort of graduate education they were for the most part expecting and hoping for, Marvin is caught by surprise. Marvin had sensed a call to ministry in his senior year at Stony Brook. He prayed and fasted over his decision and reread the *Autobiography of Malcolm X* in order to connect "with those who had these spiritual sojourns." He has obviously taken the decision to attend seminary quite seriously. Yet he is not especially aware of what seminary life might entail and not particularly familiar with Christian beliefs and traditions beyond his own Baptist church. For example, despite his Baptist upbringing and obvious commitment to the black Baptist church, he applied to Notre Dame's Department of Theology. He does not seem to have considered whether this was a setting appropriate for his ministerial education. He just knew of Notre Dame's national reputation and really didn't think it made much difference where he went as long as he got the M.Div. degree. Furthermore, Notre Dame seems to have sparked an expectation of his own imagining that seminary would be a kind of monastic basic training, an existence of isolation, spiritual contemplation, and strict regimentation in which young *men* are introduced to a special fraternity that will lead them to a higher moral and spiritual plane.

"I did have," he says in his first interview, "the naive, mystical concept of what seminary was about, basically due to media and literature of what seminary life involved. I thought it would be very disciplined, somewhat on a military line. Union wasn't that much different from my own undergraduate background. That was very distasteful." He expected seminary to be "somewhat rigidly confined in terms of keeping a watchful eye on your behavior, your actions, and the way you express yourself. It would be different than the secular world." What he found was that "you can come here and feel free to do anything you want and just study the Bible. That did turn me off. I'm still trying to cope with it, because a lot of the things that I believe in become somewhat disjointed. I do not find that appealing. . . . I think that when you're doing the biblical work, preparing sermons and speaking in a religious, spiritual framework and studying in that same framework, these distractions can upset. At least it upsets me to a large degree."

Further, he is not particularly pleased with the manner in which his courses are taught. He is having a difficult time perceiving that the Bible can be studied with a critical mind without losing reverence for its source and message. He notes, "I was basically surprised, still am to a large degree, at the way the biblical material is dealt with. People twist and juggle the material to conform to their own questionable beliefs. . . . [The material is] dealt with in a very insensitive, callous manner in a lot of my classes. There are only two classes where I really feel that the religious spirit of the professor is being portrayed. Not that he's proselytizing, . . . but the fact that you can see that the person has some religious background and does conform to certain moralistic beliefs within his own lifestyle."

The reality he has found at Union is that of a liberal-leaning, co-ed graduate school in which men and women share bathrooms in the dorms and students are expected to study the Bible and the history of Christianity from an academic and critical point of view. Non-believers and traditional believers sit alongside Pentecostals who sit alongside Unitarians. When it comes to sorting out the requirements of their faith, students at Union are largely left to their own devices, though here and there they make connections with individual faculty or other students who serve as mentors and companions. Although Marvin lives on campus, as a native New Yorker he is able to both enter and leave Union's world. Sometimes he appears to be an onlooker to what is going on at the seminary, picking and choosing among the various aspects of the seminary's life.

A difficulty that many beginning seminary students face, especially those raised in noncritical traditions, is how the Bible is treated, in the scholarly process, as something other than an object of devotion and piety. Many students experience biblical criticism and exegesis as cold, impious, and troubling to the foundations of their faith. Certainly Marvin admits to such a response, although even at this early date he asserts, "I'm pretty much solidified within my own beliefs, my own concepts. [Professors presenting the critical method have] . . . tugged at it and pushed it a little, but they really haven't upset it. I'm somewhat immune to it. It just leaves me a little uneasy at times. I can see it having drastic effects." However, he balances this concern with the realization that his home church (Cornerstone Baptist) and the church he serves (Abyssinian Baptist) offer a counterweight to these critical challenges to his faith. Moreover, he goes on to add, "The people around me, my mother and a few other friends of mine, are very religious, so . . . I'm in constant contact with the framework that enables me to keep a good grasp on what I'm about and who I am. It would take more than just class to upset that, which I'm very grateful for."

Despite the deflation of his expectations, he seems to adjust well to the reality of Union and finds ways to engage the knowledge offered while not becoming spiritually disoriented within his own faith. This ability to hold onto core beliefs while continuing to deal with new information and outlooks probably requires a combination of stubbornness as well as a mature desire to comprehend and be intellectually flexible. It is also aided by the fact that Marvin remains deeply committed to his role as an assistant pastor at Abyssinian Baptist Church, one of the most influential black churches in New York, and the nation for that matter.

"Sunday I'm in the church most of the day. Sometimes I go home Sunday after church or Sunday evenings, since my church is unique in terms of the black church. We don't have too many evening services. I usually use that to visit other churches in the evening or go back to my home church. I know they have evening services. I like to hear other ministers preach and other religions, other cultures, and just listen to how they interpret the Gospel and how they present it."

When Marvin considers the role he can play as a pastor in the lives of others, the challenges that his faith faces in seminary seem less distressing. "A minister," he says, "is looked upon as setting an example." Then he goes on to tell how a former college roommate of his had "called me up about two weeks ago and told me about how he had become very religious and is restructuring his own life, and he thanked me. I said, 'What are you thanking me for?' He said, 'You know if it wasn't for you I wouldn't be doing this.'"

Marvin is quite proud that the example of his disciplined manner of living can carry real moral and spiritual force with others. "It's not as if I'm proselytizing. I don't believe in that. But I do believe that your actions are proof enough that there is something in religion that is very beneficial."

David

David's experience of his first semester, like Marvin's, challenges the boundaries of his own assumptions and experience. He says that he was advised by his church leaders to attend a different seminary, perhaps a Hispanic one or a more evangelical one, or at least one of his own denomination's theological schools, but he wanted to go to Union for several reasons. One, it is located in New York, his hometown; two, he has known about it since his early teenage years when a Union student had worked at his Presbyterian church; three, he recognizes it to be prestigious; and four, he understands that Union is going through a transitional period. "I thought it would be a good idea to come to something that is reshaping itself again, to find itself and what it is really in life."

Having come from a college that was theologically liberal, he thought it would be a good idea to continue his rebel ways at another liberal institution. He feels that Bethany College had challenged his faith but that "what happened in Bethany helped my faith become a little bit stronger. It didn't hurt at all. I felt like coming to Union I would continue that growth in my faith." He believes that Union is going through a chaotic period and that, by attending, "I felt like I was coming in to help." Such an assertion sounds a bit self-important, but it fits with other statements he makes about his need to serve. In a similar vein, when asked about his expectations for attending Union, he says, "One of my desires all the time has always been, of course, my people" (meaning Hispanic people generally and Puerto Ricans in New York in particular). David speaks here with the increasing self-confidence of a grassroots leader who finds himself in an institution that is far more connected to the established order than he might at first have imagined.

David further expresses a desire to see "something like Union itself, as an institution, to be involved in a community, in the Spanish community, and to realize the need of the Spanish people, beyond just an academic need." Related to this, he hopes Union will emphasize practical preparation for ministry alongside its emphasis on academics and scholarly inquiry.

Shortly after his first semester, David is already demonstrating his announced inclination toward resistance and nontraditional forms of study by taking a course on the history of the Jewish people, which is offered not by Union but by the Jewish Theological Seminary, just up the street. He explains that he was told he could not take the course because he lacked an appropriate background in exegetical method and biblical criticism. But he argued for his right to take the course and used his religion courses at Bethany as examples of appropriate preparation. During his discussion of the course on Jewish history, he expresses an appreciation for the ways in which it has expanded his horizons, saying, "It's the first time I've ever encountered the idea that Christianity is just another form of Judaism." The limits of his own cultural experience are expanded by this sustained involvement with the Jewish community. In fact, at one point he admits, "I never realized that the Jewish people had so much resentment toward the Germans."

Other classes that he is taking are the fieldwork course, which he considers not practical enough, and a course on South American liberation theology, which seems to open his eyes to a new way of looking at Christianity's role in society. He asserts repeatedly, though, that the courses at Union cover the same material he has already studied at Bethany: "A lot of the stuff that I'm given here is repetition to what I've taken already. I don't want to take Old Testament, because I had that already. I don't want to take New Testament; I had that already. There's no need to repeat those courses." While David asserts that he has had college courses similar to these courses at Union, he does not probe the extent to which the content and aims of the seminary's courses are different from the undergraduate ones he has taken. In a way, this protest permits him to distance himself from what might be required if he were to fully engage the biblical courses. He gives the impression that he has wrestled with these issues as far as he is willing to go. This theme continues in different ways throughout his years at Union as he puts up with what is expected of him but often distances himself from any serious engagement. The fact is that the seminary is a limited part of David's life, which is centered primarily in his church and the Hispanic community. There are a few other Hispanic students at Union, but David does not have much contact with them. He comes and goes not unlike a solitary figure, valuing what the seminary can give him but limiting at the same time how it can actually shape his life.

Ruth

More like Marvin than David, Ruth is taken aback by the disorienting experience of studying the Bible and Christianity from the critically rigorous perspective employed at Union and most other seminaries. She expresses the fear of losing her faith when confronted by the critical approach to faith in Union courses:

"I guess a lot of times I feel pulled, and different things are pulling you. I feel good about it. It's just that I'm also trying to hold onto certain basic things that I came here with. . . . I don't mean to give the impression of something being pulled away, but what I feel is in terms of simple, basic faith in Christ. I feel that's what got me to this point, and I know that's what's going to keep me going on. I look at my mother, my family, Black folks. I feel it's what's brought them, looking at it historically. So I want to hold onto that in its simplicity. I don't want to lose that."

At another point, as if convincing herself that the doubt and confusion she is feeling are bound to have a good outcome, she says, "I feel good about the classes, to an extent. When I say that, I mean in terms of the scriptures. A lot of things that had not occurred to me, are not a part of my background, have been opened up, and I feel good about that. I don't feel it's taken away from my faith at all but, if anything, opened up some things."

She also feels that the diversity of views and lifestyles accepted at Union is difficult for her to handle. Yet she wants to learn to see the world in a more complex manner. "I want to be able to deal with some of the other issues, homosexuality, that kind of thing, and be able to look at it." In other ways, however, she feels that the diversity that she herself represents, that is, her African American culture, is not as well represented as it should be.

"The one thing I'm struggling with, along with some other black folks dealing with black churches, is the part that Africa had to play in terms of Christianity, in terms of African religions and the influence they may have had on Christianity, to get a feel for that . . . [but] . . . it doesn't come. It means doing that kind of thing on your own. It would make it easier and more enjoyable if it was a part, not only for the benefit of black students, but for all folks, for a wider perspective."

Ironically, while feeling the need for a more authentic black religious experience at Union, Ruth has also found, much to her surprise, that some black male students are openly critical of black women attending Union and hoping to enter ministry. In a conversation, she says, "with a particular person, . . . that person was telling me that they don't feel like I should be here or be involved in thinking about ministry." In the years to come, most of the women in the study will face attempts to bar or limit their efforts in ministry.

Throughout her years at Union, Ruth lives in her own apartment in the Bronx and commutes to the seminary. Like David, the other off-campus student, this provides her some more stable place out of which she experiences the sometimes bewildering world of Union.

Anna

Anna finds similar discouragement in the African American community—on campus and off—but she is more willing to express her dismay than Ruth. After entering Union, she says, "I had a hard problem finding field placement. See, the black Baptist church has not accepted and will probably be the last to accept women in the ministry. The only reason I got licensed was because my father's a pastor and that church licensed me. Many of the pastors here told me they didn't want a woman and to go somewhere else. I was sent here and there, and a lot of the brothers that worked in churches didn't want me in their church. I was just going back and forth. Finally, my father knew the minister that I'm working with, and although he doesn't really accept it, I'm there. He doesn't let me do much, but I think at least it's a starting point, and I did want to be in a black Baptist church, so that was sort of like a sacrifice I had to make. That was really a disappointment to me in terms of the relationships of the brothers and sisters. For the guys to come off that way really bothered me. For a while, I was trying to figure out what kind of rationale I could give them until finally I decided that I didn't have to tell them anything. As long as I felt that God wanted me to be here and this is what He wanted me to do, I didn't have to explain to anybody else. I feel better about it now. I just don't deal with it."

While Anna shows herself to be quite articulate, especially concerning her likes and dislikes, she tends to reveal little about herself. She also demonstrates a marked restraint when dealing with faculty and other students, especially white women. This posture may arise from the fact that she is not sure how much she can trust them; she feels their experience is markedly different from her own. Further, like Marvin and Ruth, she is never quite comfortable with the lack of explicit piety that so characterizes the Union community and that stands in such marked contrast to her own upbringing in the black church. Like Marvin and Ruth, Anna finds the social atmosphere at Union almost amoral. Although she certainly did not expect the cloistered atmosphere that Marvin anticipated, she is surprised by the coed dorms, the widespread drinking, and the acceptance of homosexuality.

"Everything is okay at Union. I don't feel that there's any morals, any ethics, any anything. People live together, dorms are coed, people get high, everybody drinks, lesbianism is okay, homosexuality is okay. I get the impression that Union is scared to say no to anything."

While it is clear that Anna affirms Union's liberal stance in theology and social action, she is upset by what she considers the seminary's laissez-faire approach to personal morality. She is not naive about the social and cultural changes taking place throughout American higher education, but she has not expected the same to be occurring at a theological seminary. She is puzzled that the school can be clear about the ethics of war and peace, economic and racial justice, but not provide normative expectations for individual moral and sexual behavior. Without being explicit, the school, like many other liberal institutions of the period, seems to be acting on the assumption that ethics is about personal responsibility toward one's self and others but with no particular corresponding norms regarding specific sexual and ethical conduct.

In fact, she is quite conflicted in her views about life and ministry. Although she asserts that she is "not into feminism per se," she is upset that most "of the brothers here have not accepted the fact that women should be in the ministry." She appreciates that, after talking with "the few black women that are here," feminism has "awakened me to sexist language," but she also wonders "if there are any masculine white men in the class. All of them are so submissive to me."

One thing she does miss in the classes she attends, she says, is "a Christian orientation" and by this what she seems to want is more focus on how the Christian life should be lived. Anna comments, "I think it goes back to the morals and ethics and everything. Maybe they don't want to touch it. Somehow, I guess, I had really expected that orientation."

Sarah

Sarah expresses a similar criticism of life at Union when she explains how she would advise someone else about Union.

"It depends on who was asking me," she says. "If my college roommate was asking me [Sarah went to an evangelical college] I'd tell her, 'No, don't come here.' She couldn't handle it. She's from a very fundamentalist background, and she couldn't handle it. Old Testament, that's one thing, but the way she deals with the Bible and Christian faith, this would blow her mind. She'd either have to block most people out as not Christian or not her type of Christian and not associate with them much or totally change her ideas. Either one would be a shock to her."

To survive at Union, Sarah believes, one must be mature. "Spiritually, emotionally. Just dealing with the city. I think it's good to have some practical experience. I don't think it's good to come here straight from college."

Despite the fact that she was raised on a farm and grew up in a religiously conservative community, she is excited about coming to New York. "There's no place like New York City for all the opportunities that one can have here."

When asked to be more specific, she says, "Well, there's the National Council of Churches, World Council of Churches right next door. There are a million churches here. There are a million social agencies. A lot of organizations centralize here in New York City. There are millions of people to work with." Yet when she first arrived at Union, "before anything officially started, when I arrived to get my key for the apartment, it was so cold and unfriendly. I was ready to leave. I was really ready to go home. . . . Nobody seemed to bother with the fact that people were waiting outside to unload my things. It was a cold reception. . . . I'm surprised I'm still here."

Fortunately, after classes started "things began going up. I felt like I could get my feet on the ground when I enjoyed classes and then started to interact with more and more people in the seminary and get to know them."

When asked how she would now define Union, she says, "Diversified, in one word. That's what it is. There's the whole spectrum. There are conservative evangelicals and there are those who would call themselves agnostic or atheists or whatever. There's everything." She doesn't seem to be put off by the school's diversity. After all, it's one of the things she came to Union for, to expand her view of the world. But she does see a drawback to the diversity.

"I don't think that Union has the possibility of really becoming a really close-knit community. I don't think you can expect people with such different points of view to be buddy-buddy. I don't think people are nasty to each other too much around here, but I don't think that real close community is possible."

Certainly Sarah would know about community. After all, she comes from a denomination that prizes community among its valuable attributes. But Sarah is ambivalent about the Church of the Brethren. While it feels comfortable to her, it also seems restrictive. One of her reasons for attending Union and being in New York City is to free herself of what she sees as the negative aspects of community. Therefore, when she is asked how her first semester at Union has affected her, she says, "I think that I have broadened my perspectives. I have a better understanding of how theological enterprises take place, sometimes amusingly. I've changed, just in living with the people that I share the apartment with. That has changed me, and living in the city has changed me probably more than anything."

Chris

Like Sarah, Chris has come to Union and New York City to broaden his experience. Chris is a Southern Presbyterian—in fact, the only Southerner among the eight students. He is also, at twenty-one, the youngest, and both his youth and his Southern heritage color his perspective. Yet New York and Union present him with what he believes are unique opportunities. Regarding his first semester in New York, he says, "I've been to two plays and an opera, and I'm going to the *Messiah* and the *Nutcracker* next week. . . . I love reading the *New York Times* every morning. I like getting out. That's what I really like about the fieldwork, is just getting out into the different racial and socioeconomic backgrounds of my church. [He is doing his field-work with a small, multiracial congregation in Manhattan.] Most of them are really poor. I like that kind of diversity. I thrive on different people's backgrounds. I love going down to shop in the Village. I like eating out at different kinds of ethnic restaurants; I've been eating out a lot. I like both the cultural part of it and just getting to know the kind of common middle- and lower-class people that are in the church I'm working with. I thrive on it. I love going into apartment buildings and looking at the people and the situations they live in and what they're thinking about and what they worry about, what their really personal struggles are."

He had originally considered going to Princeton or Yale or Union Theological Seminary in Richmond. He particularly mentions in his first interview that he liked Union in Richmond because, "It was smaller, and I felt a little more human." But he also perceived Union at Richmond to be far too focused on practical training and too closely tied to the Southern Presbyterian church.

It took Chris a while to even consider applying to Union in New York City. As he explains, the reason for this was "mainly because of the bad reputation and the bad press that it had gotten. You know, the financial situation. This was the time when New York City was going down the drain.[1] There were a lot of progressive ministers in the South who were saying Union has just completely folded or is close to it and is not worth consideration. Specifically what got me interested in Union was the announcement in August '75 that Don Shriver was president. . . . I didn't know him, but I knew who he was as a denominational figure in the Southern Presbyterian church. I had read parts of his book, *The Unsilent South*, when I was in the tenth grade, and I had been to a National Ministries Conference he had led." Besides, the fact that Union is in New York "played a big part in my decision."

Chris also finds appealing Union's "attempt to mold Christian-ity in the environment of New York City, in the challenge of the financial crunch, and of the tightening of the quality of life here, everybody having to live a more austere life, not in a puritanical way, but out of necessity. I felt like the people at Union Theological Seminary were dealing with lifestyles that, for the most part, a lot of people need to deal with and are going to need to deal with. . . . I was impressed with the way they nonchalantly and subconsciously did that. It wasn't a self-righteous thing. We are creating a new life-style; we are the way of the future. It was a kind of freedom of intellectual quest, a freedom of thought and freedom of religious search and expression which impressed me as being a place where I could interpret my Protestant heritage."

On the other hand, Chris feels that "all that Union Seminary is able to say to the world or the church at this particular point is, 'We accept everything.' In a way that's a noble and courageous thing to say, but in a way, that's a very weak thing to say. Sometimes I wish it could say something a little more definitive than 'we are pluralistic.'"

While Chris is impressed by the diversity he finds at Union, especially the inclusion of "the Pentecostal and evangelical traditions" and feels that he's found "a real freedom to explore where I am within the Christian tradition," he is also troubled by the lack of a singular point of view at the school.

"What are we as Protestants going to say about the old Protestant values that have come down to us and which are no longer accepted? To me that's one of the real challenges of Protestantism today. What do we say about our traditional values which have been undermined?"

Chris, like most of the other students, is both drawn to and critical of Union's diversity, openness, and apparent unwillingness to define any normative institutional commitments that encroach on inclusiveness and individual liberty. Without saying so explicitly, Chris, like others, seems to be aware that behind the inclusive commitment a liberal orthodoxy of sorts exists at Union that is not so open to more conservative theological beliefs or ethics. The seminary culture, in effect, does have normative criteria that censor beliefs that run counter to the dominant liberal inclusive ethos. The difficulty is that this stance does not easily admit an orthodox mindset, even though less radical and less liberal students feel its enforcement in subtle and not so subtle ways.

These eight students, therefore, find themselves entering, not the homogeneous, monastic environment that Marvin was anticipating, but a seedbed of theological pluralism and societal inquiry. They must find their own ways to absorb and respond to the academic and cultural milieu in which they are now expected to exist. At this stage, they are exhilarated and threatened by the freedom that their new circumstances provide them. Some of them fear for their faith, yet they also know it must be tested if it is to withstand the challenges of a lifetime in ministry.

Multicultural issues are seldom far from any situation described at Union, and neither are they in most schools or congregations. The issues of racial identity, gender, and sexual orientation are immediate and on the minds and in the hearts of students, faculty, and staff. Matters of class are quietly avoided and seldom dealt with directly, although there is a dim recognition that such questions are troubling. But they almost never claim much space in the life of the school. Anna, Ruth, and Marvin are acutely aware of racial dynamics and are constantly on the alert for signs of prejudice. While they appreciate the efforts that Union has made to deal with racial matters and the steps it has taken to recruit more African American faculty and students, they are quick to point out how tentative these efforts seem at times. On another level, some of the unexpected aspects of this issue are the ways in which black students are surprised and often shocked by the lack of piety among white students and what they consider the laxness in their moral standards and behavior. This gets more complicated, however, as black women confront black men about their sexist attitudes, especially the prejudice against women in ordained ministry.

David's issues are not necessarily the issues other Hispanic students will face as their numbers at the school increase in the coming years. He enters Union as an older student, and this fact also must be recognized in thinking about his experience at the seminary. He expects Union to be more oriented toward the practice of ministry, practical things, and he resists dealing with the kind of academic demands that the seminary places upon him. At the same time, David also perceives the reality that the school has little recognition of Hispanic culture and the needs of Hispanic churches. In fact, he says that he would like to help the seminary learn some things about this culture, but he seldom gets a chance. The fact that he spends little time at Union, other than going to classes, compounds the problem of how much, or how little, he feels himself to be a part of the community.

In later years, Union does not give up on its aspirations to be a multicultural institution. Limited by fiscal restraints and the protocols of tenure, it takes a long time for the school to realize, even approximately, the goals it set to achieve higher numbers of students and faculty from minority communities.

In the coming semesters and years, these students will be further confronted by Union's diversity and New York's disparate communities. They will also be challenged by Union's academic rigor. After one semester, they do not yet feel overwhelmed by their course loads—the thousands of pages of required reading, the dozens of papers they will need to write, the tests they will need to pass—nor are they yet overwhelmed by the fieldwork they are expected to do in churches around the city, nor the part-time jobs many of them will take on to help make ends meet, nor the distress of watching their student loans ratchet up, putting them deeper and deeper into debt. All of these stressors will grow and accumulate with each passing academic year, and they will further challenge each student's stamina and faith.

chapter 4

The Middle Years of Theological Study

I feel like my mind is almost stretched out of shape. — BETH

As THE EIGHT STUDENTS COMPLETE THEIR SECOND SEMESTER AT Union and throughout the following year, the students begin to find their own way—identifying courses and teachers they like, negotiating fieldwork, sorting through alternatives in ministry, and confronting their own personal questions. During the first several semesters, Union's academic and cultural demands combined with official and unofficial outside activities start to weigh on the students, and each student must find compatible ways to accommodate those demands.

The eight students may be full-time students at the seminary, but they have found significant relationships and communities outside the quadrangle. While the seminary's architecture expresses order and discipline and implies a common life, such attributes are suggestions merely, not a reality. Students are free to choose an array of courses built around a core curriculum. Attendance at weekly worship in the seminary chapel is itinerant. A few see it as their primary liturgical involvement, while for others among the eight worship in their fieldwork churches is all they really care about. The pub created and run by students attracts some of the eight participants. It is a setting that feels like their own with a freedom from what little constraint they experience in the rest of the institution's life.

The eight have differing opinions of their fellow students, but all of them are narrowing down the field of men and women with whom they identify or with whom they are developing some degree of trust. The same thing is happening with their attitudes toward faculty as they sort out the teachers to whom they feel drawn and the areas of study that appeal to them.

Beth

Following her second semester, Beth continues to appreciate Union because it provides her with academic challenges, opportunities to explore what is important to her, diversity in the faculty and student body, freedom from conformity, and a sense of community. This last perception is in marked contrast to several other students who struggle to find community at Union. But most of those live off campus, whereas Beth lives in a campus dorm, and that may be a key to feeling part of the Union community.

Feminism and the impact of feminism in her life and at Union are important issues for Beth. Whereas some other more conservative women have an ambivalent attitude toward feminism, Beth is quite certain of its value but also willing to discuss the way in which it is applied—for better and for worse. In an interview held in May of 1977, she says, "I think the whole feminist issue is very important, but at Union it tends to get pitted against academic excellence. It always seems you're supposed to give up one for the other. . . . I'm becoming increasingly aware that it's not just a matter of not discriminating against women any more but that our whole perspective is really patriarchal. . . . The question that's pertinent to me now is to what extent is Christianity a patriarchal religion? To what extent does it really speak to women? Although I think the male professors here are very qualified, they definitely do have a patriarchal perspective. That has to be challenged. What I'm saying is that this whole thing of thinking that the problem with finding a woman professor is that she's less qualified is a false issue. I think it's very important that we break through that.

"[We] just need more of a woman's perspective. It's not a peripheral issue. Both men and women have these two modalities—feminine and masculine. If we're in a society that completely negates the feminine, then that affects all of us. It affects our definition of human beings."

Despite these concerns and criticisms, Beth remains positive about Union: "I know a lot of women in my feminism class found Union really oppressive. I personally think it is one of the few places we have in this whole country and probably the whole world where you can come and get in touch with these things. I think that people who think Union is so bad haven't been out of school for very long. Having been out of school and in a work situation and living situations, Union to me is an oasis."

The one area in which Beth says Union fails (and she consistently expresses this belief throughout all the interviews) is that "there is virtually no opportunity for spiritual growth . . . no course offering on things like prayer." Other than that, though, she continues to believe that "Union for me, and I bet it has been for other people, is just the chance of a lifetime." She says this despite the fact that her husband has taken a job in western New York, 230 miles away, so they are now spending much of their time apart. She asserts that such time apart allows her to build self-confidence and independence. By the end of the following fall semester, however, she acknowledges that such a periodic and long-distance relationship leaves her feeling less than settled.

During the summer between her second and third semester, Beth moves to be with her husband. There she has the opportunity to help coordinate a summer Bible camp, and she begins to feel at home in this new place. Thus, continuing in her second year turns out to be far more difficult for her than she had anticipated.

"I had a very hard time getting started," she says. "Part of that was because I felt completely fragmented, because I was trying to establish a home in two places. I felt doing the studying was very important to me. I mean, if I hadn't wanted to be here so much I would have left, because it was that rough at the beginning."

At the end of her third semester (December 1977), she also has concerns that spending so much time apart from her husband is putting pressure on their relationship. The demands of school work also seem greater:

"I think last year was more of a hobby year for me. This year I'm literally getting to the nitty-gritty, and I'm putting in a lot more hours. I'm being pulled a lot more than I was last year. I mean last year I felt like I was being challenged but, this year, I feel like, like my mind is almost stretching out of shape." This increasing sense of pressure is not uncommon for most of the students as they finish their third semester in seminary.

At the end of this semester, Beth decides that she needs to solidify her ambivalent relationship with the Episcopal Church. She is feeling enough commitment to pastoral leadership that she is considering ordination. "I'm not ready to be taken under care, but I am ready to start asking the questions, and I don't feel like I have a home, a church home," she says. She doubts that she would want to do parish work (although that is exactly what she ends up doing throughout her career) and asserts, "I want to be a church bureaucrat. . . . I don't like having the one-to-one responsibilities of people."

This ambivalence toward the church and parish ministry will continue throughout her life. In its best moments, the ambivalence provides a creative tension; in other moments, it often devolves toward confusion about her life and work. Although she is a person who has a natural tendency to look inward, she has often courageously committed herself to movements and issues that try to overcome injustice and inequity. She values her privacy but has a keen sense of the public dimension of her call to ministry.

At this time she also articulates her priorities: "The three things in life are my studying, my husband, and my relationship with the church." Later in life, she will add her son to the list. Other than that, the list will remain surprisingly consistent and clearly defined throughout her career.

Beth concludes the interview following her third semester by offering a number of insights into the pressures placed on her marriage by dorm life and her time spent apart from her husband. "Union is very exciting, but it's also very unsettled. I'm somewhat aware that there's sort of an anything-goes mentality here, and I find myself being somewhat guarded. I mean, especially being married and being here by myself. I feel like it has to be pretty established what my values are and that kind of thing."

During the interview at the end of her fourth semester, Beth indicates that she intends to take a year off from school and do an internship at an Episcopal church in western New York. She says she feels the need to "give myself some space so that when I do my third year of study in here I'm fresh, because this year I felt stale all the way through. I've done a good job, but I just haven't felt the intensive enthusiasm. And I don't, especially writing a thesis, I want to be fresh. I want to explore how I feel about church and possibly get more of a sense of direction about what I'm looking for, in terms of a job, when I finish. I want to give my husband and I a chance to be together, and those are the main things."

Beth is feeling worn down by her academic work and her long-distance relationship with her husband. As if in reference to this emotional weariness, she once again expresses concerns that "in terms of spiritual growth . . . there could be more course offerings . . . , for example, prayer. In terms of worship, there are a few in worship I know, and these could be offered not only from the historical perspective but also from the perspective of depth psychology and theology."

Additionally, she wonders if the seminary could not do more to be of help in resolving the issues facing her as she seeks to find a way through the challenges of work, calling, and family. She is not sure how she will balance being a priest, a minister's spouse, a feminist, a social activist, and a person of faith.

"I don't think that we really get down to the questions of the interior life, in terms of spirituality, in terms of our own psychology and what that means in terms of relationships. I think that we are so achievement-oriented and so busy, and I hate to get on my tirade, which is what it's become this semester, but the epitome for me is William Sloane Coffin.[1] I mean I just have no tolerance for that man, at this point, because I feel like he is just the epitome of what we need to throw in the trash and just start all over with. He's the classic example of sort of show business theology. . . . I know he's a brilliant man, fantastic preacher. But you know what I say to people is, . . . he's just a little bit too much on the exterior."

Beth is clearly looking for more grounding in the path she has chosen. She is trying to find models of persons who have experienced some of the things she is facing and found a way to live with authenticity and spiritual depth amidst competing demands. Her pointed criticism of Bill Coffin, who was highly regarded by many students, is perhaps a sign of her disappointment at not yet finding such a model in ministry. And so she ends her second year at Union, feeling that she is at a turn in the road, not so much a point at which she will decide whether or not to become a minister but one at which she needs to decide how to answer her vocational call while being true to herself. She has not yet sorted out how the call to ministry that she feels and essentially accepts fits her own nature, the truest sense of herself. It is not that she thinks that one cancels out the other; she just wants more understanding of how these different dimensions of who she is will relate to each other.

Chris

Quite in contrast to Beth, Chris sees in Bill Coffin the sort of minister he would like to be. Besides that, Chris's fiancee enjoys Coffin's sermons. During the May 1977 interview, Chris mentions his fiancee for the first time. He states that she has moved to New York to be near him, and is living in an apartment while he lives on campus until their wedding, which is planned for that summer. He gives the reason for their conscious decision to live in a nearby apartment complex and not in the married couples' housing provided by the seminary: "We'd rather have hardwood floors than linoleum." He also says that it gets him away from Union. When asked to explain what exactly he wants to get away from, he says, "Part of what I'm getting away from is maybe the intensity and the inwardness and the self-analysis of this community, the concern with analyzing itself and improving itself."

In fact, when asked in December of 1977 whether he is participating in any sort of analysis or counseling (a common thing among

Union students), Chris cuts the subject short and merely says, "I'm so biased against that stuff."

His attitude at this time toward Union is conflicted. He appreciates the academic opportunities that Union offers. He is also learning to appreciate its cultural diversity as well, although he chafes at the lack of openness to more conservative and traditional viewpoints. Chris appreciates the opportunity to live in New York and partake of the cultural life of the city. In fact, during his first year, many of his most positive remarks pertain to his enjoyment of the city rather than the seminary.

Chris struggles with the tension between his idea of Union and the changes he sees taking place in the school. For example, he believes in a classical theological education model that he sees as threatened, and he is opposed to Union's lack of a traditional grading system, which he had says leads to "academic sloppiness." He also complains, somewhat proudly, that other students think he has a snobbish attitude.

Later in this conversation he mentions that his brother-in-law was thinking about applying to Union in New York, and in response Chris describes how he would advise his brother-in-law and others:

"I'd probably sound very negative. I would just want them to know what they were getting into, and [if they] still wanted to come, I'd say, you're not going to find another place in the world like it."

Toward the end of this interview, after his second semester, Chris speaks about the positives of Union, but he couches those positives in contrast to the Southern Protestant tradition in which he grew up. He reflects, "I knew there was something lacking in my own tradition and in my own personal acceptance of my tradition. Once I've come up here and been exposed to the different traditions and the diversity up here, I can locate specific events in the past which were the source of my questioning and which may have been confirmed positively or negatively particularly in the Southern white culture, which was moneyed and which fashioned itself as liberal. I guess it is, compared to the rest of the South. But the church is institutionally so strong down there, and the minister is still, I think, a very respected, important person in the community and can very easily be involved in an ego trip. It has been good for me to get up here where

those kind of props don't exist and those assumptions are challenged. . . .

"I knew there was something more than what white, Southern,
Christian society could offer. It's been hard coming up here, but I'm
glad I did. I'm glad that I'm making that gain. I don't know how it will
function back in the South. I really do feel different."

When Chris returns for his third semester, he and Laura are married and are living together in their apartment off campus. He has
returned, he says, without "the sense of enthusiasm and excitement
that there was last fall." Having, as he puts it, "made my peace" with
Union, he expresses his intention to focus only on school. "But the
expense of that or the price of that," he says, "has probably been further isolation from people." He also mentions his marriage as a cause
for his sense of isolation. He mentions again his snobbishness and
remarks that he and Laura have limited their associations to a few
friends. "But other than that," he says, "there's just not much involvement at all."

He then speaks of "events that have happened that I really think
are bad." He does not like the controversy over the search to name
new professors in Old Testament and Systematic Theology, because
he believes these appointments may be made in a way that is detrimental to the classical tradition. The searches have politicized the
seminary community as various groups try to influence the appointments. He asserts that he is willing "to let the feminists have their
day and to let the minority group activism have its day, although I
am more in sympathy with them than I am with the feminists. But
when they start talking about affirmative action in faculty hiring,
that sends shudders up my spine."

When asked whether he has made his worries known, he says, "I
make my feelings known whenever there's a forum for it. I don't refrain from saying that, although there's really not the opportunity. . . .
But if I were, if I had a forum, if I were on a committee and that kind
of stuff came up, I would really, really fight."

He speaks some about the church in Brooklyn where he is doing
his fieldwork and says, "It's been good to have the parish involvement. There's a lot of people out there that I really like. It's a different
situation, and I still kind of feel like an outsider in terms of the kind

of church experience I'm used to in the South, and I guess that's to be expected."

When asked what he thinks about as he takes the subway to Brooklyn, Chris comes up with an array of thoughts that express many of his concerns for the future of ministry generally and his vocation specifically. He says, "In my off moments, I always think about . . . how important the institutional church really is going to be in the future. And that's mixed with a homesickness of coming out of a part of the country where it is strong and the minister is a more respected or more important person than he is up here. And I guess, deep down inside, and I don't really fear this, but deep down inside I think probably that the secularism that has, if that's what's destroying the churches up here, will be, you know, invading the South more and more and more. And that my experience maybe twenty or thirty years from now as a church person will be more like my experience up here, which makes me think it really is worth it to stay up here, because you're going to learn things up here to possibly avoid the mistakes that have been made, that can keep the church strong."

Chris then compares what he feels is the sterile freedom of ministry in the North with the loving but more narrow-minded South. "I think there's a real freedom up here. . . . The question is whether that freedom is to such an extent that that's why the churches are dead up here—I mean, if the minister is so insignificant that nobody gives a damn what he's doing. There's probably a moderate position somewhere, because this concern about the pastor's morality in the South is a demonic thing, but there's a beauty to it in that at least the people care. Whereas, up here if you're out running around or doing whatever you're doing and nobody cares, there's kind of a sadness about it."

He expresses worries about his own ability to be a good minister, which he connects to other concerns about himself and his marriage. "I think about my own personality in relation to a local congregation. Am I maybe just too stuffy? Am I maybe just too removed or aloof or cold to people? Maybe the role of the minister really is to be a jolly person and, you know, not think too deeply. . . . I guess being married, when you really do have to start taking into consideration another person, makes you realize that you might be able to make some adjustments as one person. But when you have a family, whether it's just a wife or seventeen kids, that they count and that your definition of work and your self-image as to how many hours a week you work and how important a person you are and how successful you are, all those things now have to be taken into consideration if you've got another person or other people that share your life. You know, in college I could study until two in the morning if I wanted to. I was just free from responsibility for other people. And for better or for worse, I'm not anymore."

Soon thereafter Chris mentions the feminists at Union and how much he dislikes them, but then he goes on to say: "I think I will be able to go back to the South or the church, wherever I go, and have a clearer perspective on the relationship between the church and the gospel, between the church and politics, between the church and the ideology, between the church and gay rights, between the church and divorce, sex, abortion, all these things that up here I guess I found them just immoderate, and I have a more clear definition on each of those issues."

Chris's anger toward feminist attitudes and actions evidence feelings that lie within him. The extent to which his language and emotion toward feminist students and faculty connect with other conscious and unconscious trigger points in his own life is not explored. It is evident, though, that theological, personal, political, and ideological streams converge in the issue of feminism and cause him to speak so forcefully. As he articulates this strongly held feeling against the feminists, Chris tries also to see the positive benefit of this being one more experience he can bring back to the South with him—an experience that has caused him to be aware of positions and attitudes he would probably not have seen or sought out in such a dramatic fashion had he remained in the South.

Chris begins his interview following his fourth semester speaking about the courses he took during the semester. Generally, he seems pleased with the courses and more comfortable with the academic side of his efforts than his fieldwork. In fact, at one point he suggests that Union's emphasis on the practice of ministry is misplaced, that students should "take one course in homiletics, one course in counseling, but make the rest of your seminary education academic."

This opinion is in sharp contrast with most of the other students, who feel that Union should offer more, not fewer, opportunities to develop knowledge of and skills in the practices of ministry.

Much of the rest of the interview is given over to Chris's concerns about his workload and his hopes for his upcoming internship year. Specifically, he is feeling overwhelmed by what seem to be the endless demands of work and school responsibilities: "I've just got to break out of this cycle, you know, of fragmentation, working and trying to study at the same time. . . . It's the number of hours. Although I realize that I work a lot more than most students. And that was by choice this year. But I really wanted to try to get a good parish experience in New York, and the one that I had this year was satisfactory, but I wouldn't classify it as good. And I think anytime you work in a parish situation, no matter how low you are on the totem pole, it's always going to be more hours than is written in the job description, and there's always going to be just day-to-day worries and telephone calls and things like that, where you can't limit it to a given number of hours. . . . I was working about 30 hours a week, and I think, you can't do that and go to school. . . . I'm worn out. It's taken all my emotional and intellectual ability to go to school here and live in New York. And I really need a year off from that."

When asked to discuss his sense of fragmentation, Chris says, "I guess if I had to put it in a nutshell, what my frustration is with both New York and Union is the lack of smoothness of personal relationships—the tension, whether it's dealing with a store clerk or fellow students or whatever, and the constant pace. I think it just drains you. I think it's healthy, but I don't think it's healthy for very long, and it's something that I need to break from. I need more of the collegiality of the church, both the ministry and the laity, you know, in the South to kind of keep me going and give me some support."

He also talks about the need to maintain a certain lifestyle. "Laura and I spend a hell of a lot more money, I think, than most people our age. But one of the reasons we spend that much money is the attempt to have some of the comforts of life that I find just so lacking in this city, that make life more bearable here. . . . We don't have to live in quite the nice place that we do. . . . We spend more money on clothes and more money on, I guess, furniture, you know, fixing up our house and things like that that most people don't, but those are just basic things that I want to have."

Chris is looking forward to a year away from school. His plan is to return to the South where he will be the campus minister at a university medical center. "In addition to that, I'll be—about a day and a half, two days a week—I'll be acting as the presbytery's hospital visitor. . . . And then the third thing I'm going to be doing is, I get the chance to preach once a month at a small Presbyterian church which, the minister there is just an old friend, who is an old fiery Southern evangelical orator who has a perfect record on civil rights and activism. He's kind of a mixture of a Southern evangelical with a liberal social conscience and just a great, great preacher. He just called me up and said, 'I want to give you coaching.' So he's going to bring me down there once or twice a month and let me preach and go over the sermon. So it'll be a good year.

"I basically see it as a year for me to receive some strength and some renewal—emotional, spiritual—from a more familiar culture. . . . I'm talking about the strength that comes from friendships, from people that you love, from people that you're close to. . . . I'm looking . . . to go back to the South and compare it with new eyes, having lived up here for two years, and in a sense, to find what in the South I think is worth redeeming, fighting for, saving. . . . Having lived up here, I think I can go back to the South with clearer eyes to determine what parts of the South that currently exist I can now affirm and fight for, what parts of the South as it currently exists I can be a prophetic witness against. And that's why I left the South, to come up here and get that perspective, and I've gotten it. For that, I'm eternally grateful, even though it's been hard."

So Chris finishes his second year at Union with a need—like Beth—to find spiritual and emotional renewal. Unlike Beth, however, Chris exhibits no doubt about his ultimate choice of a vocation in the denomination of his youth. He does, however, continue to express uncertainty about the cost and rewards of being at Union and living in New York City.

David

At the end of his second semester, David is still working full time and taking a full load of courses. In the following semester, however, he plans to enter the ISTEM program (Inter-Seminary Theological Education for Ministry)—an alternative program in which students studied and practiced ministry in various church and community contexts outside the seminary—so he can concentrate on the practical preparation for ministry, which is one of his primary concerns. As he says, "I find that when the seminary tells me what I need for the church, it's not what I find that the church needs from me." By enrolling in ISTEM, he feels he can actually reduce his workload, because he will not be duplicating the work he is already doing in the parish. "My work with the church," he says, "house calls, hospital calls, and my regular work, which consists of twenty-five hours of the ISTEM program, before was extracurricular; now it's also part of the studies."

His description of ISTEM leads to a prolonged discussion of the need for Union to become more involved with the Hispanic community and to deal with more practical issues of ministry. Although David appreciates the outreach Union has made to various Hispanic cultures in South America, he believes that "Union needs to deal with the Puerto Ricans right here in the City of New York. We are an entirely different entity from those coming from Puerto Rico. I think it's about time that they [Union] would begin to create a dialogue with the communities that are immediately surrounding the seminary." After all, when Puerto Ricans are in their homeland, he says, "they're very religious people. They come to the United States, and they completely lose that to the point that you see them in the streets drinking, playing dice, playing all these kind of games. But the church is the last thing that they think of. Yet at home the church is the first thing. Why? What causes that when they come to the United States? What freedom does the United States give them, or what kind of fear do they have of the church? I'm struggling with that personally, I know, to deal with that in the community in which my church is, because I cannot relate. That to me is a theological problem and a big theological problem."

When asked what Union could do to improve his own experience as a student, he immediately emphasizes the need for more practical training. "Expand the practical theology department to a three-year program instead of a one-year program, to a pastoral counseling center where those students who . . . are doing practical theology outside can come and meet . . . with the different professors from different fields and help us develop this sense of the responsibilities of our job. Golly, I didn't even know what to do when I visited a person in the hospital! I almost put my foot in it my first visit there. That could have been detrimental to the church. Thank God the person who was next to me held me back, thinking that I was doing right. If I had somebody to meet with, to counsel me, I would not have gotten into that situation."

Despite some criticism, he continues at this point in his student career to speak highly of Union and its "liberal viewpoint" and asserts how important it is that he has learned about the feminist movement and the gay community. He also appreciates the many great theologians who have been part of the Union tradition, including Dietrich Bonhoeffer, Paul Tillich, and Reinhold Niebuhr. He wishes, however, that there were more casual points of contact between students and professors outside of the formal relationship of the classroom.

By the end of his third semester, David has had a chance to participate in the ISTEM program and seems quite positive. As he says, it is "very good for a person who's going through his Master of Divinity. It puts you in a situation where you have to learn your techniques." He asserts that since he had so many religious studies courses in college he has already covered most of the introductory course material at Union and indicates that he decided to drop all of his courses in the second year except for his church history course and focus on ISTEM, where his own context and ministerial responsibilities are actually part of the work of the program. He says, "I felt like working in the field full-time as a minister. I needed something that was more viable to me." He thus demonstrates his commitment to practical, hands-on ministry, but his decision to drop courses also implies perhaps a certain unwillingness to meet the academic standards expected at Union.

Nevertheless, he continues to lead his own church and through it participate in his local community—joining his neighborhood block association, providing a Golden Age meeting place for older people, and even offering the church as a polling place for voters. He also went to Puerto Rico during the summer, preaching and giving speeches on the Puerto Rican experience in New York.

He mentions a plan to enter an exchange program whereby he would spend six months ministering in Puerto Rico, while a Puerto Rican minister would do the same in his parish. This plan apparently never comes to fruition. Nevertheless, he seems highly confident and upbeat. When asked to evaluate the quality of Union academically, he says, "I evaluate it very high." However, he asserts, "when it comes to the religious aspect of the Bible studies and Bible work at Bethany, it's equal to Union." Once again, he clings to what he feels are his previous accomplishments and rejects or diminishes Union's expectations of him, perhaps because those expectations have not been presented to him in ways that seem applicable to his experience and thus fail to give him the confidence to move forward.

After more probing, he returns to early themes about the shortcomings of Union: It is isolated from other educational institutions. It is isolated from the Hispanic community. It is, in fact, isolated from most of the neighborhoods that surround it.

At the end of his fourth semester, David continues to be quite positive about the ISTEM program, which "has been a very good experience. It's shown me that what I want to do can be done." Speaking of ISTEM, he asserts that "putting the practical line of theology and theory together makes a beautiful unity." He also continues to promote his concern that Union is not practice-oriented and suggests that professors and active ministers should coteach certain courses to help students understand the practical application of academic studies: "So when you leave the seminary, you don't just go out with just a book. You also have some experience background. I mean that's one way of doing it in the classroom."

David remains committed to parish ministry, and that vocation increases as he serves as a pastor. In fact, when the practice of ministry is addressed directly at Union—for example, in ISTEM—he seems fully engaged in learning. It is the more traditional classroom-oriented courses that constitute a worry for him. Because of his upbeat manner and attempt to remain as positive as possible, it is easy to miss the fact that after two years at Union signs are appearing that he is going to have to confront these academic issues in a more direct way than he has to this point.

Marvin

By the time Marvin completes his second semester at Union, he is beginning to feel overwhelmed by the demands on his time, and he speaks of doing better time management.

"What happened," he explains, "was that I got caught between the church and the seminary, which really calls for an extremely large amount of discipline. Being able to balance the time is very difficult. . . . I did not know how time consuming it would be, how demanding it was. With my own pride and wanting to do a good job at the seminary and in the church and not sell myself short on this side and not neglect the needs of the parishioners on the other side, I caught myself running between the two. Then what happened was at the end, for the last two weeks, I finally had to just stop and make a decision. Luckily the church had reached a slow point. There wasn't that much activity going on that needed my immediate attention, which was fortunate for me. . . . Finishing up the second semester, things worked out pretty good. I'm pretty satisfied in terms of not going to pieces at the end, but still in all, I think this past year has been one of direction and knowing what it is going to take. . . . I was green to so much, green to the church and to seminary. Now I know what is necessary to be successful in both and I think I will more or less sit down this summer and evaluate myself, know how I work best, under what conditions, and become a little more disciplined."

As do several other students, Marvin feels that Union does not place enough emphasis on practical training. "There's not that much leniency or consideration for those who are working in a parish setting. It seems as if the atmosphere of the seminary is saying, 'You're either committed to one or the other.' I mean in terms of myself, enjoying the theological arguments and the philosophical aspects of theology and religion which the seminary introduces you to and trains you in and more or less grooms you in that aspect, this is what

I think the seminary caters to more so than the minister that is leaning toward the practical field, parish ministry."

Nonetheless, he feels that he has learned and grown at Union. He
speaks of visiting with some people on Park Avenue: "One lady was a
Christian Scientist. Another fellow just had a good understanding of
religion. He had been through most of the major religions—Catholi-
cism, Hinduism, Protestantism. He had a good working knowledge
of what they were about. He was very well traveled. He talked. I felt
at ease, not totally, but more than I think I would have ever been
had it not been for Union. I think it is just the atmosphere of Union
and the fact that the classroom situation, the type of discussions that
take place, the readings, all of that came together. I think that really
made me aware of the effect that Union had on me, being able to
sit down in a situation that I would have never felt comfortable in
before and interact and have my ideas respected and thought about,
challenged, and do the same thing for someone else. That made me
feel good."

On the other hand, when asked what Union is doing for black
students like himself, he says, "I think if they are coming to Union
to find themselves as a black person, they are making a big mistake.
Union will not help you in terms of that. You have to have a good
understanding of who you are, what you're about, before you come
here. I'm speaking personally, not with theology or anything like
that, just who you are, being a black person or anyone from any ethnic group or any minority group." Students should not "come here
searching for something or running away from something, thinking
that this will solidify you."

From the challenges of being a black student at Union he briefly
segues into some of the difficult realities he is beginning to face in
parish ministry. "Coming here black, already you're coming out of
a tradition, already you're coming with a certain amount of questionable handicaps, maybe. You're expected to relate on an academic
level, plus meet the needs of the parishioners. It's unique because the
average church person does not see the minister as having too many
real human characteristics or qualities. You find it hard to tell someone, 'No, I can't make it. I can't attend this affair, because I'm tired.'
. . . A fellow minister friend of mine told me that that's one excuse

that parishioners do not respect. . . . You find yourself spreading yourself thin even when you do not want to."

During summer break, Marvin marries and runs a children's summer camp at Abyssinian Baptist Church. He and his wife have moved into Van Dusen Hall, the campus housing for married couples. Having a settled home life and one year of seminary experience, Marvin feels comfortable going into his second year at Union. As he says, "There's a little more self-esteem there, confidence there."

He continues to feel some discomfort with the liberal orthodoxies that tend to prevail at Union. However, while he sometimes complains about feminists and gay rights advocates, he also indicates that he is trying to understand their points of view. He is learning to be more open-minded and willing to listen before he speaks.

Because of the time demands placed on him, Marvin is far less involved with seminary activities—including the Black Caucus and the financial aid committee—than he had been before. In fact, he expresses a certain bitterness about the cost of attending Union and the minimal amount of financial aid he feels that he is receiving.

"Financially, yeah. I'll go back to that 'cause that was a shock for me. I had to pay a tremendous amount, and I will next year in terms, you know, of just going to school. And to a large degree that has made me very, I don't know the word to express it, but that has really upset me, you know. And then as I talked and researched the problem, I found that this is the philosophy of Union. . . . You're taken care of pretty sufficiently during the first year, and then for some reason or another, you're expected to come upon a gold mine by the second year. Then your funds are considerably cut the second and third year. Now, I do not know what they expect. . . . I think they do expect the church to supplement the education here, and some churches may do just that. But I know in my own church, unless you really are preaching on a regular schedule as a guest minister in other churches, then you will not have that kind of income."

Combined with the money difficulties are the demands of church members who don't understand the pressure that young seminary students are under. "I can spend 40 or even 30 hours a week in the church . . . , and that does not necessarily tell the members of the congregation that you are there," he says. "They like to see you in the pulpit. They like to hear you throughout the worship service, presiding and things like that. . . . They expect to see you there on Sunday, because you're their minister. They enjoy you, and in my particular church, they love young ministers. That has been their tradition. And even if they don't see me at . . . Friday night prayer service, some of them are—I won't say they get upset—but they express it like, 'We missed you Friday night,' and things like that. . . . You preach and you get to know them personally. If you're doing a good job, visiting them and things like that, then they remember you and they adopt you. The older members feel you're their son. The younger members feel that you're like a big brother. . . . So, it's a tremendous personal level that we are on, and at times it has tremendous rewards. But then at times you are expected to always be charming. . . [even when] you don't feel like it."

Following his fourth semester at Union, Marvin continues to be pleased with its academic standards, but he feels that "the practical aspect is kind of played down, separately and overtly. There isn't room for it to be applied in an actual setting. It's strictly from an ivory tower perspective. . . . You can't really relate it to the common person. . . . How do we take what we've learned in the classroom and apply it to actual settings? If you wanted to stay in Union for Ph.D. work and write books so that theological students will read and understand, fine, perfect, but if . . . that is not in your plans, then you are lost as to the necessary tools to lead people. As far as the black community goes, we need more scholars, true. But we also need competent leaders out there doing theology. . . . It's like a doctor staying [in academia]. You know the black community needs black doctors, so if a black doctor emerged and stayed in the schools teaching students, then the community never really thrives off that doctor's achievements, especially if that black doctor is teaching white students."

Nevertheless, he continues to affirm his decision to attend Union, and he feels that his new academic learning has enriched his preaching even as he strives to keep his sermons simple and convincing. "It's like a lawyer going to court," he notes. "He has to know both sides of the argument. And he's not going to take to the judge anything that's going to weaken his client's defense. But he's only going to take those things that are going to enhance it and help it. . . . When I walk in my community and see brothers and sisters on the corner strung out on drugs or even selling drugs, I have to tell them something that's going to kind of make them think about what they're doing and see if they can do something better. . . . But it has to be something where I can bring them into the office and not only preach to them and talk to them in a very down-to-earth fashion, because theological language, at that point, is not going to do them any good. They don't understand it and they won't even take time to listen to me. But if I can relate to them on their level and somehow take what I learn here, reshape it so that I can have a convincing argument, and then deal with . . . some social concerns and social awareness and some leadership ability where I can counsel them and direct them to loans and scholarships and people who can give them jobs and things like that, . . . you know, as Jesus did. He not only preached, but he fed through the miracles, as we look at it. The people didn't sit there hungry listening to him. But he fed them and talked to them."

All in all, he feels that he has a strong understanding of his priorities. He says, "I've got the church, the marriage, and school. But you know one thing that I think I have got a pretty good grip on is the worrying aspect. I don't worry as much as I used to, but I just go ahead and do what has to be done, and a lot of people tell me that that's not only reflective in my character and my way of doing things, but they can feel it, that I'm not as tense and as tight as I used to be. . . . I think I'm a bit more open-minded. . . . One thing that I've learned here, in order for things to happen, in order for change to occur, people have got to get along better, and there has to be a way or means of sitting down and arguing and debating things out in an open fashion."

For Marvin, therefore, his second year at Union Theological Seminary ends on a generally positive note that, as he says, may reflect his character as much as the lessons he has learned during the preceding two years.

Anna

In contrast to Marvin, Anna feels rather low about her experience at Union. Although she asserts that she has grown and remains committed to Union, the tone of much of her conversation at the end of her first year is less than affirming. As she says, "When I came, I think I was a bit naive about life and about the temptations and hassles that life brings with it. I was used to temptations and hassles but not in the extent that I experience here. Here it's been almost insurmountable trials in terms of Union, in terms of the black community. Just trying to exist here as a black woman at Union has been a big, difficult problem for me. . . . I'm just coming to the conclusion now that whatever happens, happens for a purpose. I feel comfortable. I feel that God wants me here. I don't always understand why, but I feel that this is where I belong. I have decided now that beginning next year, I'm almost clear that I have to find another kind of constituency to identify with within Union.

"I do feel one good thing. I feel good about the black women group that has gotten started this year. It's really been helpful, I think, for all of us. It's a support group. That's one thing that I really hope continues. I'm going to really try to get into that. In terms of the Black Caucus, . . . I'm not saying that I won't be involved, but I don't feel like being in the mainstream of things. Not now. I don't see where it's benefiting me.

"As far as Union, I never see myself fitting into a white constituency. That's neither here nor there. It wasn't expected. As far as the white women, I did go to a couple of meetings this semester with the Women's Caucus. I definitely decided that that was not what I wanted to be about. . . . It's just not me. I don't feel comfortable. I don't feel that Union is doing anything to make my space better."

When asked if she has found any support from the black faculty, she says, "I think they have tried to be [supportive], but they're so busy with other concerns that they don't really have the time to be pastoral all the time. I think some of them feel like it's putting them in a position that's kind of shaky. We're in the process of trying to heal the problems that have happened between the black faculty and students. . . . I feel like there is maybe one person on the faculty I can talk to. But as far as the problems that I was experiencing as a black woman, I don't think they were sensitive to what I was going through. . . .

"Now that this year is ending up, everybody is asking me if I'm coming back, as if I had given the impression that I wasn't, particularly to faculty members. I felt like they expected me to give up: 'Well, she's not going to last.' That bothered me because there wasn't any effort on their part to try to make it, to talk to you or try to see what the difficulties were. It was just, well, she can't make it, so we'll let her go. I felt bad about that."

Anna continues to be critical about certain aspects of her experience at Union, yet she is surprised to hear that some students and faculty assumed she would not be returning after her first year. She wants her time at Union to be a success, but she has yet to find a comfortable fit with the institution.

She goes on to say, "I like my classes, for the most part I do. . . . I like . . . classes [that have] related the black experience to me . . . in a way that I never had experienced. Preaching tied it all in for me, made me realize how important it is to study Old Testament and New Testament and to know how to do exegesis and all this, so that you could formulate a good sermon or become a good preacher. . . . I feel that the professors I have had have been really genuinely concerned about me."

She did not, however, like the courses that followed a seminar setting and emphasized discussion, saying, "I feel it was a waste of time. They could have been useful, but I'm not a talkative person. I always felt that when I got in there, everybody would talk and then say, 'Well, Anna, what do you have to say?' I felt that if I had anything to say, I would say it. I felt like all of my evaluations said, 'Anna did good work, but she's a very quiet student. She never said anything, and I felt she had a lot to offer.'"

Anna relates many of her doubts to being a black person, particularly a black woman, in a predominantly white community. One of the problems, she says, "is being everybody's token. Every day I just get surprised that so many white people know my name that I don't even know. They just come up to me, 'Well, Anna, I think you should. . .'

And I'm looking at them, well, who are they? How do they know my name?"

At the end of her third semester at Union, Anna speaks of her summer project, which was a study of black women in ministry. She stayed in New York and worked with her theology tutor on the project and seems fairly pleased with the study, which she hopes to see finished during the current semester.

In her search for a greater sense of connection with the city, Anna has also found a new church, Convent Avenue Baptist Church, which is one of the prominent black Baptist congregations in the city. Although it is not part of her official fieldwork, she now has a position on the church's staff. She was recommended by another Union student who was leaving the church, so she "went and talked to the pastor. He told me that I could start, you know, working there on the staff of ministers, so that's what I've been doing this semester, and it's really been a great help in terms of experience."

Aside from that and a minimal involvement with Union's Black Caucus, she is focusing primarily on her school work, taking a course on black music and folklore, a course on women in American church history, a course on education in the church, and another on depth psychology. She was surprised that the psychology course was not pastorally oriented, but has enjoyed it nonetheless. On the other hand, she continues to struggle with a sense of isolation, which she describes in her reaction to the course on women in American church history.

"Whenever I'm the only black student in the class," she says, "especially in a small situation like that, dealing with women, I think I'm always on the defensive. Because I always realize, at least at Union, how they treat you when you're in those kinds of situations, and my suspicions were all true. I just felt very uncomfortable in there, like a novelty." She then comments, "I noticed that we were not talking about black women at all until the end. And then there was a special section on minority women, and every person in the class was expected to do an oral presentation on one of the topics in the syllabus, and of course, everybody else picked what they were going to do, so I got black women in the church, which, you know, wasn't bad for me, because that's the only thing I'm interested in anyway. But I felt that in order for me to discuss a topic like that, of black women in the church, I had to have a certain level of trust. And I feel that at Union, they always want you to reveal yourself without gaining the trust, and I just have a hard time opening up to people that I really don't trust."

When asked about her future plans, her tone turns more positive, and she discusses the possibility of working on a Ph.D. and perhaps entering pastoral counseling, although she definitely intends to be ordained in the American Baptist Church as soon as she graduates.

However, her tone turns sharply negative again when she begins discussing a faculty search committee on which she has served and that, as she says, "caused me all kinds of hell and really just messed up my total image of the people here at Union. I was put on the theological search committee, which I applied for late because I didn't even realize last year that they were looking. . . . I talked to . . . [another student] and some people on the appointments committee about it, and they were very happy that a black woman would apply and all this stuff. And then, after the committee was chosen, I later find out that they're unhappy about the fact that I was chosen. They really wanted the other two people on the committee because they could work together. . . . And people thought that I was too, that I would get overwhelmed by the males on the committee and that I wasn't feminist enough, really, is what I was hearing. . . .

"Immediately I was just definitely down on all white women at Union, because that's what I saw it as, the white feminist group. It . . . went so far as they had been meeting with Shriver to tell Shriver how it was with this person. They had one black person whom they had gotten to meet with them, a guy, and he said he wasn't aware of what all was going on. He got in the meeting with Shriver, and he told me that they started talking about me: 'And Anna's not this and she's not a feminist, and we want this and blah, blah, blah.' And he said that that's when he finally realized what was going on, and he stood up and told Shriver that he didn't want to be a part of this. He wasn't aware that they were trying to kick me off or that they weren't satisfied with me. And it just makes me think that there's a group of women on campus who are very hostile. If they don't think you're feminist, then they don't want anything to do with you. It has built up a great mistrust for me of white women, and I really have to work through that, but I don't think they did anything to help."

She then begins to speak about the lack of black women at Union, but adds, "Do you really want black women to come into this kind of situation? Would I really want to put another black woman through this? And I really haven't worked that out in my mind yet."

Anna's tone following her fourth semester at Union is far less negative than her tone following her third semester. She begins by complimenting the excellence of some of her courses, especially biblical and theological courses, but then goes on to criticize the lack of practical training at the seminary. "I don't think that there's a basic thrust at Union for pastoral, parish work."

When asked about her thesis topic, she says, "I'm going to do it in the theological field, preferably something on feminist theology in terms of black women." Expanding on this topic that seems to elicit such paradoxical responses from her, she says, "I think that feminist theology has become such a big thing now, and all the conferences and things that I've been to have always criticized the black woman for not really getting involved in the feminist, you know, struggle." She even suggests that she might "go into a Ph.D. program in that area—if I go into a Ph.D. program."

She talks of getting more involved with her new church, working with the new members committee and the sick and shut-in committee and teaching a course for children. At the same time she is continuing to disengage from Union: "I was becoming disenchanted with Union. I felt that the less I had to do with it, other than taking classes, the better off I would feel about it." Nevertheless, she says, "I don't regret coming to Union. . . . I think that I have become a much more mature person as a result of what's happened to me here, not necessarily in just the classes but in dealing with the politics here and just the whole thing of living alone in New York. The whole thing has been one of growth to me, and I don't think that I've gone backwards. Even though I might be disenchanted with some things, I think they all have virtually helped me in making a better person of me."

More specifically, she says, "I think the Black Caucus has been, even though there's been a lot of disappointments, it's helped me a lot. The whole idea of interaction and dealing with the brothers has

been very good for me, even though it hasn't always been positive.
. . . Also, I think that the experience of dealing with white women
here has been interesting, and I think that it's enlightened me a lot.
Whereas, I was really blind and had heard things, now I can say from
experience I know this and this. And I also realize that, you know,
you just can't group them all in one group and leave them there. I
love the courses here. I really have enjoyed my courses. That's one
complaint I haven't had. And I have really appreciated the black faculty that's here. And they've probably been the best thing to me."

Anna acknowledges that feminist perspectives and theology have
been a powerful influence on her. "I have learned through my experiences, here at Union, that I, as a woman, am worth something
and that I'm not, you know, I'm no longer satisfied with taking the
back seat of things." However, despite her words of appreciation for
feminism, Anna returns to speak about her distrust of white women.
She says, "I still think there's really no active dialogue that goes on
with black women and white women, and I don't know what the
real reason is. Perhaps we just can't get together. And I guess I feel
my hostility is probably really personal." She then goes on to say that
although she would like to have at least one woman reader for her
thesis, "I really can't think of any woman here on the faculty that I
would like to read."

She clearly prefers the counsel of the black professors, yet even
there she concludes that Union comes up short: "I've had disappointments, in terms of some Black professors, in that I think that,
well, we've discussed it. One thing that has happened this year is that
black faculty and students have really been very close this year, and
we've had a lot of dialogues at their houses and stuff. And one thing
that they keep stressing is that they really don't have the time to pastor to us, but you know, it's sort of an inevitable position that they're
put in, and that's really been a problem for me, because I think of
all the problems that Black students have had, that they really need
somebody to talk to. And I've had a lot of friends here who've almost
been on the brink of going off, because there's nobody here that really has the time."

Thus Anna ends her second year at Union feeling that she has
grown personally and academically but in many other ways feeling

disappointed in the school and distressed about her relationships with many students and faculty.

Sarah

During her second semester at Union, Sarah finds herself becoming far more acclimated to the seminary and the New York experience than she had expected, saying, "To think that I would actually feel at home in New York City, I guess that's a little astonishing." Although she is making more friends, she continues to complain about the lack of community at Union. She would like to see Union, for instance, provide "more ways that people would interact more freely. Oh, and another thing, have more encouragement of faculty interaction with students on other than a classroom level."

Sarah offers an even more specific example of missing community in the communion service at the seminary. The service lacks the kind of close relationships that characterize her memories of Brethren celebrations of the Eucharist. Holding a communion service without a connection to such Brethren traditions as the Love Feast and feet washing makes it seem a tepid event.

She doesn't care much for the practical theology course she had enrolled in, but she enjoys her fieldwork with the American Friends Service Committee, dealing particularly with "the issue of battered women."

Despite growing more comfortable with New York and Union, Sarah indicates her intention of spending the next fall semester at Bethany Theological Seminary in Chicago (a school affiliated with Sarah's own Church of the Brethren), but when fall semester rolls around, Sarah is back at Union. She had spent the summer doing ministry with a Pennsylvania congregation she had not visited before.

As she says, "It had its good points and its bad points. But in June it seemed to have more bad points than good. . . . It was terribly unsettling for me to go to a place where I knew no one. Standing up in a congregation where I knew no one and living in an apartment all by myself was something I'd never done before, and I don't care to do it again. I mean, it's one thing to live like in a university or whatever community by yourself . . . rather than going to a community . . .

where everyone already has their group set and you're coming in as an outsider."

The experience has left her feeling unsettled enough that she is starting to question her desire to enter parish ministry. Further, it discouraged her from following through on her plan to attend Bethany for a semester or two. After all, such a plan would have required her to uproot herself again and go to another new and potentially isolating environment in Chicago. Besides, she has a particular young man at Union that she wanted to come back to. By returning to Union, she says, "I felt like I was coming home. Yes, it was a release to get away from what I felt were negative pressures in the summer." During her summer ministry, she felt that she could not "express feelings of exactly how I felt about things and beliefs and stuff, rather than have to think, 'Well, I'd better not say this because actually it will sound a little bit too radical, and I might get this person upset and that person upset.' That was a pressure that I felt over the summer, that I couldn't quite be totally honest about how I felt about everything." Besides, she says, New York "has unlimited opportunities. . . . I mean, as far as fieldwork."

After the summer's unhappy experience with parish ministry, she wonders whether she might be more inclined toward work on a Ph.D. and teaching or perhaps doing agency work, such as "some organization for prison reform or maybe even an organization dealing with battered women, similar to the work I did last year." These doubts about parish ministry and inclination toward agency work will continue off and on throughout her tenure at Union, though she will end up going into parish work immediately after graduation.

In spite of the openness she has experienced at Union, Sarah worries, "about the apparent reactionary feelings about feminism. There's a lot of negative feelings." She is upset by a fellow student "calling feminists a hatchet group" and adds, "It's really kind of sad, for me at least it is, that that is happening here, because I know that happens at home in conservative, rural Pennsylvania. But to have this nasty attitude towards feminism here at Union Seminary is sad." Her concern about a conservative turn at Union will continue throughout her stay. Nevertheless, she enjoys most of her courses—although the workload seems at times overwhelming—and she even begins to appreciate the course on practical theology.

At the end of her fourth semester she mentions that she has grown in confidence, although when pressed for a reason for the growth she says, "I don't know what's behind it. I guess being here longer. I talk more in seminars this year than I did last year." She also asserts that she would like to see Union put more emphasis on personal growth, but once again, when pressed for a more detailed explanation, she has few specific recommendations to offer. She does, however, relate her personal growth to feminism and again asserts, "I have kind of felt this kind of conservative trend around here. It has really bothered me. . . . I've had some really rotten encounters. You know, I just couldn't believe that a student here at Union would not have a better understanding of sexism than they did." She then identifies a particular male student "who perhaps for me epitomizes sexism around here" and also a female, "a new student this year who claims to be a feminist but exemplifies so much of what I consider sexism. She falls right into the trap of playing the cute little doll, sex object, that for me is sexism. She plays right into that and plays it to the hilt but yet claims to be a feminist, and that just irritates me."

Sarah's response to the issues swirling around her is personally involving. She does not take much time to reflect in a sustained way on her experiences, but she knows how she feels about them. The feminist issues become a way of bringing together many of Sarah's longstanding questions about her church, her family, and herself. In fact, she indicates that she is planning to do a thesis on a history of women in her hometown congregation. She also indicates in passing that she began therapy in the fall and discusses her feelings about the experience:

"I like more reciprocity in relationships, and it's just so strange to me to have somebody sit there and listen and not be listening to them in return. So it's very strange for me. Plus I'm not accustomed to spending money like that." But then she adds, "It's probably given me a little more courage about certain things," such as helping her express anger when appropriate.

While obviously more at ease in the cultural and academic milieu of Union than are Chris or Anna, Sarah sometimes finds it difficult to articulate the exact reasons for both her negative and positive responses toward Union.

Ruth

Ruth ends her first year at Union trying to resolve an issue that she will struggle with for years to come—that of being a black woman trying to enter ministry in a predominantly white denomination. As she says, "I've been looking at leadership within the Lutheran church, in terms of black people. There's not that much." Further, she's been told that "a lot of times when black people go through the Lutheran system, in terms of being ordained, that they come out with a messed up mind. Whereas they may have had certain dreams for black folks in the beginning, that has changed. It's made me think about if that could happen to me. Am I willing to take that kind of risk? If that is what happens in that process, do black people need to be involved in the Lutheran church at all? Maybe we need to try to come out of that and come into something that's our own. . . . That's constantly there in my mind as I'm going through, step by step, but I don't feel at a point right now where I want to forget about the Lutheran church.

"I've been talking to some of the black leaders, people that are working in the national offices. If anything, some of the people in the national part of it haven't offered the kind of support that I thought I would get by being here at Union. From one man in particular, he felt that 'you should be in a Lutheran seminary.' That's what they want you to do, go through that system. He really didn't understand why I might want to be at a place like this."

Not going to a Lutheran seminary will remain a sticking point between Ruth and the Lutheran church for the next several years. But when she is asked why she has decided to continue at Union rather than switch to a Lutheran seminary, she offers a number of defensible reasons, including the school's location on the East Coast in New York City, the opportunities for ministries in urban churches, courses at the seminary that raise important issues such as women in ministry, especially black women in ministry, and the presence of such diverse groups as the Gay Caucus. Moreover, she likes the way in which students have a voice about what goes on at the school. She doubts she would find these things at other seminaries.

However, she feels that Union is not a "place of fellowship, where you feel like you can come to worship as well. That I don't feel here. I don't see it at all. In terms of my spiritual life being nourished in that sense—worship and fellowship—that I don't get here at all." And while she certainly appreciates Union's commitment to diversity, she worries that "in the midst of so much diversity" there are "so many things that pull you." It seems to her that such diversity makes it hard to "hold all of what you are together."

This worry leads to concerns about a lack of community at Union, although she admits that part of the problem is the fact that she is a commuter who does not live on campus. Further, she does not seek involvement in Union's many committees but would rather find community through her fieldwork at her home church, among, as she says, "people that are struggling."

When asked how she might reflect in later years on her first two semesters at Union, she says, "I guess it's been a year of many questions, deep soul searching, and trying to be honest with myself about who I am and what I can and can't do, how I, as an individual, am functioning in terms of the gospel." When asked about specific occurrences that have caused her to reflect, Ruth refers to "a talk I had with a brother on campus where he told me that he didn't feel that I should be considering ministry at all, because I was a woman. It was the first time that it hit me and shook me. That was one thing. Another would be a talk that I had with my fellow students about coming from a Lutheran background and not understanding certain things about black church people, feeling that because of that I was funny. . . . The conference that I went to in the fall on black women in the ministry began to cause some things to formulate, some questions to rise." Finally, she refers to an incident at her home church. "We had been doing some very shaky planning for a Christian ed program, and the day came for it to open, and hardly [any] of the kids came. Having to sit down that day and realize, okay, you might see certain things that you feel people need or that should be done, but if the people are not seeing or feeling that need, then you're wrong. Maybe you're wasting a lot of energy and time."

All of these things leave her wondering about her vocation.

"I'm still pulling some things together. It's still not clear. I don't know how it's going to be for me. . . . I don't get from Union any model of what the minister should be."

Despite these doubts, Ruth returns for a third semester at Union and, in her December 1977 interview, she is glad she has remained at Union and will spend the academic year at the seminary rather than going to one of the Lutheran schools she had considered. When asked what she sees herself doing after graduation, Ruth speaks of being a pastor, perhaps in New York, but almost certainly on the East Coast, "working with the congregation of people." But when she is asked if she foresees herself as an ordained minister with a parish church, she says, "Can I have another possibility?" It turns out that she is still holding on to the thought of returning to teaching in elementary school, the job that she had and loved before entering seminary.

She then begins to express doubts about her vocation and worries that she might not have the emotional strength to persevere in ministry:

"One thing is realizing how much right now, in terms of the work that I'm doing, I need support and sometimes not seeing that in the future, not seeing, you know, marriage in the future, not seeing the people that I'm around, being there in the future and wondering, you know, will I be able to make it, will new areas of support come up that will really nourish? I don't know. . . . Will I ever, do I have the skills to really make that be? I know it's a gift, but to be able to taste it."

As her fourth semester at Union ends, Ruth seems open to the idea of attending a Lutheran seminary. "I don't know where yet. But I guess I've gotten hooked up with one of the Lutheran seminaries out in Berkeley, California." Her intention is to do a year's internship and then "in September '79, spend a year out there." Yet she continues to resist, even resent, having to fit Lutheran requirements. "I've been struggling with that a little bit, because . . . they're saying now that it's required, that you have to do it that way, and I guess part of me just doesn't want to let them say that to me. . . . I feel like they need me, and part of me just doesn't want . . . to be their little nigger. Do you know what I mean? Do what they say and stuff and just invalidate what I feel has been good preparation for me, for the ministry and so forth."

When asked why she continues to commit herself to the Lutheran tradition, she says, "I feel a need for black ministers in the ALC [American Lutheran Church] for black congregations and because I believe that Lutheranism, with the ideas of grace and all that, not necessarily Norwegian or German culture or whatever, that it can be understood in the black tradition or Hispanic. And all the cultural things that come from our people can be used to express that same idea during the worship."

When talk turns to Union, she voices concerns about the lack of practical training offered by the seminary. Aside from actual pastoral work, she feels that she needs to learn organizational skills and bookkeeping skills, such as "how do you deal with a church budget?"

While she continues to praise the "diversity of the community" at Union—"it's been vibrant here"—she also asserts that her work at her church feels more significant to her than her studies at Union. Yet she also admits feeling very inadequate in certain aspects of her church work. "It's like, just yesterday, I was, for the first time the only minister at church and had to lead worship and just do everything, and I was so scared." When assured that she probably did quite well, she responds with a glum, "Yeah, it was alright." Then she adds. "I don't like planning sermons. I don't like getting up in front of people. And maybe it's because my time is so pulled. I don't have time to sit down and really reflect upon, you know, usually I leave it until the last minute and stuff. I don't know. Maybe because it takes a lot out of me, too. I just really don't, I struggle with it a lot. I wish it was something that I didn't have to do. And I guess I don't feel like I do it well. Some people, you see, they're so vibrant and they know how to give examples and stuff, and I just feel like, you know ..."

Here she stops, and when asked to make some final comment about Union, her response is filled with emotion: "What is here in this building, you know, these courses, degrees, all that stuff, don't mean a thing when you get down to it, if you don't have some kind of awareness of how to just—I don't know how to say it—be down with just everyday folks, that being here in these walls and stuff don't make one bit of difference if that is not a part of your life as well. I don't care whether you're teaching or what, because you teaching isn't going to mean a thing . . . or be worth anything unless you've either taken some time to do that, be involved with, you know, just some down folk, or constantly do that along with your work. I guess that's what I feel like. People at my church, in a community like that, you know, they don't give two cents about some of the stuff that happens here, and if you're talking about ministering to people like that, then you need to be finding out . . . what are folks, you know, struggling with."

So Ruth, a young black woman, committed to helping her people, serving God, and exploring ministry within the white-majority Lutheran church, reaches the end of her second and perhaps final year at Union in a state of profound uncertainty. It is a condition that will continue far longer than anyone might have expected.

Tim

At the end of his second semester at Union, Tim is articulate and confident. His general tone is that of a young man who feels certain of the possibilities that lie before him and sure of his ability to seize whatever opportunities present themselves.

Like other students he complains that at Union "there's not enough emphasis on the practical." But he gives this complaint a different twist by pointing out the amount of effort he is putting into his fieldwork, both during the academic year and during the summer break: "I'm going to be working at the church again next year the same amount of time and really putting exactly as much work as I am right now, and yet I'm going to get at least two points less credit for it next year. That just doesn't even make sense to me. I don't understand. I think it's ridiculous. I think also, in a situation in which I'm going to be the minister of a major church for the whole summer, putting in at least 40 hours a week, I ought to be able to get more than two points of academic credit."

In fact, the church's minister is taking a six-month sabbatical and has asked Tim to take over during his absence. This is both a flattering and an intimidating situation, for Tim feels that he is still navigating the early passages of his own religious journey. For example, he continues to be troubled by Union's exclusive attachment to Christianity, even though he knows that it is a Christian seminary. As a curious, idealistic young man of the 1970s, Tim craves opportunities to explore all spiritual traditions and is disappointed that Union does not provide such opportunities:

In the spring of 1977 he comments, "I find the seminary to be, in terms of worship, a very uninteresting place for me. I learn a lot from it, but I find it to be very, very unhelpful for anyone who deviates from the particular Christian emphasis. That's not necessarily wrong. I mean, it's a Christian seminary. But I find that difficult. I also find that, academically, it is a very Christian-oriented place. I find myself very frustrated sometimes, trying to do research for other possibilities, other answers, which just don't occur to people."

Despite these and other criticisms, Tim continues to be positive about Union and his commitment to parish ministry.

As he concludes his third semester at Union (December 1977), Tim offers a glimpse into the energetic and multifaceted life he is currently living.

Besides his load of courses at Union and the course on Jewish history that he is taking at the Jewish Theological Seminary (JTS), he is also working about fifteen hours a week at his church, and he is working two part-time jobs. "I have switchboard at Van Dusen, and I work at the Pub on Thursday nights. . . . It really cuts into my studies heavily. For example, I work at the Pub Thursday night from 8 till 1, 1:30 sometimes, and I have the JTS class at 8:30." He needs the work, as do many other students, to help pay expenses, but he also seems to enjoy a life filled with action. He usually plays rugby on top of his other activities: "I've played rugby, I think, ten years. And I am terrifically fond of this particular team that I've been playing with." But "this year I have not been playing, because I just simply cannot handle it this year. And the reason for that is the fact that my girlfriend is now in the East. She was in California, and now she's in Pennsylvania [at Swarthmore]. That's another, obviously, very important aspect of my life. And it was a choice between her and rugby, and it was my girlfriend."

In the midst of all these activities, Tim appears to be easily handling his courses and continuing to question the limitations of traditional Christian views: "What I've found among an awful lot of
students, which is very hard to describe, is two things: one is that
they tend not to question their own assumptions and they also tend
not to try to listen to other people's faith or what they're about. . . .
A lot of people tend to be rather exclusive in their religious beliefs."
He goes on to complain that "our discussions here tend to talk about
theological issues of judgment, righteousness, and a lot of things
which are all very, very good, but they don't seem to talk too much
about the human realities of weakness or about pain, of guilt and depression. They seem in a way to deal with people on a very superficial
level." When asked why he thinks this to be so, Tim says, "I think it's
because most people don't try to understand what other people are
talking about and what their faith is, what's their stand. They don't
put themselves in the other person's place."

When asked about his future goals, he says that he sees himself
"in the church, as a parish minister, yes, probably an urban church.
That seems to be the flow of where I'm going at the moment. And
involved with largely a traditional parish ministry with emphasis on
preaching, counseling, community action, those three things."

Despite his willingness to question theological orthodoxies and
explore other faith traditions, Tim never seems to doubt his commitment to traditional parish ministry, saying at one point, "That's
not a question for me. . . . I'm going to be a parish minister." He does
not anticipate that the model of the minister as teacher and seeker
is already growing less tenable in the popular culture of the church.

In the interview following his fourth semester, Tim discusses his
planned thesis on Sophia Fahs, an important Unitarian Universalist
figure, which sounds like it will be a good fit for him, but the project
eventually falls through, and he switches in his sixth semester to a
nineteenth-century female leader, Margaret Fuller.

He also talks extensively about the tensions he perceives between
feminists and traditionally oriented male students on campus and
offers some specific examples: "There have been several incidents
which have sort of set me to thinking but nothing terribly significant.
One small incident has caused me a great deal of thought, which was,

I'd noticed that in the elevators in Hastings Hall somebody, several somebodies, had been consistently defacing any sign that was put up by the Women's Center, and it was getting . . . to be really gross stuff. So I put up a sign saying please don't do this. We don't appreciate it. . . . And invited other men to sign my sign. Well, eighteen men did sign it. That sign within four or five hours was torn down, and so I put up another sign suggesting that I could put up signs as long as they wished to tear them down. And so I went up there, and some more men signed it, and then it was defaced. I left it up there for a day or so. It all happened within about forty-eight hours.

"The person who tore the sign down was sort of feeling bad about it and came to me and confessed about it and said he had not been the person who had defaced the signs but had gotten angry at my sign. And I had always had a feeling that this person smiled too much, but there was something behind that he just wasn't getting out in the open, and that kind of indicated to me that I was right, because it just takes a whole lot of anger to suddenly just feel the necessity to tear something down and run off. But I believed him that he hadn't been the one defacing the signs.

"So the second sign got defaced. It was up there for a while, and then I came in one day and both signs were torn down. It had been up about forty-eight hours total. And there was a sign in their place from someone in the Women's Center. And it was a really snotty sign, asking us to please stop our childish game. And that really annoyed me. That was uncalled for. If they had wished to be constructive, they could have been constructive. That was not constructive. And it sort of made me realize that on both sides, the side of the men and the side of the women, there is such an underlying edge of bitterness and anger, such an enormous chip on the shoulder of so many in the seminary. It really shocked me. . . . There's a sort of ragged sourness in those people."

When asked to describe possible reasons for the conflict between the men and the women at Union, Tim offers the following explanation: "This is a very general, wild guess. I don't have any evidence for it. I suspect the place is kind of unique in one sense in that it is both within the pale of orthodox Christianity and yet it's right on the edge, so that it attracts both the speculation and rebelliousness of people coming from the background of traditional Christianity and people coming from other directions, which makes a very varied community. There's a lot of pressure on people I think to come up with their own theology. People feel a lot of pressure. There isn't a focus to the community in the way of theology. . . . I'm not saying there should be either. I'm just saying that there isn't. And it is an additional pressure on people. A lot of people bring with them certain kinds of ambivalence about their own past—maybe one reason why they want to go to a place that is neither totally orthodox nor broken from it. . . . It's just a feeling that we attract an awful lot of people who don't fit into a single mold, who are in a sense rebelling against that mold. . . . They don't yet have a personal statement which would either find them inside or outside."

As have several other students, Tim perceives that one of Union's strengths, its openness to diversity, which means being willing to tolerate an extreme range of views, is also one of its weaknesses. Being one of the more liberal students, however, Tim seems to prefer Union's openness to any change that might lead to a more cohesive though limited institutional identity.

By the end of their fourth semester, most of the students are struggling with their vocational understanding and their relationship with Union. Several have found that Union's commitment to diversity has made it difficult to find a sense of community or theological coherence at the school. What they see are numerous sub-communities and caucuses that speak of some generic sense of community, but trying to designate where this ideal community might be found is seldom successful. They point to what they consider *laissez faire* attitudes regarding feminism and gay rights, and they view these as being in conflict with more traditional understandings of church and society. Others, however, appreciate greatly Union's experiment in diversity and its efforts to cultivate a sense of community made up of many different groups and points of view. Rather than seeing these diverse viewpoints as negative, they see them as positive expressions of the pluralistic world in which we live. They are willing to put up with the rough edges for the sake of the freedom of perspective and experience they value deeply.

Regardless of where they stand on this issue, all have searched for ways to allay their concerns, some by taking even greater advantage of the opportunities for diversity available at Union, participating passionately in the various causes and concerns that fill the school's hallways. Others have anchored their lives in their home churches or the churches in which they do their fieldwork. And a few simply focus on their academic work and avoid the rest of seminary life.

All contemplate their call to ministry with varying degrees of hesitancy and certainty. Few doubt that they are meant to enter the work of the church, but a few, like Ruth, still wonder whether parish ministry is the right vocation for them. They hope that their remaining time at Union will provide the experiences and insights they need to make the right choices.

The pressing issue of diversity is never really resolved. Dealing with the kind of diversity that is often reduced to a collection of groups is frustrating for those seeking something more than toleration. Their search for some common thread that will serve as a point of commonality is frequently a dead end. Retreat to one's own private community is one option, and the effort to impose a definition of diversity for everyone is another. Each of us tends to place limits on the diversity we seek or celebrate, often leaving out those with whom we disagree or frankly do not like.

For a school or a congregation, there comes a point at which the celebration of diversity needs some definition of what it means and how all voices may be heard and not just the ones we favor. Taking the tack of dealing with diversity as simply a matter of making room within existing structures never goes anywhere. Some institutions at this point simply pull back from including new groups into their midst. Many institutions, though, begin to realize that hospitality toward those we have seen as other than ourselves involves our own transformation, and this is never an easy thing to do. Expanding the cafeteria of possibilities—different options for worship, different courses of study, different forms of social life—only goes so far. If there is to be something more than just diversity for its own sake and we seek a truly participatory way of being, then the hard work of building that kind of institution has to be initiated and sustained over many years. If there is a motto for this kind of approach it is the one from Eugen Rosenstock-Huessy that I have often relied on: "I respond even though I will be changed."[2]

chapter 5

Reassessments and Moving On

I have a stronger sense of who I am and more self-confidence.
. . . I feel freer to move and feel better in myself, better in my
body, which affects my whole life. — SARAH

AFTER TWO YEARS AND FOUR SEMESTERS AT UNION, ALL OF THE students are thinking about what lies ahead. They are looking at what shape ministry might take in their lives after graduation. The questions and issues moving through the seminary's life have receded as the students begin to reclaim the sense of calling that brought them to the school in the first place. Some are taking a year away from Union in ministry internships; others want to press on and complete their degree requirements in the coming year. All hope to resolve soon any uncertainty that remains regarding their calling and the work of ministry.

Anna

One student who remains in school is Anna. Even so, she asserts that the thing that is uppermost in her mind is "what I'm going to do when I graduate." She intends to graduate at the end of her third year at Union and be ordained during the summer in her father's Baptist church. Despite the fact that the black Baptist church is not particularly open to women ministers, she is determined to persevere in this denomination. As she says, "I've decided that if God called me to do something like this, then I'm going to do it."

As the chaplain of the Black Caucus, she was determined during the recently ended semester to "develop a more congenial relationship with . . . the black church community." So at her instigation, the caucus conducted a youth revival in various local black churches. Much of the organizational work fell to her, and she is especially proud that "we did have women preaching." Many of the congregants were surprised by the prominent role played by women, but they "seemed to respond favorably," and Anna "got a lot of good comments on it. At least that was one of the things we wanted to make them aware of, of the women, and the other thing is that they realized that we were not so into academics that we could not relate to them."

During the revival, Anna found herself for the first time in a leadership role with men in ministry. In this regard, the revival "was a real learning experience to me, because it was my first time working in a powerful position over men. The hassle that I went through, you know, with the church, with the youth minister there, with the guys, just trying to get them to listen to me and get them to do what I wanted. . . . I don't think I was as forceful as I should be. But I know now what I have to do, which wasn't always clear to me in the beginning. I am more aware of the obstacles that are before me when I graduate, but I'm also more equipped to deal with it now than I was when I first came here."

In this sense, Anna believes that Union has helped her grow as a person. "When I came here, I was basically naive and shy. . . . My four years at Spelman were really a very sheltering experience." So her time at Union has opened her up to a more complicated view of the world around her.

Similarly, she feels that her work at her fieldwork church has given her some needed exposure, but she then complains that "things at the church are just kind of stale right now." A new young minister has been added to the staff—"a favorite son of the church, very popular, you know"—and she feels that he and a new female minister have supplanted her at the church and reduced her opportunities to participate. Therefore, she has spent time preaching in other churches, if only to have opportunities to practice her skills. Nevertheless, she continues to foresee difficulties in finding a position as a minister. As she says, "I preached this past Sunday, and I was telling them that this is my last year, and people have come up to me and asked, 'Well, what are you going to do? Do you really want to pastor? Is that what you want, really? I thought you were just working here, you know.' And I realize that even with the deacons that I go visiting the sick with, they question me, and . . . they haven't the faintest idea what I'm really doing."

Despite the sense of resolution on issues that have bothered her and insights she believes she has achieved, Anna remains ambivalent about many of the experiences she has been exposed to. For instance, when some of the women in the Black Caucus decide that the men in the caucus are not being responsive to the needs of women and decide to split off into their own caucus, Anna does not join them.

"I was called the traitor, because I was being with the Black Caucus and going, so I decided to quit altogether. . . . I couldn't walk through the halls without somebody rolling their eyes."

When asked about her experiences interacting with white students at Union, she confesses that she has not had much contact with them. "In fact," she says, "I think that this year has probably been the first year that I ever really spent any time, and that was through . . . [the] class in parables." During this course, the students were divided into groups and asked to produce skits (or exegesis presentations) that personified various parables. According to Anna, the process "forced us to get together, and we really got a chance to talk and argue about what we believed and what we didn't. And it was really my first chance to get to know people that I'd seen for three years."

When asked to characterize her response to the experience, she says, "It's been alright. It's been good. I just see the white students of my group that were in that class as being, well, I'm not sure that they're Christians, you know. I mean, I always feel like I'm the only Christian in the group when I get in with them, because . . . they don't want to moralize about the gospel, and we have to argue about what the parable means. By the time they get through with it, it's all, you know. . . . Maybe I'm just too fundamental. . . . One time, one of the groups did a skit about Jesus being one who associated with all the outcasts—the outcasts being homosexuals. . . . When they got through there, they asked who had problems with it, and I told them that I did, because even though Jesus associated with the people who were outcasts, Jesus didn't condone what they were doing. He always told them 'Go and sin no more.' He made them aware of what they were doing. . . . Most of the white students in the class don't like to get into that. They don't like to moralize or judge."

She concludes, however, that she "really enjoyed getting to know the people. I really did. I thought that was good. And now, when we speak, it's different."

When asked why she is on track to graduate in three years when many other students require four or five, Anna acknowledges that it has been difficult to maintain her schedule, pointing out that she is taking five courses this semester while also beginning to write a thesis. But then she adds that "the other reason I'm graduating is I do not have the money to stay here another year. . . . I think that most of the other black students in my class are trying to, because we all know that we don't have the money to stay here."

Financial pressures are a reality for all of the students, but they are especially critical for the black students. Even though Union was relatively generous in its financial aid policies, over the years, because of institutional fiscal constraints, it had to cut back in the amount of aid it could provide students. Because many African American and other minority students generally came to seminary with minimal financial resources, they felt the cutbacks more acutely.

At the end of her sixth semester and third year at Union, Anna has remained true to her plan. She has completed her thesis and is now looking for a position, either as "an assistant in a church, particularly a Baptist church, or some kind of chaplaincy in a school or a teaching position." She also speaks periodically about doing counseling, or more specifically, marriage counseling.

She has applied for numerous positions, and through the influence of Gardner Taylor, the civil rights leader and pastor of Concord Baptist Church of Christ in Brooklyn, Anna has received more than twenty letters of interest. She has also been on three interviews: one in Indianapolis, another in Boston, and a third in White Plains, New York. The pastor at her fieldwork church, however, "has been very quiet through the whole process. He has said very little and has helped me none at all. And I had gotten to where I was very upset about it." Then, on a recent Sunday morning, "he stood up in the congregation and told the people that I was graduating. 'We need to pray for her, and I have one request that you pray, that if it is the Lord's will that Anna remain with us next year . . . we hire her as full-time.' I almost fell out, because he's let me do all this work, go through all this, and has said nothing."

Nevertheless, as Anna points out, her church "is a very good church and a very established church and has given me a lot of exposure being there. I'm getting to the point now where I know the church now and could possibly do some things in it." So she is certainly giving the fieldwork church serious consideration, even though she believes that the minister there has not been as supportive as he should have been.

She has also been asked to speak at Union's upcoming alumni/ae banquet and describe her experiences at the school. While putting together her notes, she confesses that "I have been very detached from the community a lot, and even the black community. . . . I was chaplain of the Black Caucus, and that's literally what I did." Rather than being deeply involved in the Union community, she feels that she has focused more on ministry.

"I spent a lot of time in the churches. . . . And I preached more than ever. I have been preaching like maybe three Sundays out of a month. . . . In fact, in April, I was in Indianapolis the first Sunday; I was in Montego Bay, Jamaica, where I preached there on Easter for a week, and then the next week I was in Boston, and the next week I was somewhere else. . . . I had a lot more preaching opportunities this year, which I guess I should be thankful for."

Yet she insists that Union has provided her with a "very good background in Bible" and valuable introductions to various aspects of theology, including liberation theology and black theology. "But I think the one that has made a definite impression upon me is probably feminist theology, which I think . . . since I discovered it here, I spent my whole time here either reacting to or against it."

Anna continues to express herself as someone who has learned despite her resistance to ideas that threaten her sense of how the world is or should be. While feminism has opened her mind and sharpened her perceptions of society, she still questions its applicability to her and other black women. She expresses the hope that black women will begin to put their own stamp on feminist thought and theory.

As if defining her relationship to the ideological and social movements surrounding her at Union and her unwillingness to commit wholeheartedly to any of them, Anna asserts, "I guess I joined my own movement."

She completes her final interview at Union on perhaps a slightly rueful note, acknowledging that perhaps she has held herself aloof from other people at Union and missed out on possible connections and opportunities. While she has made friends and had valuable experiences with other black students and with black professors, she expresses disappointment that it was not until her final semesters at Union, as she was writing her thesis, that she began getting to know some of the white students in the community and actually sitting up at night talking with people on her hallway. She explains, "A lot of people I never thought knew I existed started talking to me. 'Are you graduating? What are you doing?' And it seemed to be that, even though I have not been really that close to them, at least I felt they had definitely made an impression on me, and I guess I made one on them. And then the fact that I was asked to speak at the alumni banquet, . . . I did not expect that at all. I was like, 'What? Me? Are you sure?' That really surprised me, because . . . I just didn't think that would happen."

David

Unlike Anna, David will not complete his degree at the end of six semesters at Union. In fact, it is in the midst of his sixth semester, spring 1979, that David shares the extent of his academic struggles, particularly his difficulty completing written assignments or expressing himself adequately through the written word. He reveals that he dropped one course, because he did not write the required research paper, despite the fact that he had attended every class. He was able to complete another course, because the professor was willing to help him "struggle through my problems in understanding the exegetical methods." These are the same exegetical methods that he had previously insisted he had learned in college. At this point, David begins to realize that the work he had done in college, while preparatory, was not equivalent to the work he is expected to do at Union. He mentions, for example, that he has difficulty separating opinion from critical analysis.

For the rest of this interview, David seems uncharacteristically subdued. It is almost as if he confronts for the first time the gulf that exists between his expectations for theological study and what the school itself actually stands for. In this regard, he speaks of becoming less interested in education as he becomes more involved in his denomination.

"It's still one of the top priorities," he says, "but my involvement with the denomination requires more of my time. Why I'm doing it is because I see a need of my presence in different areas to help my people, to be understood by my denomination. And the ministers that we have around are not ministers who are well equipped in the sense of understanding English well enough to dialogue with these people. A lot of them can't speak English at all. And those that could, unfortunately, do not have . . . the proper education to defend issues that can be brought up. And so, therefore, I find myself going to many meetings, trying to protect, if I may use the term, my people's needs."

Soon, however, his remarks express a sense of discouragement. He fears that he may not graduate and thereby fail to be the Hispanic example of achievement he believes he is expected to be.

"To quote one of my professors in my undergraduate days: 'You've got to remember that you are going to be a leader when you get out there.' And that has put a heavier burden on my shoulder."

Although David had originally endeavored to find a place for himself at Union, he now seems to have given up that struggle, having concluded that the seminary is not a place that recognizes his gifts in ministry and has, from his perspective, only passing interest in the practice of ministry itself. Moreover, David is now confronting head-on his difficulties with written English and written Spanish. What the public schools had deferred or ignored in his writing skills has placed an enormous burden on him as an adult, who is now held accountable for making up this long-term deficit. He is at times, as might be expected, perplexed and resentful, yet he does not consider

turning back. When discussing what he feels are the flaws in the re-
medial course in writing he is being required to take, David indicates
that the class makes him feel inferior: "I don't even write anymore.
I'm afraid to write. . . . I can't say English is my language, but I can't
say Spanish is either. . . . I don't know if I could even write again.
I can't even write a newsletter for my church in Spanish." Despite
these discouragements, he intends to move forward.

At the end of his seventh semester, David talks about his continuing work on the M.Div. degree. As always, he is as much involved
in outside activities as he is with course work. In fact, besides his
responsibilites as a pastor, he has also spent the past year being the
president of La Junta, the Hispanic association of Disciples of Christ
in the Northeast. Whatever his lack of academic skills might be, he
does not lack energy or determination. He intends to graduate at
the end of the academic year, taking four years rather than three to
graduate.

When asked about his response to Union, he is more critical than
in the past, although he focuses as usual on the lack of practical
courses on ministry and on the fact that his expectations of seminary have not been fulfilled by Union: "Let's put it that way. . . . I was
expecting Union to be more of a challenge and not in the academic
affairs but more in the practical affairs of the ministry, to force me
to see and seek the needs of those who are outside, the need of those
who I'm going to be administering to, instead of seeking and finding what my mentality can develop out of those rhetorical and logical people who have written books from centuries and centuries on.
. . . That is what I'm saying. I was expecting Union not only to get the
systematic theology but also to get a practical theology as well and
have those two gel together in such a way that it would launch me as
an individual and me as a pastor, and it didn't do that."

In his final interview, spring 1980, David offers a number of criticisms of Union, stressing once again the lack of outreach to Hispanics and the lack of practical training. He also says he feels isolated
from the institution, although he admits that working full time and
not living on campus make it hard to be involved. In many ways, he
has spent large portions of his life being an outsider, in some instances by choice, in others through circumstance. While some students

who share David's experience of being raised in Puerto Rico and New York City face similar language issues, other Hispanic students do not and are involved in the life of the school with more rewarding academic achievements even as they deal with the complexities of finding their way in the seminary's majority culture.

David concludes the interview by describing his upcoming marriage and plans for the future, including the possibility of being involved in theological education at some point.

Chris

Returning to Union after a year's internship in his hometown, Chris begins the interview following his fifth semester on several positive notes, evincing less of the weariness that seemed to dominate his outlook at the end of his fourth semester. As he has hoped it might be, his internship "was a renewal of roots after all. After some rough years up here, it was a very healthy year. It was a good year. . . . About 75 percent of the time was in campus ministry. . . . That was the main assignment, and that was basically what I was paid to do. But in addition to that I did about three afternoons a week of hospital visitation . . . , visiting Presbyterians who were from out of town in area hospitals. It was not CPE [clinical pastoral education]; it was not anything sophisticated. It was simply a one-time short visit. And then I would go back and visit people again if they were in the hospital for longer than a week. I would just make a Wednesday afternoon round of this specific hospital.

"Kind of an addition to this work for the . . . presbytery, was work that I did at a Presbyterian church on the weekends. I would go down there about every other weekend. I had no specific responsibilities other than to be an apprentice and get an exposure to the parish work and preaching and polity and program and all the things like that. . . .

"So it was an intern year that had kind of two poles. One was doing an urban campus ministry in a graduate setting of health, and the other was being an all around ministerial apprentice in a traditional, small-town, Southern congregation."

Chris then goes into a good bit of detail describing his internship, particularly his work at the ecumenical campus center, which had been completed in 1970. According to Chris, the center had languished during the intervening years, and he now takes great pride in his role in bringing the center back to life.

"It was successful partially because I was so young. I was the age of these students. Three or four of them I had gone to high school with, and I think just having somebody young there in ministry. . . . We offered them programs that were general in nature and that I think related to some kind of humanistic, sometimes even religious level, to their tense technological scientific orientation that they have at medical school. . . . I think we just created an hour break for them in the midst of their demanding and dehumanizing education."

Certainly Chris's commitment to ministry was reaffirmed by the experience: "I have always had the feeling that if you go in and do a good job, a competent job of developing programs that meet the concerns that people have, . . . the people will respond. And they did. You know, it was just phenomenal the amount of response we got. . . . The fact that I went down there and just had that kind of good old institutional success, I mean, the way we define success, in terms of numbers of bodies in the building, people coming to the programs, people I got to know, to meet with, even on a deeper level than sponsoring a program, all those things, reaffirmed in me that, even in today's world, that can be done, that the ministry and Protestantism does not have to be something that is auxiliary or secondary or on the fringe of society. I had kind of a whole other theological rejuvenation of the desire to relate the gospel to what I call the mainstream of the center of life, to people's vocations to their responsibilities, to what Bonhoeffer calls their successes.

He then goes on to assess his year spent back in the South in comparison to the time he has spent in New York: "I had grown up in this kind of Southern nurture of the church that's kind of a churchly society. . . . Even though it was not an oppressive, fundamentalist type of society, but it was still a church way of society. And of course, up here it is not. So I was interested to go back there after having lived in this kind of society. And I found that it was refreshing to get back to that, and then in a lot of ways, having been up here, I found a lot of things about that churchliness that I didn't like—some of the . . . easy luxury in which the church exists down there. They can fight over the most mundane and picayune kinds of things. You know the presbytery had a $300,000 budget surplus last year. I mean the church still has so much momentum down there. . . . I think ministers down there have no conception of . . . , say, the degree of disintegration in bourgeois traditional Christian morality. I don't think that they can conceive the fact that people in seminary live together, . . . the degree of divorce rate and the uncertainty of personal life up here, the intensity of feminism and gay rights and things like that. They're not so much opposed to it as that it's just beyond their experience."

When asked whether he would like to return to the South, he says, "I want to go back to what I would call a more normal, wholesome existence." He then affirms his previous opinion of Union.

"The quality of education that is offered here and what I would call the traditional theological disciplines in biblical studies, theology, and historical studies is excellent. . . . The rest of it I'm not so sure about. You know, I wish we could have that kind of education in a more productive environment, a more personal environment. You know, the other half of that is my resentment, which sometimes borders on bitterness, which did not abate down there [during the internship]. . . . The degree again of feminism and of gay rights and of liberation theology and . . . [the] kind of dug in and alienated urban environment that Union has . . . just seems so far removed for me from what about 95 percent of the people in this country go through. And I just, you know, it was kind of hard coming back, and I'm really tired of it now."

Thus, despite his positive experience of the previous year, he is already returning to his frustrated and disaffected attitude toward Union. He dislikes what he calls the culture of alienation among the students. He recognizes that some students have legitimate, historical reasons for feeling alienated, but many others, he believes, do not. These thoughts bring him, once again, to question his decision to attend Union.

"Yale is really where I should have gone. I think I realized that the first year I was here. I could have gotten in there, and I turned Yale down to come here. And why I did that I'll never know, other than I think there was something romantic . . . to want to be in the city. But that excitement just wore out pretty quick."

He then offers a list of ways to improve Union, a list that reflects—less in its elements than its implications—his generally conservative attitude toward theological education. He wants more classically oriented professors, he wants to reinstate a system of grades, and, as he says, "We have got to get better students, . . . who are more committed . . . to an academic model than a therapeutic model of learning. . . . I don't know if those kinds of students, the kind of student who is committed to the institutional church in America and to preaching and to theological dialogue within the church. . . but wants to come to an ecumenical environment and get the best education, I don't know if they are around." He then adds, "That's why I feel like such a minority."

In his final interview at the end of his sixth semester (spring 1980), Chris once again begins on an upbeat note, talking about his thesis on Karl Barth and Dietrich Bonhoeffer and his upcoming job as an associate minister at a Presbyterian church in the Southwest. He will join two other ministers at the church and will be doing youth ministry and some campus ministry at the local state university. He will also have the opportunity, he believes, to "preach like fifteen or twenty sermons a year, which is good for a third person on the ladder."

When asked, however, to reflect on the person he was upon entering Union and the person he is today, his thoughts take on a harsher tone. He says that he has become "a lot more hardened person," although he asserts that this hardness has been a change for the better "for the most part." He feels that he is "more realistic about life and about the church and about what people can do, what I can do. It would be the best of that. I think the worst of that would be in the sense that . . . a drain on some compassion, a drain on maybe some patience. I'll just have to leave it at that. Part of the clarity that I've got is, well, it's frankly a rejection of a lot of what I've seen up here."

When pressed to clarify some of his criticisms of Union, his thoughts turn harsher still. He says that the challenges that have confronted him at Union have "made me learn to hate, and I really have." He asserts that what he hates "is hate itself, because I feel hated. . . . The challenges here are, to me, challenges to an ethic of middle class American life that, because it is hated by those who are making the challenge, it has made me hate them. And it has really made me more defensive of that kind of life. And that's hard. I think that once I get back, I'm going to begin to see the negative characteristics of that life. But right now, I'm defending it."

Chris has kept most of his feelings about Union to himself. He has seldom voiced his criticisms openly because he feels this would simply embroil him in the controversies that he has so little use for. He chooses to remain a bystander to much of what goes on in the life of Union. He is certainly not unaffected by the seminary's various conflicts and protests, but he has decided not to engage them directly. All of these experiences and feelings, however, he intends to carry with him as he returns to the South and enters pastoral ministry. As he says, "I have not fought people here, because I felt I was here to get an education, but I'm going back to the church and I'm going to fight."

While Chris would not identify himself as part of Nixon's silent majority or the Reagan revolution, he shares with many other Americans at that time a wary response to the changes wrought in recent decades. He identifies himself as traditionally moderate in contrast to the ideas of the radical left. When asked to identify more specifically the things he would fight against, Chris offers as examples the ordination of homosexuals, liberation theology, and the far left of the Democratic party.

So Chris, who arrived at Union considering himself to be a liberal thinker (at least in relation to the social milieu of his upbringing), concludes his seminary career feeling highly critical, even resentful, of what he believes to be Union's culture of radical and unrealistic ideologies. He has discovered that his brand of liberalism is seen in the North as a form of watered down conservatism, but he feels strongly that the Protestant church in the United States will only damage its own viability by embracing a Northern liberal agenda. As he leaves Union, he is looking forward to returning to the South and to forms of ministry and ethics that make sense to him. Chris, however, also leaves feeling alienated in ways that at times seem more intense than the issues of seminary life should warrant. Yet he does not follow these feelings of distress in a more inward direction, at least for the present.

Finally, for all of his uneasiness about Union and the ideologies he so distrusts, Chris, as much as any other student, appreciates the city and appropriates it as another school for learning that often heals and makes up for, to some degree, what he finds missing in Union itself. He embraces the cultural, artistic, and lively neighborhood life of Manhattan and finds there a genuine diversity in contrast to what he sometimes regards as a chaotic, even manufactured, diversity in the seminary community.

Sarah

In February 1979, Sarah describes a great deal of turmoil in her life. She has broken up with her boyfriend only two weeks before, and that has clearly left her emotionally shaken. She also describes some difficulties that will require her to scale back her large thesis project.

"I was going to do it on [the] local history of women in my home congregation back in Pennsylvania, and I'm not at all sure that that is going to work. I was going to go home at Thanksgiving and get a lot of interviews done, a lot of information. And things fell apart. Problems and problems at home. It just didn't work out. So I might not be able to do it. There's the problem of everybody wanting me to do it a certain way. . . . My parents. People in the church. You know, 'Be sure you include this. Don't forget this. If you don't say so and so you're going to hurt somebody's feelings.' So I don't know how I'm going to handle all that."

Her disappointment over the thesis, particularly the pressures placed on her by her parents and home community, leads Sarah to discuss the growing conflict she feels between the conservative values with which she was raised and the increasingly liberal values she is coming to embrace. Unlike Chris, she is moving away from these traditions of home and exploring a new sense of herself. "I'm a different person from what I was at eighteen. . . . My parents tell me I've changed tremendously." And she agrees. "I feel like shaking [people from my hometown] and saying, 'Hey, I'm not the eighteen-year-old little girl that you saw going off to college.'"

"Here," she says, meaning Union and New York, "I found more people who can accept what I am saying and thinking and doing. I don't have to keep constantly tempering what I'm saying."

This growing conflict also affects her attitude about job possibilities after she graduates. She continues to have doubts about parish ministry, particularly the overwhelming demands she foresees such a vocation placing on her time and emotional resources, especially if she returns to her hometown or a similarly conservative locale where she will have to stifle her more liberal thinking. She fears feeling "confined" and "boxed in," just as she has felt during her summer ministry work in conservative locales. And yet, she has turned down agency jobs with the American Friends Service Committee and the Presbyterian Church and says, "I wouldn't be surprised if, in a couple of years, I did go into the parish as an associate." But then she adds: "I don't want to preach every Sunday."

All in all, she describes her current state as feeling "like everything is flying apart" and expresses distress over a controversy in which Union did not promote a particular faculty member she holds in high regard. "It may sound very bitter," she says, "but institutionally this place seems to have gone conservative or something."

Therapy, which many students find helpful, seems to be going well, and she says that she has learned a lot about integrating her thoughts about mind and body, particularly through her participation in two courses—one on sexuality, the other on dance. As she says, "I learned a whole lot about myself and how I feel about myself in my body, and that all fits together. . . . I always thought—I mean, I knew intellectually that this wasn't right—[that] the intellect and rational stuff was better, and body was . . . something you had that sometimes gave you some aches and pains. No real appreciation for my body, and I've somehow integrated that a bit. . . . I see myself as more of a whole person. I was reading for another course . . . some scripture verse about God creating us and it was good. And all of a sudden that occurred to me that that included my body. And I thought, 'Oh, yes!' So there have been a lot of good things."

When asked to summarize her reactions to her time at Union in May of 1979, she describes Union as "rather a lonely place" without "much community." But she also affirms the many positives of her experience. "Here you are allowed to be anyone you want to be, which has been very freeing for me." She describes the broadening experience of attending Union, citing her increased "breadth of understanding," including her growing understanding of gay people and various women's issues.

She also returns to the theme of mind–body integration—"getting more sense of myself as a total being." Therapy and courses on body movement and sexuality seem to have led her to a personal break-through and "a great boost to my ego. . . . I have a stronger sense of who I am and more self-confidence. . . . I feel freer to move and feel better in myself, better in my body, much better in my body, which, you know, affects my whole life."

She also refers for the first time to her missing eye, an injury caused by a childhood accident that has obviously been a source of vulnerability throughout her life, even though—with her prosthe-sis—it is not easy to detect. As she says, "I am not going to let any-body put me down for how I look anymore."

Although Sarah has many questions and uncertainties about the future, she seems upon graduation from Union to be someone who has an emerging sense of herself—tested within the challenges Union has presented her over these years.

Ruth

Like Sarah, Ruth begins her interview feeling discouraged. In fact, when she first sits down and is asked how she is doing, she begins to cry and must be given a few moments to regain her composure.

As soon as she is able, Ruth begins by describing her previous year, which was spent doing an internship "at a church in Newark, a largely Hispanic area, a good number of black folks also. The church was tri-racial. A good number of elderly white folks who had been there, Black, and Hispanic. . . . I'd never dealt with white folks who were trying to hold on, keep control of the church. . . . And that was kind of interesting to see how some things I could handle and some things I wasn't able to."

She had arranged the internship through a Lutheran seminary in California and had intended to complete her degree at that semi-nary rather than return to Union, but her continuing conflicts and misunderstandings with the two branches of the Lutheran church—American Lutheran Church (ALC) and Lutheran Church in America

(LCA)—seem to have changed her mind. As she relates, "I'd done some writing to the head of the board of theological education. He said if I could get one of the ALC seminaries to be willing to certify me while I still was at Union, fine, go ahead. He did not encourage that. He thought I should spend time at a Lutheran seminary. But if I could, go ahead. I visited the seminary in Ohio . . . and met with the president and some of the faculty there. And they really felt . . . I've been doing things my own way all the time I've been going to Union. I did my internship at an LCA parish rather than an ALC one. I got connected with another seminary and not with them, and it seems like I've been doing things all along my way, and now it's time for me to get in line and start doing things their way. You know, they don't want to be used, they told me. Some of them said some things I could understand, but the attitude was one of treating me like a child, like, 'certain decisions that you made may not have had any sense, or you don't understand them' or something. And there was no willingness to try to understand, I just felt. They felt it was a painful discussion. So did I. And I didn't feel that I was being treated like an adult. So that was that one side."

She also reveals that she has recently broken up with a serious boyfriend in New York and that has left her feeling free to go to California to attend Pacific Lutheran Theological Seminary and fulfill the expectations of her denomination if she chooses to do that. But in the end this is not what she wants to do. She would rather remain at Union and try to find some other way to move through the ordination process in the Lutheran church.

When asked for more details about her internship, she says that she was given opportunities for "leading liturgy every week and preaching once a month and more often, like, during Lent. Visiting, making home visits, hospital visits. Teaching Christian education, first communion, baptism. Basically those kinds of things." She says that she enjoyed the activities, although, "the visiting was hard for me, because I felt hesitant about going to people's houses. But I see that as an important part of ministry."

She felt that she had good rapport with the church members, but she did not care for the attitudes of the clergy that she met in Newark:

"I met a few that as far as their attitude towards the people, was very paternalistic, you know, where some of the few who were willing to come to the city to minister to these people, and, as far as teaching and everything, it was very basic Christianity, kind of basic Christian teachings. I didn't feel enough attempts were made to understand and incorporate the people's culture into the life of the church."

When asked about her feelings about being ordained, she says, "I still struggle with it, whether I want to pastor or not. Only the people that I've worked with there, the people at my fieldwork church, have been very firm. It's just some fears within myself, you know, confidence that I can handle a church and be able to be pastor to a congregation of people." She talks about going back to teaching or "doing some chaplaincy services or something, that kind of thing." Then she adds: "I feel very tired."

She says she has been feeling "a lot of pressure. And there's been a lot, as far as my personal life, a lot of things that I have been going through."

When asked where she finds emotional support, she says, "There are some female friends I have at my church who are around my age or a little bit older." She also mentions her family but quickly retracts that possibility. "I mean that's a whole other [thing], and I want to stay away from that. It's like putting yourself into a whole lot of other stuff." As far as Union is concerned, Ruth sees it as an academic institution where she takes courses but has almost no connection with other students. She has made some friends in the Black Caucus and the Black Women's Caucus. Otherwise, she describes Union as being a marginal part of her life.

Ruth, then, who has always struggled with her feelings about herself and her vocation, is ending her years at Union in the midst of personal questions that she seems unable or unwilling to articulate entirely. Although she has a network of friends with whom she can share her issues, it appears not to be extensive and seems to exclude her own family. She remains committed to ministry but uncertain whether she can or even wants to assume the responsibilities of being a pastor.

Tim

Tim begins the interview following his fifth semester (Fall 1978) by announcing that he has begun psychoanalysis.

"Five times a week," he says proudly. "I want to do a classical [analysis], dig in and see what's going on. Freudian, by choice—classic couch and everything. It's really sort of funny, because I can see myself doing all the sort of things I always read about that patients do."

When asked how the analysis is going, he says, "I don't think it's ever what you'd expect. Huge emotional jolt, because you're dealing with yourself at a very basic level five times a week, and it just gets, it brings up all kinds of stuff, and it's very confusing, but it's interesting." He then acknowledges that the emotional demands of such intense analysis have affected his other relationships, particularly that with his girlfriend, which he believes is coming to an end. Nevertheless, he seems to be able to separate his academic life from his emotional life, because, as he says, "academically it has been one of my better semesters."

He is still doing his two part-time jobs on campus as well as his continuing work with a Unitarian Universalist church in Brooklyn, while also taking a full course load and going through his denominational ordination process. As in previous semesters, he seems to have no lack of energy, and he is becoming "a lot clearer in my own religious beliefs, where they are. I am a lot clearer on what ministry is and why I am in it." He adds that his participation in CPE (clinical pastoral education), although emotionally demanding, has provided him with a great deal of clarity:

"I'm not sure that one thinks of CPE in positive or negative terms. It was a good experience, since I learned a tremendous amount. It was a really difficult experience, too. A lot of emotional involvement. A lot of shock. . . . Not only were we doing a lot of death counseling, we were doing a lot of rape counseling, crisis counseling in the emergency room. . . . And then we had an intensive group process which is fairly difficult." In fact, the emotional intensity of CPE was the impetus that got him into therapy. It made him realize "that I really had a lot of work to do within myself."

Although school is going well, he seems to be confronting for the first time the practical challenges of trying to become a minister in a denomination as small as the Unitarian Universalist church.

In the same interview at the end of his fifth semester, he states, "We've got 182 in seminary right now, and we're graduating about thirty a year looking for parishes, and we've already got a market that's got too many ministers. We've only got about 500 churches in the United States that pay full-time salaries."

Tim spends a lot of this interview talking about the relationships among students at Union, especially within the dormitory settings. On the one hand, he is gratified and flattered by the unofficial leadership position the younger students seem to assign to him. People congratulate him for the work he does and thank him for his participation. "I've also had people come up and bring me things that they think I should read, and they want my comment. I like it, but it's, I don't know where it comes from. It is kind of nice."

Later during this interview, though, he expresses more concern about the "very active sexual underground here at Union. . . . People's feelings do get shaken up, particularly through experiences like CPE, and when that happens, it tends to get expressed sexually." Tim includes himself in this charged atmosphere of sexual tension—the same atmosphere that makes many students uncomfortable and that Beth refers to when she describes her struggles to clarify to other students her personal boundaries based on her marriage vows.

Tim ends this interview by discussing the behavior among the more traditionally oriented male students in the dorms at Union. He feels that these students, being confused by provocative new ideas and challenges to their long-held prejudices and assumptions, are lashing out (in graffiti and other ways), particularly at women, especially those they perceive as having feminist leanings.

"When you have a community of people who do not well understand their own feelings about their own lives, they put a tremendous amount of emotional energy into something like this . . . , which could be better dealt with inside themselves, which is one reason why I am in analysis."

The need for self-awareness is an important issue for Tim. He sees the need for it in himself and wishes that more students would strive for it, so they could better identify the sources of their fears, resentments, and anger. Tim believes he is achieving a degree of self-awareness, and though he may not be as fully aware as he believes himself to be, he is always a seeker and sometimes the finder of critical and thoughtful insight.

Tim's final interview at Union occurs after he has graduated (Summer 1979). He talks about his thesis on Margaret Fuller (a key reformer and leader in nineteenth-century transcendentalism) and her relationship with Ralph Waldo Emerson. He mentions his engagement to be married and then speaks with some pride at being asked to help lead the communion service at graduation. He describes it as "a fascinating experience for me. It completed the circle, because in the beginning when I first came here, I felt very uncomfortable with the Eucharist, because I had stopped taking communion when I was quite young—six years old. And when I came here, I just didn't feel comfortable taking it and didn't. I'd come to the point toward the end of my career [at Union] much stronger in my understanding of communion and took it wholeheartedly, maybe not with the understanding other people had but enthusiastically. So to end up at the end of that time being one of the ones that celebrated communion for the class was a good experience for me, a strange but good experience for me."

Beth

Beth is one of the students who chose to spend a year doing an internship after her second year at Union, and the interview takes place in Fall 1979. The year away seems to have done much to relieve the worn-down state of mind she was experiencing at the end of her fourth semester.

Her work was done at a once wealthy and prestigious Episcopal church in western New York. But its neighborhood has deteriorated, and the most reliable members of the congregation are leaving. Like many such churches, it is running urban outreach programs even while it is losing its sense of parish life. In fact, one of Beth's roles was to "develop the internal structure within the church, hopefully to pull in young adults," but as she says, "people from the age of twenty-five to forty, who are not involved in church, very often are not involved because they don't want to be. It is a very fine line between trying to provide something that they may be interested in or just seeming like you're trying to get them into the church because you need warm bodies." After all, she points out, her husband, the minister of a Presbyterian church three blocks from her church, started a young adult's group that got "more young adults involved in the church on a temporary basis, but it didn't seem to create any interest in church life. If anything, they wanted to avoid church topics, because they didn't want to be too churchy."

As the young adults showed little interest in church participation, Beth focused her attention on the children, many of whom, she says, had suffered from "the total lack of Christian education going on in the church." As an example, she says, "I taught a confirmation class for six months, and these were fourteen-year-olds who started in the class and didn't know the difference between the Old and New Testament."

Nevertheless, Beth is pleased with her evolving experience in the practice of ministry and her reaffirmation of the Episcopal tradition in which she was raised and is now engaged in its ministry. She is deeply drawn to the liturgical tradition of the church and knows she is not pulled in the same ways toward her husband's Presbyterian tradition. This returns her to a struggle she has had before.

"It's very hard for me to feel comfortable relating to a church in the role of a minister's wife. It just evokes . . . a lot of hostility, and I can't sort out just the reaction to the role from my reaction to the church."

Despite the challenges she has experienced, Beth is obviously committed to her call to ministry and announces that she has begun the process of ordination. Yet even as she states her commitment, she remains conflicted about certain aspects of ministry. "I am not interested in parish work overall," she says. "I also don't like all of the having to be congenial all the time. My relationships to people, I like to relate to them not simply on a superficial basis. I just don't have the patience for that. I'd rather either be by myself or with people I can feel comfortable with and probing things that are important to me or that I can feel . . . very much at ease simply being myself." She particularly dislikes "the lack of privacy" and that parishioners seem to "transfer all their parental needs onto the clergy. I would prefer to have much more of a professional relationship with people. I don't like them calling me at home. I don't like being expected to go to graduations and birthday parties and all of that. Not that there is anything wrong with that. I personally don't enjoy that part of it."

Beth has a probing, analytical intellect and feels stymied by what she perceives as the occasional banalities of social interaction. She is more inwardly directed than many students, which means that interacting with other people, even when it is pleasant, can leave her emotionally exhausted. As Beth says, when explaining her difficulties meeting the seemingly endless needs of parishioners, either as the pastor herself or as the pastor's wife, "I just need enormous amounts of solitude and privacy. . . . This was a major, major problem last year. We lived in a house next to the church. Our phone number was the church phone number. People had seen the former minister as kind of a pal, and consequently, there was no understanding on their part of the manse being a home and not an extension of the church. I think it's hard for anyone, and for me it was just about devastating. . . . It just created all sorts of tensions with me. And then my husband tried to deal with it in terms of suggesting to people that they, if they're calling for routine business, to try to call between nine and five. And he talked about how the manse is a home and everybody needs a place for spiritual retreat and so on. Well, they almost fired him. . . . I'm not kidding. It was really frightening."

Nonetheless, she and her husband survived this scare, and Beth clearly enjoyed her year at her Episcopal church, particularly the challenges to her intellectual and organizational skills and the opportunity to share her life full-time with her husband.

Returning to Union, Beth is focused on completing her degree and becoming ordained. She admits, however, that after a year away from school, she at first felt disoriented and out of place at Union.

"I felt overwhelmed all over again by the diversity. I had two feelings. First of all, I felt that I was being pulled in a million directions and that I was going to be pulled apart. Then the second thing was, I felt enormously isolated, because I didn't really plug in anyplace. Those were the kind of two feelings I had—very inadequate, very alone. Once I got on track with my studies and I got back into what I was really here for, it's not a problem for me, but it did surprise me coming back how hard it was."

She then expresses again her continuing commitment to the Episcopal Church and her acceptance of its creedal statements, such as the Apostle's Creed, that gave her so much difficulty earlier in her adulthood. As an example of the reality of these creedal statements, she says, "I could feel it in the work I did last year with kids in the slum neighborhood—really awful conditions. I was trying to give them food because they were hungry . . . but also trying to communicate, kind of an entangled reality and connect with that in some way, too. And to me it wasn't just being nice, it was the whole thing of incarnational theology."

"There is something," says Beth, "very exciting about the reality of the gospel."

Marvin

Marvin concludes his fifth semester at Union feeling positive about his accomplishments but also a bit uncertain about the future. As he says, "I'm like in two different stages. I'm looking toward my future, knowing that I'm graduating in May and yet not overlooking the work that is necessary to see that that does come about." He describes himself as being in "a dazed kind of state, not knowing what the future is holding forth in terms of our leaving here but knowing that leaving here is part of what is in store."

"It's kind of scary," he continues, "because you leave here with a freshness, having graduated already twice, I guess, and . . . not really knowing what the next phase of your life holds for you. It leaves you somewhat perplexed, because when you leave an institution, you . . . are kind of in a dream world for a little while, like winning a race. All of a sudden, you are a winner, but after a while, you have to come down off the cloud and then what is next is winning again and being successful continuously in the things that you do."

He knows that he will be entering congregational ministry. He has no doubts about that. And though he is not certain where he will start his career, he has the assurance of being offered a position at Abyssinian Baptist Church, where he has done all of his fieldwork since entering Union.

When asked about the preparation for ministry that Union has provided him, he agrees with most other students when he says that "the academic discipline is something that is a tremendous asset in terms of any kind of parish ministry. The skills and the tools that one gains here cannot be underestimated to any degree. But as far as a direct connection otherwise in terms of being able to be a good minister or pastor, then Union has totally missed the mark on that." As far as Marvin is concerned, Union has failed to "teach just basic parish ministry kinds of courses—what is necessary in terms of funerals, you know, marriages."

Marvin also feels that "Union is not really sensitive to the needs of blacks on the whole or black men in general. Right now the shift has been toward women, and there's been a semi-focus on black women, and there has to be some means of stability." It bothers him that black men seem to have a diminishing role at Union and that feminism has become such a dominant ideology at the school. Although Marvin tries not to couch his criticisms in a hostile tone, his frustration is evident.

"Right now society tends to, you know, they are having this major struggle over women, the ERA and all of this. The black male is screaming out, you know, don't forget us! The black female is being pushed ahead of the black male which is really doing an injustice to the black community as a whole, dividing it perhaps more than what the media already sees it as being."

He is also highly critical of the financial pressures placed on black students in particular, explaining, "One major problem that I have . . . in terms of being black in the United States and being a student in any kind of decent institution, there's not a time when you can actually relax in terms of financial pressures, because the black community does not have the financial security which allows them to relax. Any major financial change in my own lifestyle would automatically disrupt my education altogether. And I think this is true for many [if] not all of the black students. If there's no financial bankroll that I can lay back on, if I am in need of a couple of hundred dollars at any unforeseen time, I can't just pick up the phone and say, 'Mama, I need some money.'" He then reflects on the poverty in which he and so many black people were raised: "I've come from the bottom. So there's really no struggle or nothing new to me in terms of this."

When asked what enabled him to weather the challenges posed by Union, he is quick to identify them.

"Well, God, first of all. I have to say my mother, who played a major part in my life. Then my wife, who is another support mechanism for me, and the church. Going to church every Sunday and being able to recharge my batteries, analogously speaking, has probably gotten me through."

In the last interview before graduation, Marvin states that "your hermeneutics may be good, but then how do you parallel that to the contemporary situation where you feed the people upon hearing it or speak on their level, so that when they leave the church, they want to return again . . . that that was a good message that will get me through the week and enable me to look in a very optimistic light at many of the problems that I will be dealing with daily. That is lacking—strong emphasis upon preaching. The technicalities, in terms of preaching, that's not here."

He reiterates some of his concerns about feminism and his worries about his student loan debt but remains confident that his vocation in ministry will come to fruition. As he says, "If it's part of God's plan to see that I pastor, then that situation will be provided, . . . not that I have a very lackadaisical attitude about it. . . . But I just feel that I don't want to be too zealous about my own career. There's something out there for me, and when the situation comes, I'll know it. . . . I think with the number of people pulling for me for pastoral situations"—he names Abyssinian ministers Samuel Proctor and Calvin Butts—"something will unfold. It's only a matter of being aware of the situation and knowing that in terms of suiting my own needs when it does transpire."

He then adds, "Going through Union is like going through a puzzle, a maze, . . . even going shopping. There are some things you know you must purchase and other things you should perhaps leave on the shelf. I purchased a lot, and I know when I leave here, there will be a lot of things I'll just leave on the shelf. . . . It's been the most difficult yet the most rewarding time in my life, these last three years.

And . . . a tremendous amount of growth in all aspects has taken place on my part."

In the spring semester, 1979, Anna, Marvin, and Tim will graduate. Since Sarah has not yet finished some requirements, she will go on to serve a church and then formally receive her degree the following year after completing what remaining academic work needs to be done. The others, because of internships or other reasons, have extended their time at the seminary. Most of the students—even those graduating—remain uncertain, if not about their actual calling to ministry then about the manner in which they will enter that calling. Some have felt renewed by internships that have given them a year of practical experience in ministry; others have gained emotional insight and self-knowledge through psychotherapy. Some have been enlivened by Union's commitment to diversity and find here the kind of community that will inform their ministries in the future. Others continue to be let down by a seminary culture they feel gives second place to traditional beliefs and ethics or ignores the needs of their particular ethnic group. Some are simply tired of the continuing conflicts within seminary life. All, however, as the end of their theological studies come into view, look forward, if with some trepidation, to moving beyond this institutional world and taking their next step into the work of the church.

As they consider their experiences of seminary, they mostly understand the points and counterpoints that make up the life of the school. They seem to recognize that their expectations are always going to be somewhat in conflict with what is actually happening at the school, and to this extent there is a reluctant admission that the seminary culture is more complicated than some of their opinions about how to change it might suggest. In dealing with *alma mater* (literally, nurturing mother), the students may want more than she can provide. As one of Beth's preferred psychoanalysts, D. W. Winnicott, might say, they have to settle for a "good enough mother"—not a perfect one, but at least one who provides the basic things they need for learning and their own growth.

The use of the feminine to refer to educational institutions, especially theological seminaries, pertains to the formative aspects of
education. However, this particular institutional mother at this particular time was wrestling with her own self-definition, and there
was conflict over all of this. In this regard, the anger often directed toward Union's outspoken feminists came from many different
conscious and unconscious sources, just as the feminist community
itself included many different elements within its own protest and
advocacy. All of this made for a heady mix not open to easy resolution or facile solutions. Whether it was a creative environment for
teaching and learning is a primary question. For some, the continual
conflict within the seminary was diametrically opposed to the kind
of thoughtful conversations they had imagined at the center of theological education. Yet these same conflicting dynamics, the battle-
like discourse, was for others a remarkable means of teaching and
learning.

The school's ongoing fiscal issues affected both students and faculty as financial aid was less than hoped for and professors felt the
daily frustration of what one professor, Raymond Brown, once described to me as the "annoyance of small economies."

As we will read in the following chapter, most of the eight affirmed the extent to which their experience at Union did indeed prepare them for the world in which they would serve as pastoral leaders. The issues that confronted them at Union were similar to the
issues they would soon confront in their own ministries, so there is a
sense in which their theological education was a kind of harbinger of
things to come. What they learned in dealing with life at Union was
something they have carried with them over the long haul.

While congregations once expected homogeneity or at least diversity around a commonly agreed upon core of belief, they now
have to deal with a multiplicity of beliefs where there is little held
in common except the community itself. Pastors are challenged by
the expectation that they can manage this pluralistic institution and
find some way to maintain harmony among diverging points of view
and expectations about worship, mission commitments, and shared
governance. Given the pressure to increase membership or at least
staunch the loss of members, pastors are under significant pressure

to be all things to all people. This has always been the case to a certain extent, but the "people" are far more divergent than they were a generation ago, and they are not quiet about it either. Given such a context, the ministers educated at Union in the midst of cultural challenges surprisingly similar to the present at least had the opportunity to develop their own practices of ministry in anticipation of a vastly changed environment.

chapter 6

Years in Ministry

I love ministry. I love what I am doing. — DAVID

EARLY IN 2004, I BEGAN CONTACTING EACH OF THE EIGHT. IT HAD been many years since we first met, although off and on through the years, I had seen their lives from afar. In a few instances, I had actually spoken with a few of them as our paths had crossed. In 2004, however, I began arranging times to meet with them and find out what had happened in their life and work since we had last talked. In the next few years, I was able to schedule visits with all of them in the various places they lived throughout the country.

At this point, the eight are moving into the senior years of their lives. One is old enough to receive Social Security benefits, and the others realize that that day is not so far away for them either. All have taken circuitous routes to arrive where they are now, both in their personal and their professional lives. Now, they relate to me the details of challenge, disappointment, service, and achievement experienced in the decades since their graduation from Union.

Sarah

Sarah appears for this interview having just returned home from a bicycle ride with her husband. She lives in a middle class suburban development where lawns are neat and the streets well maintained. She lives several miles from the church she and her husband once served in this small Pennsylvania college town. Her house is comfortable and elicits a warmth that matches Sarah's own welcome.

Sarah begins by describing her first ministry as a young associate pastor at a Brethren church in a small town in Florida. It was there, she says, "I was ordained in a wonderfully celebrative service with huge butterflies hanging above the altar." She was still uncertain at the time whether a congregation was the best place for her, but the Florida church was unique. Composed largely of retired clergy and long-time Church of the Brethren laity, it was a congregation with a keen sense of the church's mission. Sarah remembers, for example, how one church member went out of his way to remind her that social justice was a crucial part of the ministry in which she was ordained. Moreover, the congregation consciously claimed responsibility for helping Sarah learn the ropes and discern the nature of her work and calling:

"There were numerous older members in the congregation who were now retired, having served the larger church in a variety of ministries. They were my gracious and loving teachers. I remember one elderly, tall, white-haired, soft-spoken gentleman who came into my office one day and talked about justice for the poor. He had worked in India for many years and had been an executive for Agricultural Missions. Now he was actively involved with the National Farm Worker Ministry in Florida. He had come to introduce me to this ministry and to invite my involvement. I was pleasantly surprised that this soft-spoken gentleman was speaking so powerfully about his understandings of justice, which were so much in tune with my own understandings. I had come to this obscure little town in Florida and found such richness of spirit."

There, too, she first evinced (without being entirely aware of it) her talent for quiet empathy when visiting the sick and dying and when leading funerals and memorial services. She refers to this aspect of her work as a "ministry of presence—being rather than doing."

"At that time," she says, "I did not know that this was one of my gifts. . . . I did not value this gift as much as I do today."

Sarah looks back fondly on her time in Florida and sees it as a time that helped her overcome self-doubts and the anxieties that accompany public speaking. In a way, the Florida congregation was a school of ministry, a place that helped consolidate the more academic learning of Union and made it relevant to the everyday life of the church. At the same time, her learning was personal, and she found here a more confident sense of herself and her gifts in ministry:

"It was in Florida," she notes, "that my self-esteem and confidence was built as the congregation welcomed and nurtured me. In summer pastoral internships, I had become physically ill . . . every time I had to preach. I managed to do okay, and people said my sermons were fine, but I did not think I could preach regularly if I was going to become sick prior to every time I preached. It was so different in this Florida congregation. I soon realized that while I still got the jitters prior to preaching, I was no longer experiencing those other symptoms. It was grace, pure grace, that this congregation offered to me, and their grace allowed me to preach with greater confidence, knowing that if I messed up, they would forgive and give me a second chance (even a third chance). Their grace allowed my gifts to flourish."

Although she did not do everything right in Florida and there were bumps along the way, particularly wariness among some congregants about having a woman minister, she could not help but be reassured by her first extended experience in ministry. She also appreciated the open-heartedness with which the lead pastor, Ron Petry, shared responsibilities with her and encouraged her to see herself as part of a team rather than a rung in a hierarchy.

After serving in Florida for less than two years, Sarah became Director of Volunteer Services for the Church of the Brethren. In thinking about this time she states, "I was excited about the peace and justice aspects of the program, which I continued to love during my tenure there. What I didn't realize was that I did not fit well into our denominational culture." Unlike others in the Brethren tradition who see the culture expressing humility, quiet service, and a genuine sense of community, Sarah sees the culture as one that avoids dealing with conflict, values harmony above other virtues, and often devalues individual initiative and passion.

Although Sarah enjoyed working with many fine colleagues at the denominational headquarters, she was "not allowed to express differences with any degree of passion. I had to repress passion. . . . That was identified as the Brethren way. . . . I was not fully aware of how my soul was being squeezed."

During the latter part of her time on the denominational staff, Sarah fell in love with her future husband, who had also been a staff member. He had been recently divorced and eventually left the staff to become pastor of a small congregation in Chicago. He and Sarah were later married at his church in Chicago, and Sarah commuted to denominational headquarters in Elgin, a suburb of Chicago. She continued working on the staff for another two and a half years. After Sarah became pregnant and gave birth to their daughter, however, she decided to resign from the denominational staff. As Sarah says, "It was too difficult having a young child and traveling as much as I did. One year I was on the road 110 days out of the year."

She and her husband soon left Chicago and moved to the suburbs of Washington, D.C., when he was called to a new pastorate in Maryland. There, wanting to help with the family income but not wanting to return to a formal church position, she decided to open a day-care center in their home.

"The day-care center was open ten hours a day, five days a week. I did this work for five years. . . . This was the hardest job I have ever had, yet I received the least amount of recognition. I experienced the reality of working class America."

Sarah felt at the time that she was providing a valuable service for the community, but the "realities of how day-care providers are viewed and treated was a real blow to my ego." On Sunday, she says, "I was the pastor's wife—an identity I have never enjoyed. During the week, I was the babysitter in most people's eyes and was treated as such." In the course of these five years of declining self-esteem, she occasionally did supply preaching and other part-time church work. "These periodic opportunities were like oases in the desert of these five years."

In 1993, she was called to lead a nearby Brethren church on a three-quarter time basis. The congregation was small, partly because the conservative members had split away. The self-esteem of the remaining congregants was about as low as Sarah's own self-esteem, so working together, they helped build up one another.

"In this setting," she says, "my gifts of listening and encouraging were utilized and appreciated. . . . Although I was only at the church for four and a half years, I believe that my need for increased confidence and their need for healing (and also increased confidence in themselves as a good congregation) were met. When I arrived the congregation often blamed themselves for the split and troubles they had experienced. As an outsider, I was able to lift up their strengths and their gifts and encourage them to be who they are as a congregation."

In 1997, Sarah and her husband "were called to be copastors [for] a nearly 600-member congregation in a small college town in . . . Pennsylvania. I would never have guessed that I would return to rural Pennsylvania in a pastoral position." She was disappointed to have to leave her Maryland congregation, but in retrospect she believes that "the work I needed to do there was accomplished."

In Pennsylvania, says Sarah, the "congregation prided itself (although we could never use the word pride because that is not the Brethren way) in being progressive." Its progressive activities included opposing the Iraq War before the invasion in 2003, sponsoring peace rallies in D.C., being a sister church with a congregation in the Dominican Republic, and building a Habitat for Humanity house. The congregation was well known throughout the denomination and could be classified in ecclesial culture as a high steeple church. In August of 2004, however, her seven-year ministry in this congregation ended as she felt compelled to resign in light of a continuing conflict in the life of the church.

"So what could go wrong in such a great congregation?" Sarah asks. "Why did I leave this congregation after seven years, feeling defeated and worthless?"

The crux of the conflict was Sarah's willingness to accept without hesitancy gays and lesbians into the congregation. Although the congregation had been quietly proud—in a kind of low-key Brethren way of being proud—of having some gays and lesbians in the fold, Sarah's emerging public acceptance of the gay members became troubling for other church members. An issue that had been managed with a sort of don't-ask-don't-tell policy among the congregants now became a source of open conflict, and Sarah became the catalyst and scapegoat.

In a series of incidents that eventually erupted in a full-blown congregational conflict, the precipitating event was an invitation

Sarah received to serve on the Brethren Mennonite Council for lesbian, gay, bisexual, and transgender interests. Because she knew that
her participation could raise controversy, Sarah asked the executive
committee of her church if it would be acceptable to them that she
serve on the Council. When they gave their permission, she point-
edly asked them if they would support her if she were criticized in
the congregation. She received verbal affirmation from each person and thus felt that she had managed the situation effectively to
avoid conflict. However, some days after the meeting and after Sarah
had accepted the Council's invitation to participate, the chair of the
church's executive committee told her that he had not spoken during the meeting because he, in fact, did not support her participation. Such unwillingness to express disagreements openly, which
she categorizes as passive–aggressive behavior, was to characterize
many of her frustrations in the conflict that would follow in about
six months.

The issue intensified when Sarah invited a lesbian couple in the
congregation to bring their adopted child to the church's next dedication ceremony. "I had said, you know, 'When we have our next baby
dedication, I'd be happy to have you participate.' And . . . they were
like, well, okay, maybe. So I had the invitation out there, but they had
put it off and didn't respond for, I think, for almost a year. Then they
decided, yes. . . . One of the couple had grown up in this church, and
her parents are here, and she is their only child left . . . [and] this is
their grandchild. So I think the grandparents tried to convince them
to have the baby dedicated in the church. So they decided, yes, they
were going to do that. So we sent a letter out to four couples . . . to
do a baby dedication in September. . . . Then we started getting feedback: 'What do you mean? There's two women here. What is this?' . . .
And the upshot was, two of the couples dropped out. They refused to
stand up in front of the church with this couple. But one did not. So
we went ahead and had the baby dedication, keeping the board and
the executive committee apprised of what was going on.

"So that went okay. Then things seemed to smooth out. Then in
the fall, a newspaper reporter . . . called me up. . . . She was doing an
article on churches in the area that are open to gays and lesbians. So
I talked to her. Our head deacon talked to her. A number of people

talked to her. The article came out the first Sunday in December, and all hell broke loose. . . . Some people in the church really got up-in-arms about that. And . . . there were these other churches in the area that were getting angry, and they called the district office and complained. We got letters, and I got called a reprobate. All kinds of nastiness. Then in the spring. . . we had a good board chair that year. She organized meetings for people to talk. . . . There was this open forum for the whole church one Sunday afternoon. . . . I don't remember how many people spoke—a lot, sixty, seventy people maybe. It went on for a couple of hours. Of all the people that spoke, I'd say maybe between 75 and 80 percent, I think, were open. That was kind of a watershed, because the people that were mad at me . . . and sent all kinds of nasty letters and did all kinds of things . . . they were at this forum, and . . . they realized it's not . . . just Sarah that believes this. There are all these other people in the church that believe just like Sarah does, or similarly. They were taken aback."

Time passed, and the uproar seemed to have quieted down when Sarah's attempt in a sermon to encourage mutual understanding between gays and straights backfired (specifically because one part of the sermon encouraged the majority heterosexuals to reflect on the limiting nature of their attitudes). Once again the vocal minority made clear its disapproval, and this time the leadership did not support her and did not choose to have an open congregational discussion about the issue. In a related, though supposedly unconnected action, church leaders cut the budget for pastors' salaries, and Sarah and her husband and an assistant pastor were, in effect, forced to renegotiate their positions. In the end, Sarah resigned.

Sarah continues to believe that she expressed her support for gays and lesbians in a Christian and conciliatory manner, and she continues to feel certain that she did the right thing in standing by her principles. She also feels that the root of the troubles arose as much from a struggle for power and a reaction against women in ministry as it did from gay and lesbian issues. What's more, she feels that if the church members who had disagreed with her had done as Christ teaches in Matthew 18:15— "If another member of the church sins against you, go and point out the fault when the two of you are alone"—much of the contention could have been avoided. Yet for all her rational understanding of the conflicts at this particular church, enduring the personal attacks on her character and the fluctuating and uncertain support from the church's leadership were devastating for her. As she says:

"Despite the legitimate challenges of this congregation, I still wonder why I allowed my self-esteem and worth to be so devastated. I was fifty-one years old, ordained twenty-five years ago, and I was lost." Sarah learned under trying circumstances that she was probably "not as strong as I thought I was. . . . I should have taken better care of myself."

In searching for a way of both dealing with what she had experienced at the church and finding a way to move on, Sarah later applied to and was accepted in a clinical pastoral education (CPE) residency program at a nearby medical center. This gave her a needed respite from the conflict she had endured, but more importantly it signaled a renewal of her sense of vocation.

"I didn't know if I was going to become a chaplain or not, but it was my way out of Egypt. The Red Sea opened up. . . . I did not know what was on the other side, but my spirit knew it was my way out. . . . It was a gift from God."

Although chaplaincy jobs are scarce, she was soon called to be a hospice chaplain, "starting my work there only a few days after completing the CPE residency."

Today, with her husband retired from ministry and her own ministry moving in a different direction, Sarah seems to have found at last a place of ministry that fits her gifts. As she says, "In my current work as a hospice chaplain, I feel like I have found the place that uses my God-given gift of spiritual intuition. . . . What freedom! What joy! I am finally being appreciated for who I am. I am no longer being squeezed into someone else's mold of who I should be. . . . The interfaith nature of my work is another bonus. I no longer have to try to fit into the Brethren mold, which was often so confining."

Gone is much of the uncertainty that had been a part of her life and work. Nevertheless, the bad taste of her recent past lingers, and she continues to absorb the lessons of her experience. She is not quite sure how she arrived at this point, and she cannot help replaying past events and decisions.

"Although I feel well on the road to healing today, the pain of that experience still rises within me, and I continue to wonder why I allowed this to happen to me and what I did wrong."

This kind of self-examination, though, does not have the same quality of accusation and recrimination that might have appeared earlier in her life. She now can look at these difficult questions and experiences with a kind of distance that permits her to face hard realities without being caught up in them. Life has not turned out the way she had expected, and she has reason to feel that it has not always been fair to her, but these hard truths are accepted for what they are and for how they have brought, in unexpected ways, occasions of grace and love.

Ruth

Like Sarah, Ruth has struggled with her life and her calling, although she has not been subjected to the sort of calamitous conflict that was such a trial for Sarah. Like Sarah, too, Ruth is married to a minister, and while this relationship has obviously brought great fulfillment to her life (including the birth of her two children), it has also been a factor in some of her personal and professional struggles.

It was during Ruth's nine-month internship in Newark after two years at Union Seminary that she met her future husband. "He was a newly ordained white pastor from a rural and small community background near Reading, Pennsylvania," she says, "just starting in his first congregation in west Newark, and I was an intern serving in north Newark. We met at the weekly . . . Lutheran Parish meetings for Bible study, support, and planning. Good things can come out of Bible study! We dated some, fell in love, stayed in love . . . and married in 1980. I had to go through some internal wrestling about interracial relationships, pray about it, talk to my mother about it, and recognize that my faith in Christ had something to say to me about the matter. I made the right decision.

"But marriage and our desire to work together meant much hassle and negotiation between his Lutheran Church in America denomination and my American Lutheran Church denomination, even though the denominations had already agreed on imminent merger. I had to leave the American Lutheran Church, which was a disappointment to my friends in that denomination who would have celebrated me as the first black woman ordained. Then my husband had to resign his call from the congregation so that together we could receive a call issued by a skeptical synod to the same congregation."

The couple also began a self-limiting pattern of answering calls to minister in the same church while asking for only one salary. Although their careers have been spent in struggling urban churches that may have required such an arrangement, Ruth is aware of the personal costs this decision to share one salary has made on her family. She relates, "For the first seven years of ministry, in a congregation in west Newark, we did not have children. It was mostly because of choice, maybe some because of sheer busyness and low salary. But during our two-year stint in Pittsburgh, when we engaged in a frustrating and failed new urban mission, our son was born. I believe that the relief and release from the regular demands of an active and struggling parish was a gift from God; for I was able, with a six-month paid maternity leave from the denomination, to enjoy those first months with our son with undivided attention. We returned to Newark with a one and a half year-old son, and then I gave birth to our daughter when he was three. I have much enjoyed being a parent, love my children dearly, but still find it so challenging to balance ministry and family. And at times I have felt that I have gotten lost from myself."

Growing up in an extended family with limited resources, Ruth believes that "I learned to be responsible a little too soon and also learned back then to not take too much time for myself. That shapes me even today in my life and ministry. I always have lists of things to do. I am always extending family, sharing limited resources, accepting responsibility for others. Timeouts are limited; vacations have been few. I still have difficulty setting those boundaries."

After their unhappy time in Pittsburgh, Ruth and her husband returned to Newark to become copastors of a Lutheran church where they continue to serve an ethnically diverse but largely African American congregation of about 400 members. The church is in an urban neighborhood that is trying to maintain some semblance of the stability it once took for granted. The parsonage is attached to the church itself. The building is relatively small, but it obviously anchors the neighborhood in which Ruth and her husband have served for many years.

Not long after returning to Newark, says Ruth, her mother moved to live nearby, "partly to escape deteriorating project life and partly to help with our toddler son and, later, our newborn daughter. She was active in our congregation, the only childcare provider for our children, and a regular cooked meal provider. Watching her suffer and die of esophageal cancer was very difficult for me, and I still have regrets that I didn't always make and take time for her when she was alive and well. Sometimes, when I am walking through those heart-piercing issues of intense struggle, suffering, and death with my parishioners, I hear my ailing mother saying to me, 'Can't you just give me one hour?' I try to give that hour to that parish member in pain now. And I think about my own fears and anxiety about death."

While Ruth speaks often about her shortcomings and uncertainties, she seldom acknowledges the strength of character and integrity that are evident in her life. She may carry the weight of a conflicted soul on her shoulders, but that does not cause her to give up or defer what she thinks is right and what is the faithful thing to do. And in moments of spontaneity, she radiates with joy and delight. In worship especially she is a lively and compelling presence who is able to communicate love and care to her congregation.

Ruth's experience as one of the first black women in ministry in a predominantly white and male denomination has left scars, and the difficulties of race and gender have been compounded by her steadfast commitment to urban ministry and to parishes outside the perimeters of status and the regard of some church officials. No matter, she and her husband have made a difference in the churches they have led and the neighborhoods they have served.

Marvin

In 1980, just a year after graduating from Union Seminary, Marvin became the pastor of a small Baptist church in Queens, New York, and it is in this church that Marvin remains as pastor to this very day. When Marvin first arrived, the church had about 200 members, and over the course of his career it has grown to about 1,000 members. The church where he had been raised and the one in which he had done his fieldwork at Union were both larger and more historic black Baptist churches, so his adjustment to a smaller church was not always easy.

Marvin is aware that he was once on the black church's fast track in ministry. His fieldwork experience and service as an assistant minister at Abyssinian Baptist Church was a stepping-stone toward prominence in large churches. For another minister, the church in Queens may well have been the first in a series of church moves that would eventually bring him into the higher echelons of clerical life. But Marvin got off the fast track early in his career. Instead, he has remained in the church to which he was called so many years ago. His decision to stay has been costly in some respects—of which he is well aware. The church has always struggled to pay its way, and Marvin and his family have often borne a financial burden because of the church's inability to provide adequate compensation for him. Yet Marvin has found a home in Queens and seems at peace with the choices he has made. He recognizes that larger, more affluent churches have fewer fiscal pressures, more programs, and a faster pace. As he made the transition from Abyssinian to the church in Queens, he remembers that "it wasn't one that I really wrestled with too much, because you've got to take the good with the bad."

The church reflects the urban neighborhood in which it is located. The street outside is busy with traffic. The doors are locked, and admittance is only by request through the intercom located outside. Marvin's office is large and comfortable, the space of someone who is at home in this place. He wears his hair in long Nubian locks, which he adopted in the 1990s.

He says that he was always looking for a way to wear his hair that better expressed his sense of self. "Then," he says, "I went to Africa and kind of discovered roots and found out that the priests who were part of the Ashanti tribe, they locked their hair. . . . I was with a tour group, and we were going into some of the areas and learning about the different cultures, and the tour guide was telling us about those who were caught up in Voodoo and those who were caught up in the . . . Christian tradition, so to speak, yet holding on to the African roots. Then he said, and he pointed to me, 'Now, this brother back here, his hair is locked, . . . and if we didn't know better, we would think he was a priest.' Now, he did not know I was a minister at the time. So I sent my card up, and he looked at the card, and when he saw Reverend Doctor, he said, . . . 'Oh, wow, you are a priest.' . . . That was an affirmation for me."

Marvin was further affirmed on the tour when the travelers learned in one locale about "a warrior priest who fought against the invasion of the colonists, and . . . he locked his hair and had cowry shells in it. And there's a big statue right in the middle of the town where he is just champion of the cause of independence for that particular region. He was clearly a spiritual leader." Marvin, who had, as a teenager, considered the possibility of becoming a policeman and had once imagined seminary as a place of military-like discipline, seems to have always been drawn to certain military ideals—loyalty, perseverance, discipline, courage. In fact, while serving as the pastor of his church in Queens, he also received a commission as an officer in the Navy Reserve and served as a chaplain in New York City. So it is probably no surprise to see him feeling affirmed by the image of a warrior priest.

If Marvin had had grander career ambitions, he might have moved on to more nationally significant churches. Greater ambitions, however, would have required him to move regularly, and both he and his wife like the stability they have found in Queens. Marvin refers to the story of Jesus and the disciples (John 21:6) in which disciples are having no luck catching fish, and Jesus shows them that the solution is right there before them if they are only willing to try it. As Marvin explains, "All too often we fail to realize there's good fishing right where we are. It's just a matter of shifting to the other side of the boat. You don't have to change boats but just move to the other side of the boat . . . let your net down on the other side." He then adds, "I'm in the same boat, but I am just a different kind of captain, . . . one who has truly learned."

As an example of his personal learning and growth, Marvin mentions the fact that he was one of the first black pastors to hire a woman as a full-time assistant pastor. He says he would not have likely made such a choice had it not been for the broadening experience of his education at Union, which opened his eyes to the value and equality of women.

Almost immediately after graduating from Union, Marvin enrolled in the school of theology at Drew University in New Jersey and earned a D.Min. More recently he has become a licensed funeral director and grief counselor, besides being the pastor at his church in Queens, and has some hopes of eventually opening his own funeral home as a possible occupation after retirement—both to make up for the lack of a pension and to help people deal with grief. He feels that, as an ordained minister, he is in a position "not just [to] prepare people in terms of giving them the best quality type of home-going services for their loved ones, but to follow up . . . afterward and to do bereavement counseling and to do hands on in terms of ministry that moved beyond the moment."

Marvin and his wife of more than thirty years have one daughter and two sons and are preparing as well as they can for their retirement years. He takes pleasure in being a husband, father, and minister. Over the years, he has been involved in the politics of Queens, and is a known public figure in the community. As much as or more than any of the other participants, Marvin embodies a sense of being the person he had envisioned himself to be and the kind of minister he had hoped he might become. He seems at ease with himself, his choices in life, and the mix of trials and rewards that have come his way.

Chris

Unlike Marvin, whose career and private life have been relatively stable, Chris's personal and professional life have had far more ups and downs. He has done quite well on a professional level, though his path in ministry has not been easy. His personal life, however, has brought him significant distress. The same bright, articulate young man can still be recognized in his older self, but it is a man who speaks with a kind of knowledge achieved only through difficulty.

Chris began his career as an associate pastor at a Presbyterian church in the Southwest. "I was actually the fourth person called by the same pastor-nominating committee," he says. "They built a whole new staff, and I was the last one and the youngest called and basically did youth ministry and congregational life—a very typical, traditional start. I was there from June of '80 through about April of '84. . . . Early in that time, I was divorced from Laura. . . . A year later I then married a woman from that community and congregation . . . who had two small children who were seven and five. . . . The process of divorce and remarriage probably kept me there a little bit longer than it would have for a first call type of position."

It was during the crisis of his first marriage and as part of his attempt to save it that he went into therapy and revealed a trauma that he had kept to himself since his teenage years. Chris believes now that this trauma haunted many of his succeeding relationships. It may also help explain some of the hostility and ambivalence he expressed in many of his interviews while at Union, which, though directed at the seminary's politics and community life, often appeared to carry other emotional freight as well.

Although his first wife chose not to participate in therapy, Chris continued his even after the breakup of the marriage. As he says, however, "I stopped it right before the second marriage, which I shouldn't have done." By cutting off therapy, Chris feels he delayed a more complete recovery by many years.

Nonetheless, he continued to function quite effectively as a pastor, and in 1984, Chris and his wife and two children moved to a large metropolitan area where he took a position as pastor of a suburban Presbyterian church that had about 275 members and had been founded in 1967. The congregation was largely made up of corporate managers and employees and was a church that had a turnover rate of about 15 percent each year. While the congregation had experienced a conflict that had split the congregation, a building campaign that began with Chris's arrival became a means of healing these old divisions. Chris regarded this pastorate as a very good experience, a real match between himself and the members of the church.

After six years, though, Chris was ready to make a change. The two children, whom Chris had adopted, were entering high school and middle school, and Chris and his wife wanted a different environment for them.

"So . . . after the building campaign was done and the debt reduction campaign was complete, . . . we really decided to start looking. And the churches that were looking at me at that point that seemed to respond were almost a very similar profile of old historic downtown churches that had lost membership but were not yet in the IC ward."

He ended up "accepting a call to a Presbyterian church in the Midwest. It had peaked in membership at about 1,100 in the late '50s. It . . . had been founded in 1847 and had a beautiful Gothic sanctuary." By the time Chris and his family arrived, however, the church had declined to "about 550 members and had really lost anybody under about sixty. It was an established but older congregation. It just had not been able to do family ministry much. . . . My family, my wife and children, were all from the Southwest. I was from the South via New York. So it was truly a new experience."

The congregation, according to Chris, "knew it needed some life, and I think they looked at this young minister, a young family, and saw life. . . . For about four or five years the pent-up demand in that congregation . . . led us to a really fast growth. We went from about 560 to about 750 in about five years, which is a lot in the Midwest in the mainline church in a town of 100,000 people."

In the fifth year of Chris's pastorate, a wealthy new member approached him about restoring the interior of the sanctuary to its original Gothic design. In the 1950s, the interior of the old sanctuary had been remodeled in Danish modern, which the new member and Chris both believed had been "an architectural tragedy."

According to Chris, "I basically said, 'You know, we don't want to wait until you die to get that money and do that. You give it now, and we'll go to work on it.' Sometimes I regret those words, because [the project] was one factor that led to about a five-year protracted struggle of identity and leadership in the congregation."

Chris believes that several other factors, including a slowdown in the congregation's growth and worries about the budget, also contributed to the trouble. But another factor, which is one that several of the study participants had to contend with during their careers, was an unwillingness on the part of the congregation to face directly conflict within the church. Instead, some in the congregation decided that Chris was the source of the conflict and tried to remove him as pastor. Chris, however, with no little courage and faith, led the church through this stormy time and survived back-to-back attempts to remove him (by a vocal minority) and he remained at the church until all the money was raised and the restoration of the sanctuary was begun.

"It was probably," he says, "the most self-defining period of my life—those five years. But I really came to believe that God was calling me to stay there and not let them think that they were addressing their identity issues by getting rid of the minister."

Unfortunately, he was more successful with his congregation than he was with his second marriage. According to Chris, he had jumped "out of what was one care-giving marriage into what was a rescuing and care-giving second marriage. Though I knew at the time the second marriage was not right, I was neither strong nor internally courageous enough to back out of the relationship and not go forward with the marriage."

Despite his ambivalence about his second marriage, he had adopted his second wife's two children and appears to have had every intention of making the marriage work. But after about nine years at the church, he finally came to the conclusion that the marriage had failed and that divorce was the only solution. He had only recently overcome the attempts to remove him as pastor, so he was uncertain how the congregation would react to this latest development in his personal life. "I knew in initiating divorce that I would once again face putting my career on the line. But I chose to do that, and the congregation that had only recently 'beaten me up' accepted the divorce in a remarkably beautiful way."

Despite his active commitment to renewing the life of the congregation and returning the sanctuary to its original beauty and design, Chris says, "As the project progressed and I neared fifty," he says, "I knew I needed to decide whether or not to move. I went back and forth, and prior to the project's final assurance of success, I had conversations with significant search committees in different parts of the country." He realized that he had only two to four years before his age would become a disadvantage to moving, so when the call came from a Presbyterian church in a Northeastern suburb, he accepted "what has been an absolutely delightful call."

One of the satisfactions Chris has found in his new ministry is that of being accepted as a wise and tested elder.

"When you go to the Midwest at age thirty-four with a young family, young kids, in a congregation that's dominated by people your parents' age, you go as the son. You're everybody's son. And leaving there at age forty-nine I was still the same. I mean, you don't ever change those dynamics."

Therefore, when he arrived at the new church, "It was wonderful coming here because I really came to a much younger congregation as the adult. Probably the majority of Session members here are younger than me. . . . So, that's been a true confirmation of, hey, you've been through the ranks, you know what you are doing. You know who you are and who you're not."

Another significant change for Chris since beginning his new ministry is that he has "recently married a woman I have known for twenty-eight years [she was on the staff of his church in the Midwest], a recently ordained Presbyterian minister, . . . and in a life with virtually no relationships unmarked by the specter of trauma, I have found the only true relationship I have ever really had. It is terrific, and I am happy."

With his marriage, Chris relates a sense of closing the circle, or at least one of the circles in his life. He is now in a congregation that matches his own commitments and inclinations, a church where he is valued and celebrated for the gifts he has rather than the ones others might prefer. There is a fit in his life, work, and calling that is something new for him in all his years in ministry. He has time now to gather up loose ends, which he knows can never really be tied up, but like Sarah he can explore these issues without being overwhelmed by them. Most of all, he now has time to create and cultivate a personal and professional life that expresses more integrally his hopes and dreams, now chastened by time and experience.

Anna

After so many years, Anna's voice is familiar, and her quiet, distinct words resonate with memories of the person who entered Union in 1976. She speaks with the same earnestness as before but with more reflection. She speaks directly about the secret that she did not share during her seminary years and recognizes that in many ways she barely shared that secret even with herself. She talks unhesitatingly about her life and does not gloss over the difficult times even when they might not place her in the best light.

Anna's first church, she reveals, was the same one in which she had done her fieldwork during her years at Union. It was one of New York's well-known black Baptist churches, and she chose it during her school years, she says, "because it was a big church and I was going after fame and glory and the whole thing." While doing her fieldwork, however, she often complained of the restrictions the pastor of the church placed on her because she was a woman. Yet upon her graduation, he praised her good work, and he and the church offered her an assistant pastor position. Unfortunately, after accepting the offer, she found that once again she was being relegated to what she considered minor roles in the church's ministry.

While working at the church, she fell in love with a church member who was completing a master's degree at New York University, and they soon became engaged. But the pastor, says Anna, "was not at all happy about my impending marriage, because I was a woman and needed to only answer to God. Secondly, I was marrying a man who was an actor and taught theater. This was 'demonic,' as he put it. So we were not allowed to get married at the church." They were married at Union Seminary instead and soon moved to Texas, where Anna took a position with a Baptist church.

She remained at that church for five years, and during that time both of her children were born. However, during her maternity leave with her second son, her position at the Baptist church was eliminated, and about a year later she received a call to a nearby United Methodist church. Later, Anna and her husband decided to change affiliation to the United Methodist Church, and she was appointed in the Methodist system as associate pastor at the Texas church and served there for ten years.

Her husband, says Anna, "was a great supporter of me and pushed me to attempt things for God that I never would have." Yet her husband created another crisis for her by declaring, after a few years of marriage, his own intention to enter ministry.

"I did not want to be married to a minister," says Anna. "One in the house was enough."

But her husband earned his M.Div., and the two of them served together on the staff of the Methodist church where Anna had been appointed earlier.

"People were intrigued by the fact that we were a clergy couple, especially in the black church. It was so rare." But she began to "pull back and hide behind her husband. I retreated in some respects." She began slipping into depression. After an initial attempt at therapy that she abandoned, the depression eventually returned. Not long thereafter, she was able to summon the determination to pursue these issues again. While attending a Christian wholeness retreat, she was encouraged to go into day treatment to deal with a new bout of depression. She reluctantly decided to stay and checked herself into the center run by the group that had led the retreat.

It was during this period of therapy that she finally confronted her father's sexual abuse of her as a child and teenager. Anna's behavior during her years at Union was deeply entwined with what she had said or left unsaid about these psychological wounds.

"I was not honest at all," she says, "about who I was or what I was really confronting during those years at Union and the subsequent years. . . . I was so unhealthy during my time at Union. I was living a lie. The truth was too painful, and quite frankly, I had blocked out quite a bit of it. . . . Basically, I am shy and carried layers of guilt most of my life. . . . I never told anyone at Union about my secret."

She says that during her second year at Union she tried to confront her secret through therapy, but she never found a therapist with whom she felt completely comfortable. So the secret remained hidden, and the old wounds continued to fester.

"I spent a lot of time feeling sorry for myself. I spent many days at Riverside Chapel confessing and talking to God. God was the only one that I could trust. This fact was probably the biggest element of my call to ministry."

Through therapy in her later life she has learned "that I spent years protecting my dad and trying to redeem him by being a better minister. I do believe that my call in many ways was birthed out of this experience. As a child and teen, God was my only solace and the only one that I could confide in. I loved God so much and wanted to do whatever he asked of me. The place where I was wounded became the ministry that God would use in me to be a blessing to others."

Since that time, Anna has confronted her father, who was already in counseling, and her family has also been dealing with the reality of her father's behavior. Anna has also begun a new phase in her life. About twelve years ago, Anna and her husband reluctantly left the United Methodist Church, but they were determined to start their own nondenominational church. Because of the independent nature of the church, she says, "we have had no financial support or denominational support. It has been a stressful journey, and it has required a lot of our time and effort. We have about 450 members now. But it is still very time consuming for us." The experience of confronting and working through her sexual abuse has transformed her sense of ministry, especially as it has made her more open to diverse people and their needs, particularly the marginalized and the forgotten.

"[In] our church . . . one of the things that we really teach our leaders is that people come . . . through many different ports of entry. So we don't shun gays, the homeless, or others who don't look like us. We invite them in. We don't preach against them. We don't preach against the drug addicts, the prostitutes, but we find ways we can minister to them." As Anna says, "I have been very open about my own abuse, and God has used my painful experience to help others."

David

After much struggle, David eventually graduated from Union in 1981. Around the same time that he graduated, he also married. He and his wife remained at a small Disciples of Christ church in Manhattan until 1983, when he took the pastorate of a church in Gary, Indiana, where he remained until 1989. Gary was a "hard experience," he says. "The people had left the community. It was a shambles; it was almost a ghost town."

Throughout his career, David has asserted his role in promoting the rights of the Hispanic community, "to advocate for the suffering people." He did this in New York and tried to continue such efforts in Indiana. He then describes a particular incident in which his intervention brought justice to the family of a Mexican man arrested for public drunkenness.

"The young man was taken into custody and left in a cell. . . . The next day the young man was found hanged. The poor investigation done by the court system declared that he had committed suicide. The mother and family of the young man came to me and asked if there was anything I could do to open the case and have a better investigation done. The court declared that their investigation was done under the rules and there was nothing else they could do. I called a meeting of the Mexican community and worked in staging a protest, walking through the main route, and called all the media to be present. After this the court ordered the case reopened. After the investigation, it showed that it was impossible for the young man to have committed suicide."

Eventually, one of the guards confessed to being the cause of the young man's death.

Despite such work that he did in behalf of his community, David's time in Indiana was difficult and demanding, both financially and spiritually. Yet he pressed on. "Since the church . . . was not able to cover my full salary and provide any type of insurance, I accepted a job as Executive Director of LAFE (Latin American Family Education), while continuing to serve the church in full capacity as pastor. Being close to Indianapolis, both the general church and regional nominated me to several committees. One of my achievements with LAFE was to get the senator of Indiana, Richard Lugar, and the mayor of Gary [Richard Hatcher] to appear together at the educational program graduation. I was told that this had never been done before, getting a Republican and a Democrat present on the same platform. The mayor gave the key to the city to the senator."

Ultimately, the ministry in Indiana was no longer viable, and David and his wife moved to Florida, where David became pastor of an Hispanic congregation attached to the Christian Church (Disciples of Christ). At the same time, he quickly became a leader in the community.

"The Puerto Rican Club asked me to be their chaplain and help them write their bylaws and constitution. Since I wrote it, this reflects my belief in community affairs. The [Disciples of Christ] region of Florida had few Hispanic churches, and their constitution and bylaws reflected this. Getting together with the other Hispanics churches, we organized the Florida Hispanics Convention, later known as the Southeast Hispanics Convention. I made sure that some of the divisive ideals in the Northeast were not incorporated . . . in the constitution and bylaws of this convention."

David also became a member of the National Hispanics Board (El Caucus):

"This was the forum where I voiced my opinion about issues that cause division between Hispanics and the other ethnic groups that make up the Christian Church (Disciples of Christ)." Unfortunately, this was also the caucus in which he began to hear whispers saying that perhaps he "was more white than Hispanic." David's allegiance both to his Hispanic and American background has apparently led to occasional conflicts that he has struggled to resolve.

Although his participation in the larger church has not been without controversy, he has had a long and fruitful ministry in the Florida congregation. David's church is housed in an old rural wood-framed church building. The sanctuary is small, seating perhaps at most 75 people. The congregation consists of Puerto Ricans and other Spanish-speaking natives and recent immigrants. Services are led by lay leaders with David taking responsibility for preaching and the ministrations of healing. While David had serious issues with written English and Spanish in seminary, he is able to conduct services in both languages with remarkable skill, moving with ease from one language to the other. Unlike the ebullient David who most often appeared in the interviews at Union, today's David reflects a more quiet and thoughtful presence. When I visited with him and his congregation on a Sunday morning, I was struck by his genuinely modest demeanor. He does not call attention to himself, and the people clearly love him. He has served this congregation for a number of years, working as an accountant to help earn a living.

He likes small churches, he says, because they have a greater sense of community. His ministry, however, has led to many financial challenges for him and his wife.

"If you know anything about the Hispanic churches," he says, "they don't have that much money to pay for the ministry. Especially, in my case, I've always had small congregations that could hardly afford to pay a minister. If it wasn't for my wife's salary [as a social worker], I don't know how we would have survived." To further help with family finances, David also has some pension income and his Social Security benefit, and he has also established "a business in my house as a tax preparer and advisor," which he continues to offer as a service to the community. Recently, he has become a hospice chaplain as well.

First and foremost, however, David remains dedicated to pastoral ministry. One defining aspect of that ministry is David's determination to offer bilingual services. As he says, he is committed each Sunday to do "the whole service in both languages [Spanish and English]. All translation is done by me or the person that is directing or singing." He believes that such a commitment will knit the community of the church together. Unfortunately, it has not worked out as well as he had hoped. As he says, "The church has not grown to the scale others have, and many people, when they see this, leave looking for a church that only uses one language." Nevertheless, David remains committed to a bilingual church that will unify all the members of the congregation.

"I love ministry," he says. "I love what I'm doing. I have a charisma with youth. Right now we have a church of about sixty [families], and of the sixty I have ninety youth and about thirty-five children. That's what keeps me going—the fact that all my life I have seen young people grow up, do something for themselves. Some of them become ministers. So for me that's a reward."

Beth

When Beth sits down for her final interview, she is in her mid-fifties and is the rector of an Episcopal church in upstate New York. She has changed little in appearance, and her spirit and personal presence are resonant with the person she was in seminary. She is older, of course, but the quickness of mind and the straightforward way she addresses a question are all recognizable.

"I was called here to do a parish revitalization because the parish had had a long history, about a twenty-five-year history, of conflict and divisiveness. This last conflict really almost decimated the parish. There was a question of how they would stay open. So at the time that that happened, the bishop here . . . began a whole ministry . . . to focus on two things: one was parish help and revitalization; the other was ministry in the community. . . . So he identified this parish, since it was a parish in crisis, as a parish to begin a pilot program . . . of offering diocesan support in terms of five-year grants and loans if the parish would partner with the diocese to do some things that are really necessary to create a healthy inter-dynamic within the parish, so we worked a lot on congregational dynamics. So the parish bought into that program, and . . . I came in after that program had started. The previous rector had done a very good job in terms of generating a lot of enthusiasm. I think he engendered some confidence in the parish. But by the same token his leaving reinforced the experience here of people's perception that you can't trust clergy.

"When I came in, . . . it was fairly dicey in the first couple of years, both financially and in terms of parish dynamics. Lot of . . . inclination to fight over things instead of trying to sit down and talk about how we understand each other, how we work through differences. . . . We have created what we call a campus ministry here, a ministry that really is focused beyond ourselves to the community. At the same time, we've had a steady stream, myself included, of parishioners going through Congregational Development Institute, which this diocese offers locally. . . . So we've done a lot of work on creating a different tone here—not being so critical of each other, not being so judgmental. If we have issues, we try to talk face to face about it. So the diocese comes in once a year and does an evaluation. They've been just amazed at the change of temperament, enthusiasm, not to mention the ministry that we're doing. We've also stabilized in terms of our finances and membership. We're still fragile, . . . but we are more stable than we were."

Like all of the other participants in the study, Beth has had her own challenges. She has experienced the often arduous role of being one of the early women in ministry, and she has struggled with the inner conflicts that often arise from juggling the requirements of a career with the needs of being a wife and mother. However, at this point in her life in ministry, Beth seems comfortable with herself and with her life as an Episcopal priest.

Her ministry began, after her graduation from Union, in western New York, where she was confronted with a situation that she and her husband faced throughout their careers in ministry. Not only are they both ministers, but she is Episcopalian, and he is Presbyterian. Being ministers in two different denominations has created expected and unexpected tensions.

As Beth says, "What we have tried to do has been really difficult. I'm not sure we'd try it again. I think it's been tough for both of us in two ways. First of all, for male clergy, especially when we were starting out in the '80s, . . . it was always an issue that I wasn't participating in his church. Now, for me, for women clergy, it's usually not a big issue if the men don't participate. . . . So that was the first thing that was hard. And then it's always been very difficult finding positions for both us in different places. . . . When I was ordained in '81, female clergy in the Episcopal Church were fairly new, and there was a great deal of resistance to that. So when I was ordained a deacon in '81, I did have a position, part-time, at the cathedral. But that was only because the bishop created quite a bit of pressure to make that happen.

"I did a lot of sort of networking with the other Episcopal parishes. . . . I worked closely with the other downtown churches because, as you remember, that was during the Reagan era when the social services were being cut. . . . So we enhanced the program at the cathedral with providing food for people, mainly street people. . . . Then we also expanded that to create a new program for people who were without food in their homes. So we created an emergency food assistance project that worked with suburban churches to collect food and then worked with the urban churches to distribute it. So I ran that program for a couple of years. Then my son was born in '83, so . . . I worked part time but very part time when he was born."

Beth describes the birth of their son as "a profoundly spiritual experience for me, as it is for most new mothers. But it also sharpened my theological focus. Having worked in seminary on the relationship between the inner life and the call to social justice, motherhood awakened within me an urgency about both of these things. My maternal

instincts made me keenly aware of the need to respect the 'inner being' of my child. That is to say, I tried very hard to understand what he
was experiencing and to respond to his needs from that awareness. I
had little concern with 'conformity' or 'obedience' but was committed
to providing ways for him to connect what was going on internally
to the world around him. In psychoanalytic theory, this is known as
object-relations theory. . . . I was committed to cultivating what D. W.
Winnicott refers to as the 'true self.' I thought of it as feeding the soul."

In 1986, Beth was accepted into the doctoral program for religious studies at a nearby university.

"I had hoped," she states, "that this would provide an opportunity to do further work in the field of psychiatry and religion that I
had begun at Union. . . . I was completely unprepared for the hostility that the department held for people who pursued the academic
study of religion while being actively engaged in a faith community.
I had had no awareness of the distinction between seminary studies and the academic study of religion. I also found little support for
my interest in precognitive experience in the formation of images
that shape one's consciousness and intellectual development. Interest in precognition was belittled as being interested in the mental
formation of children and therefore a 'woman's thing.' What I did
find interesting was how dogmatic people could be in their academic
disciplines while condemning religion for being dogmatic."

In spite of the hostility she perceived in her doctoral program,
Beth found her four years there productive. "I had exposure to trends
in philosophical discourse that were unfamiliar to me. I took classes
in Buddhist studies. I was introduced to the work of the Jesus Seminar, which was formed at about that time. . . . My most meaningful work during that time was in New Testament studies and Wisdom literature. This was a topic through which I could continue
my questions from seminary days about a feminist appropriation
of the Bible. The image of Jesus as Lady Wisdom is a dominant and
sustaining image in my religious life. I frequently refer in preaching
and teaching to the image of Lady Wisdom found in Proverbs 8 to
talk about God's delight in humanity and to suggest an image of a
God who dances."

Eventually, though, the negative aspects of her doctoral studies began to weigh heavily on her, and Beth decided to withdraw and concentrate on earning an income to help support the family. As she says, "I have no regret about that decision."

Although her next position began with high hopes, it did not end well.

"At the time," she says, "I was on the diocesan staff as the coordinator for youth ministry, so I was at the forefront of the anxiety that always surrounds a change of leadership at the diocesan level. Youth ministry was a hot button issue in the diocese at that time. I had been hired by the previous bishop to deal with the serious dysfunctionality in that program. . . . Through the efforts of the bishop, his Canon to the Ordinary, and myself we had begun to make significant progress in reshaping the program and identifying new leadership." Unfortunately, when a new bishop came in, Beth found herself in disagreement with his approach and ended up resigning from her position.

Thus, when her husband was offered and decided to accept a position at a Presbyterian church in New Jersey, she found herself in conflict over the move. On the one hand, she was pleased at the prospect of making a change to different working conditions. Further, as she says, "we were enthusiastic about returning to the New York City area and the cultural opportunities we had enjoyed during our seminary days. We noticed at once the way in which the economic vitality created a more positive attitude toward church life, unlike what we had experienced working for the church in western New York." They were also pleased to see their son make "a fairly smooth academic adjustment within this highly competitive educational system."

Yet still she struggled.

"Although we felt fortunate to find ourselves in a part of the country that was more vital economically and which had a milder climate, I felt a deep loss at being uprooted from western New York. It was painful to watch the economic collapse that was taking place [there] at the time. I remember feeling like a refugee. The contrast between the economic struggles of people in western New York and the obscene opulence of people in that part of New Jersey was disturbing to me, especially because I felt that the wealth . . . was being accumulated in part at the expense of people in cities in western New York due to all the corporate takeovers and the outsourcing that was just beginning to take place. My husband made a quick adjustment to New Jersey. He had a job in which his talents for ministry were appreciated and cultivated. His long hours at the church made me feel even more isolated in our new home."

"This was a time," says Beth, "of emotional and professional turmoil for me. I had serious questions about my vocation in the church. I felt cut off from my husband, as we were out of sync in our reaction to this new situation. I found it difficult to fit in with people who had so much wealth. The financial pressure felt restricting and created anxiety. I came to feel that there was no place for me in the world, and I was very depressed, lonely, and angry."

Finally, she says, "out of desperation I took a job at the most exclusive Episcopal church in town. . . . The benefit to me proved to be that they did not want programming but expected quality in the preaching. I was given the luxury of spending large amounts of time in study and sermon preparation. During this five years I did extensive reading and journaling. I was also consistent in devoting significant time each day to prayer and meditation. I am still drawing upon the fertile soil of the soul that I was able to cultivate during that time. I had entered that situation with serious doubts about my ongoing ministry in the Episcopal Church. Ironically, it proved to be a springboard from which my professional life began to move forward.

"The turning of this time emerged from the emotional turmoil that I was experiencing. I was lonely and alienated from my situation. I suffered from self-doubt, anger, and depression. I was in my early forties and could not see a future that held any meaning for me, except to provide a good home for my son. I found an excellent therapist, who worked with me intensely for about four years. . . . It was hard and at times painful work, but I experienced myself as being truly a different person from it. It also gave me the listening skills that have enabled me to be effective in parish ministry."

Through her therapy, Beth says that she was able to "more readily identify what I was feeling in the moment as opposed to talking about what I thought about something. This was the first step to moving away from blaming others for the things that bothered me and toward identifying what I needed to do to have a more satisfying life."

Beth and her family remained in the affluent New Jersey community for six years, and then she and her husband both found positions in a large Midwestern city. They were concerned about moving at a time when their son was in the middle of high school, and once in the new place they realized it was a more conservative part of the country than they had imagined, more Southern, it seemed to them, than Midwestern. Nevertheless, Beth appreciated the smaller school that their son attended and the more conservative restrictions placed on teenagers generally. "Life was a lot slower there," she says. "Kids were home at 11 o'clock at night."

In this new location, Beth had her first opportunity to be a rector, taking charge of a small church in a neighborhood that was in transition from white to black.

"In the Episcopal Church, you've got to be a rector to have a career. So that was a real breakthrough for me to get that. I enjoyed the parish. It was very small. I always had great visions for it, which I could never quite get the diocese to buy into, because they . . . weren't committed to congregational development."

Beth pointed out to the diocese that, including her own parish, there were four Episcopal churches near one another. Two were predominantly black; two were predominantly white. One of each had a full-time rector; one of each had a part-time rector. She argued that by creating an alliance among the four churches and combining their strengths, all four churches could be made stronger. She received a great deal of resistance but persisted in recommending a strategy that she was certain would lead to a healthier situation. At last, the four churches came to a cooperative agreement. By this time, however, Beth and her husband had decided to look for new positions in other parts of the country. Thus, even though the work had not been completed, Beth left her parish feeling more certain than ever of her skills as a pastoral leader in the Episcopal Church.

Beth and her husband both took churches in cities near each other in upstate New York. Beth, in fact, continues as the rector of her church, but her husband is now retired and not for a reason that he would have chosen.

One rainy summer night on his way back home from a meeting, Beth's husband took a wrong turn, misjudged an unexpected curve in the road, and crashed over an embankment. The car rolled over several times, and Beth's husband could tell that he had sustained significant injuries, including a blow to the head. Nevertheless, he was able to pull himself free of the vehicle, climb back up to the highway, and find someone to help him. He was shaken up but seemed well-enough at the time. Even so, when the police arrived, he was transported to a hospital where he was found to have suffered serious back injuries. It was then, too, that the contusion created by the blow to his head began to cause swelling of the brain that eventually led to serious medical injuries. The result is that he is no longer able to work.

"It's one of those things," says Beth, "where he's chronically fatigued. He has times when he focuses very well. He does very well if he's in a very controlled situation, which he is. He's done a very good job of creating a routine for himself. He always gets up when I get up. He always makes my breakfast. When I get out the door, he does his exercises and does his walks. Then, when he's having a good day, he reads. He's got a really sharp mind, and he's able to read on his good days. But he's always loved music, so he's used this time to get some opera DVDs. So we watch a lot of opera. He watches a lot of old movies from the '50s."

Beth has accepted her husband's disability and made changes that are required in her life and work to deal with this new reality in their lives. Yet she does not dwell on their situation. Beth remains forthright and able to look at things with little blinking and a lot of grace.

Tim

Of all the participants, Tim seems the most changed. His demeanor is reserved, and he speaks in a soft voice that is at times almost inaudible. There is little energy in what he says or how he says it, although he occasionally displays glimpses of the younger and energetic Tim. Such displays, however, are quickly contained by the circumspect and careful self he now presents in conversation. Cancer, divorce, and the constant stress of dealing with a church in transition have left their mark.

Tim began his ministry in the Unitarian Universalist tradition as he had originally intended, and though he offers little information about the first decade of his career, he does say that it was during his ministry at a Unitarian church in Rhode Island that he began to become dissatisfied. He describes his years at that church as a good experience but one that was "just drying me up. I found that I really wanted scripture, and I wanted a prayer life. . . . I really wanted a deeply intimate relationship with God."

Tim has left the Unitarian Universalists and become a minister in the United Church of Christ. For sixteen years he has been the minister of an urban church in central Massachusetts. The church building reflects the once established character of traditional Congregational churches and speaks as well of the affluence and power that made such congregations significant forces in the community. Today, however, the church no longer stands in a privileged white community but serves instead a neighborhood of multiple races and ethnic backgrounds whose religious roots are evangelical and Catholic, not liberal mainline Protestant.

"For better or for worse," says Tim, "this church is the defining place of my ministry. . . . It has been eye-opening and graceful and very painful and humbling or humiliating at times. I have survived three major attempts to have me leave here. The first two times from real antagonists and the last time, my friends. The last time was a year and one-half ago, which finally only resolved itself this past spring. In that process, I went out and looked at other churches, received one offer and turned it down, made a decision to stay here, and my ministry was reaffirmed, and we've done some major restructuring of staff, expectations, committees, budget, mission, . . . [and] there is still a lot of fallout. But my ministry has been renewed and reaffirmed here after sixteen years.

"At the same time, the church has gone from an upper-middle-class white, very formal, congregation . . . to a mixed congregation, racially, in terms of suburban–urban mix, in terms of class, in terms of worship style and experience, in terms of mission. . . . We are a very, very different place than we were sixteen years ago, and we're not done.

"The major changes are three. The first is that nobody really questions anymore that we are a city church. . . . And that was a major point of contention when I came. . . . Nobody else knew about it or believed it, but our folks did. That's the first thing. And the second piece, major change, is that, as a congregation, we could . . . make decisions about difficult things, and we became an open, affirming congregation four years ago, and that was quite a process to go through here. And the third thing, which is really significant, . . . I call this congregation a Jesus-centered, open, affirming congregation. The open and affirming piece is in place. The Jesus-centered piece . . . there's some skepticism about it. But I think that . . . there is no question in my mind that . . . we are certainly a prayer-centered place or have become much more so. There is a lively, articulated, spiritual life that is no longer questioned, although there are different ideas of what that means.

"The endowment has graced us to be able to continue through a lot of these changes that would not have even been remotely possible without it. And the other thing that we have been graced with is some significant leadership, forward-looking leadership who, through a lot of opposition, finally took hold. And they are not necessarily new people. They are people who have made some huge shifts in their own faith life and . . . understanding what church is and personal mission in the world and so on."

Despite recent attempts to reframe the mission of the church, Tim describes the local demographics as unpromising.

"From the point of view of church growth," he says, "we are in a funny little cul-de-sac of cultures—Russian Jewish, Russian Pentecostal, Hispanic, African American, swamp Yankee—sort of a funny little mix of people in our corner of the city. Although we do not necessarily draw from the street, we do draw now from a much wider variety of [local] communities. We have much more . . . face recognition, for example, in the black community."

Besides the struggles and conflicts in the church, which have taken a toll on Tim, he and his wife have both suffered through and recovered from cancer. The two years of dealing with cancer were difficult for both of them, and in fact, once recovery began, Tim decided that he needed to make some "personal shifts" and went into therapy.

One result of the therapy was that Tim began to change his role as minister. The therapist, he says, helped him "stop taking responsibility for the future of the church. And what he helped me see was that . . . instead of holding all the anxiety for the congregation and leadership, I needed to be giving it back to them, which is one very strong reason why the people who were my supporters got very anxious and then wanted me to leave a year and one-half ago because I was not doing a number of things I used to do.

"We had some very considerable staff conflict, and I was not solving it. When presented with a leadership decision, I would say something like 'you know, that makes me very sad, . . . and I don't know what to do. What do you want to do?' There was a lot of my saying 'I don't know.' What happened was that leadership dug in, and it did what needed to be done eventually.

"So we have much more of a partnership now than we did before, and a much clearer understanding of what is their role and my role as senior pastor. All I wanted was something worked out."

While many members of the church felt that he was abdicating his responsibilities, Tim saw himself as forcing the congregants to take more responsibility themselves. He may also have been struggling with his own personal issues. Certainly he was struggling with a need to redefine himself, not only as a pastor but as a person. One result of this period of change was that Tim began the process of divorcing his wife, a process that Tim describes as "protracted and difficult." He says that "the congregation has been enormously supportive," but when he introduced at worship and a few social events a woman with whom he was in a developing relationship, the congregation responded with perceptible unease.

According to Tim, "Pastoring certainly had a role in the beginning and the end of my marriage. I married a doctoral student at Columbia who lived at Union Seminary, and our wedding reception was held in the Union Seminary refectory." He and his wife had three children, and, he says, "there is no doubt in my mind that the ups and downs of church life and my own ego's need to fulfill a role as pastor in a changing institution, my attempt to bridge church and family life where my family was increasingly uninvolved in my church and yet deeply affected by what happened at church, contributed to the dissolution of the marriage.

"In the end, however, I chose to leave my marriage, and my reasons have to do with being human, failing to keep work and parenting and life and relationship together. I am fortunate in the sense that because my family has not been involved in the church for many years, there was no outrage among church members at my news and a great deal of support and kindness." (As they grew up, Tim's three daughters gravitated toward their mother's Catholic faith, and after he left the marriage, all three aligned themselves with the Catholic church.)

"I work daily with my own judgment at my decision and have had to watch myself in public, because people worry about whether I am okay or whether I am planning to leave the church or whether I have broken any irredeemable rules about starting up a new relationship. I have had many private conversations and answered more questions about my personal life than I am accustomed to or wish to ever again.

"The lesson, finally, is about being truthful. Living truthfully brings pain, but it does not bring misery. Suffering, as the saying goes, is inevitable, but misery is optional."

Tim is trying to cultivate something of worth out of his own sadness, both in his professional life and in the family he is leaving behind. He has invested himself in a spiritual direction program and serves as one of its leaders. While he has found a new love in his life, and this relationship is helping him regain confidence and a renewed sense of himself, he feels the anguish of divorce and the uncertainties of being a parent in the process of divorce. Furthermore, he realizes that it is time for him to move to another church—a church that is more of a fit with his inclinations and strengths. After all these years of trying to reinvent himself to serve a congregation vastly different from the kind he once envisioned himself leading, Tim wants to be in a place that claims the spiritual and intellectual depth that is so much a part of the person and the pastor he is.

Like Tim, almost all of the participants in this study have dealt with setbacks, either in their pastoral work or their personal lives. Two in particular have revealed in this chapter difficult personal episodes that haunted their youth and followed them during many critical years of their adulthood. Yet all have experienced moments of grace and enough recognition of their worth and achievement to reassure them in times of difficulty and reaffirm their work and calling.

As we hear firsthand about the nature of ministry from the eight, it is a mix of accomplishment and disappointment. Their dreams of the life they looked forward to upon graduation from seminary have often been chastened by the actual reality of the church. They have had to make adjustments in what they do, and they have constantly had to deal with the personal issues that arise from the practice of ministry. There is a continuing effort to hold together the church they believe in and want to serve and the actual congregation with whom they live daily. While they know that the church is a human institution, they keep hoping it will be more than what most institutions settle for. Most of the eight do not serve churches that provide them with a large salary or other benefits that might take the edge off the grittiness they often experience. The unrelenting membership decline in denominations establishes a demanding context in which resources are scarce and hopes for the future are made more modest by the realities of ecclesial life.

Unlike many clergy who keep moving in pursuit of another church that may treat them better than their last one, the eight tend to stay put and commit themselves to the church they serve rather than spending a lot of time day dreaming about a more perfect place. This requires them to think about their vocation and perhaps to come to terms with the realization that ministry, especially ordained ministry, is the work of servant leaders. The language of servanthood has often been avoided, but as Robert Greenleaf pointed out, it is the center of any genuine vocation of leadership.[1]

The capacity to focus on the vision out of which an institution has been created and to see leadership as being in service to a great vision is a characteristic that makes the difference between prophetic leaders and sacred technicians. It is the kind of leadership that has the capacity to renew itself and find resources of spirit to take up tasks once again after being buffeted and tossed about by congregational life. This is not a matter of being enthusiastic; it is a matter of finding energies within that give depth and fidelity to practices of ministry. Most importantly, it requires setting aside time for practicing the kind of spiritual life that cultivates this inward dimension. Some of the eight do this with real intentionality; others do it on the run and know that this is not adequate. All of them, however, understand the extent to which the outward forms of their life need the ballast of a corresponding inward life that can sustain their spirits. Reading thoughtfully and prayerfully, preparing and studying for teaching and preaching, meditating and getting regular physical exercise, developing musical or artistic skills—all of these are some of the ways this inward life is cultivated. Going to a monastery, as many clergy do, can periodically offer a reminder of what is required, but as Eugene Peterson has suggested, creating a kind of monastic setting within one's own life works even better.[2]

chapter 7

Looking Back and Going Forward

The place where I was wounded became the ministry that
God would use in me to be a blessing to others. — ANNA

NEARLY THIRTY YEARS AFTER GRADUATING FROM UNION, THE
group of eight was invited to gather for several days and reflect on
their years in ministry. They were given transcripts of their interviews to read and were asked to put into writing their thoughts
about what they found there. Among other issues they explored
were the discouragements that have caused them at times to question their work and calling, but they also shared with one another
the triumphs (large and small) and daily satisfactions that have kept
them committed to their vocation over time.

While some looked forward to reading the transcripts of their
conversations with me beginning in 1976, others were not sure of
what they would find and were more than a little concerned about
the person they would see in the interviews. Seven of the eight were
able to participate in the colloquium. The only one absent was Anna,
who had a prior commitment she could not change. She did, however, submit the paper she had written.

Tim

"I have been told that I should write a book telling the stories of my ministry. The invitation appeals to my vanity. Remarkably, after nearly thirty years in the ministry, I still have a few things to be vain about—my stories. That's about it."

So begins Tim's reflection on his life in ministry. In the first sentence we find the tone of an old hand, a pastor with tales to tell who seems inclined to tell them. In the very next sentence, though, he tamps down the enthusiasm of the moment by reminding himself and the listener that a request to tell his stories is simply an appeal to his vanity, and he feels compelled to assert that, aside from his stories, he has few reasons to feel any vanity about his life. The final, three-word sentence—"that's about it"—reflects the tone of sardonic humility that is a dominant theme in Tim's reflection.

Referring to the tales he has to tell, Tim says, "I notice in all the stories a sense of miracle. I have been touched, moved to laughter and tears, by the long arc of holy work. I have seen prodigals welcomed, dry bones come to life, loaves multiply, water pour from the rock, a little oil sustain, stones roll away. All these in the normal human company of fear, crisis, anger, and judgment. I have had my part in the pain. I have had my part in the holiness. I am not who I was when I began my ministry, and that is a miracle, too."

Although Tim's almost sermonic description refers to several miraculous and regenerative stories from scripture, the words used to invoke these stories create a heavier tone than what might be expected. There is a spirit of resignation about all of this and not a lot of hopefulness. Tim speaks of himself as a changed person, but the change seems to be one of acceptance toward what has happened rather than affirmation of something new. The former relentless seeker now embraces the language of evangelical piety without, however, the optimistic demeanor with which it is often accompanied.

Tim then goes on to tell several stories. One is of a visit he received from two women from the church who are part of the Prayer Shawl ministry. The work of these women, he says, "is only one part knitting shawls. . . . The rest is commentary on the inner and personal life of the church and its members." Therefore, he is wary of their visit, especially because he has recently announced to the congregation that even while in the process of divorcing his first wife he has a new person in his life. Tim thus anticipates harsh pronouncements from the women of the Prayer Shawl ministry, but they surprise him by saying, "we support you and love you and hope you will be very happy."

Tim's immediate response to the women is one of grateful tears, but he does not delve into the nature of the events and conditions leading up to the visit. He simply accepts the emotions of the moment.

He follows this story with another impressionistic episode that begins by describing the varying fortunes of his church and himself. He speaks of a neck tie that he wore one Sunday that had written on it in bold letters, "For God so loved the world that he gave his only Son, so that everyone who believes in him may not perish but may have eternal life (John 3:16)." It was given to him by a Hispanic lesbian couple, and he wore it in their honor. He then discusses how the tie represents a change in his willingness to reveal publicly his spiritual commitment to Jesus, something he would not have done as a Unitarian Universalist or even as a typical UCC minister. Instead, the tie is a kind of banner that reflects the newly minted evangelical outlook that has claimed him in recent years as he has tried to reach out to the neighborhood and renew the life of the congregation. On the Sunday in question, he looked for the lesbian couple at worship, but they did not attend. So the tie, he decides, is a sign, not for them, but for himself, "for all to see—of how far I have come."

He then goes on to another seemingly unrelated story about a woman named Teri, "an African American woman in her mid-thirties," who "became a leader in the church" and tried to increase black involvement but with only middling success. Along with Teri, another African American, named Lucius, did much to improve the church's standing with the local black population. But Lucius died suddenly of a stroke, and some of Lucius's friends accused Tim of pushing Lucius "so hard in this racial potboiler that he died." One of these friends, an African American woman, appeared one day in Tim's office, drew a gun, and "confronted me with his death and the prospect of my own." Tim convinced the woman to let Teri join them. He called Teri, who came right away to Tim's office and was able to mediate the crisis. Tim concludes this section by speaking of Teri (who has since left the congregation) and her effect on him.

"I notice the absence of Teri. I miss her. I notice also that I am different now because of her. I am seldom afraid any more. And I am seldom without prayer."

Once again he lets the episode speak for itself. He does not try to complete the narrative or interpret what happened.

He next observes that "I take no magazines any more and go to few conferences. . . . I have thought about this and wondered whether I am getting like my father, who now tends to leave lights down in my parents' apartment, as though brightness is hard and shadows are easier. I have concluded that I'm not there yet. Now there is more light on the inside of me."

Despite this assertion that he has enough light inside him, Tim does not seem sure about what exactly this light is illuminating, and his language is mindful of St. John of the Cross and his own dark night of the soul.

"The arc of my own work," he says, "has moved from outside to inside. Once, church leadership meant to me knowing many and important things and out of that knowledge trying to fix the church. Once I thought that the decline of the mainline church could be reversed by better programming, more sensible structure, greater sensitivity to demographics, stronger worship, more passionate preaching, and more effective outreach." Now he looks out at his congregation on a Sunday and he can see "no natural reason for our being together." He then asserts, "If there is a common thread, it is that each person wants to know how to receive God's love. We have forgotten how to be loved. . . . I have had to disassemble everything I learned in seminary and start all over again, apprenticing myself to Jesus. . . . Little by little I have learned to open my heart, to let go of fear and judgment, and find in return I receive grace upon grace."

All of this sounds like a man who is hoping to find spiritual reassurance through a conversion of heart and soul. He is struggling to deal with converging issues—a crisis in his family life, a crisis in the church he serves, and a crisis in the changing shape of his own ministry. He is trying to stay above the churning currents of his life.

Tim then describes the time a parishioner came up to him after church, hugged him, and said that he forgave him: "He thought I needed to hear I am loved as much as anybody in the church and he was willing to let go his anger to tell me." Tim, who seems so mystified by so much else in his life, says, "I still don't know what he was angry about."

When asked whether, knowing what he knows now, he would still choose a life in ministry, Tim gives not so much a positive or a negative reply but one that defines his place in this moment but offers no judgment: "I was called into ministry to learn how to have a heart for God and to give my heart without fear. Others may well learn that lesson elsewhere, but ordained ministry has been my path. And I can now say that finally I have the heart of a pastor."

Tim's words echo Karl Rahner's graphic depiction of the ministry as a calling for persons with a "pierced heart," whose vocation is not propped up by social prestige or recognizable authority but by the service they render to the neediest of society; it is the ministry of those who know suffering themselves and try to find some means of transforming this suffering in the practices of ministry they embody in the church and world.[1]

In fact, now that several years have passed since he spoke of the things that led him to what he felt were vulnerable places within his life and left him with the often exhausting task of engaging complicated personal and professional issues, Tim realizes even more that it is time for him to leave the church he has served for so many years and find a new pastorate that better fits his theological and personal commitments. He knows, however, that it will not be easy to find another congregation.

While he has tried to reinvent his own outlook and practice of ministry in order to help his current congregation become a different kind of church in a changing community, he recognizes that he needs to reclaim a more integral sense of self and ministry. He is not trying to escape the still difficult issues he faces in the breakup of his marriage, nor is he denying the hard questions in ministry that have weighed on him, but he now seems more easily himself, more hopeful and energetic, as he expresses a renewed sense of himself, his work, and his calling beyond the bounds of what the congregation expects of him.

Anna

Anna's reflections confirm much of what she has said in her previous interviews, but after reviewing the transcripts of her interviews while attending Union, she says, "I was embarrassed by her [the Anna of 1976] and amazed at how self-absorbed and closed she was to the opportunities that her time at Union offered to her. . . . I missed the meaning of this life experience on many levels." Much of the hostility and unwillingness to participate in the opportunities available to her at Union emerged, she believes, from the acute distress she felt over her abuse by her father from ages nine to seventeen. She had largely repressed or rationalized this abuse until, while at Union, her younger sister came to visit her and confessed that their father had just abused her. Her sister's confession caused Anna to begin her own halting self-realization that was not finally resolved until many years later.

However, the abuse she experienced as a child and young person had already influenced the way in which she chose to interpret certain episodes in her life. For example, in her very first interview in 1976, she had said, "Union was the dream choice. My father had always wanted me to go to Union. When he was in seminary, it was the school to go to." But in her later reflections in 2008, she corrects this statement, saying, "He did speak of Union, but not for my benefit." She then says, "My dad was a Baptist pastor and certainly was against women being in ministry. So I risked a lot to come to Union."

"My call," she says, "was born out of an unhealthy and painful journey. My therapist used to say it was probably a neurotic choice, based on a need to fix my father. . . . I was so unhealthy during my time at Union. I was living a lie. The truth was too painful, and quite frankly, I had blocked out quite a bit of it." Nevertheless, she asserts, "My years at Union and in New York were defining moments of turning in my life. It was at Union that I confronted the secrets that I had lived with all of my life. It was at Union that I had stood twenty-six years ago in James Chapel and married my husband."

Anna speaks of the inner turmoil in her life and many missed opportunities that resulted from that turmoil. Further, she perceives that she often sought or assumed adversarial roles in which she took positions that aligned herself with some groups (such as the Black Caucus) and against others (such as feminists and the gay community). These became temporary measures that resolved, at least for the moment, the ambivalence and ambiguity she often felt about herself, the ideas that would claim her, and the work she wanted to do.

Referring to the sexual tensions and emotional distress she felt at Union, Anna says, "Dealing with the brothers daily at Union did not help. It seemed that I was always confronted with sexual advances and innuendos. . . . Yet I remained loyal to the brothers and to the black community."

Sexist attitudes, she says, have had serious impacts on her career, particularly early on. Yet a recent event provided her with an opportunity to heal some bad feelings. As she described in earlier interviews, she did not have a happy experience in the first church in which she did fieldwork for Union. She was not allowed (because she was a woman) to do much in the way of pastoral ministry. Yet, she says, "last year I was invited back as a daughter of that church to preach at the pastor's retirement. . . . It was very healing. The pastor admitted that he had mistreated me."

At the beginning of her reflections, Anna says that she is speaking in the context of "two critical recent experiences in my life." The first is being invited back to Union several years ago as part of a group being honored by the Black Caucus. During her visit she met with black women currently attending Union, and she found that "they too were experiencing the loneliness, the isolation of being a black female at Union. I find it interesting that after all these years, the issues are still the same. . . . I was able to assure them that it is worth the time and experience to stay at Union. I still believe that Union still needs to work on supporting the minorities there. . . . To be black, female, and religious is to operate under triple jeopardy." Yet for all that, she is able to assert that "the years at Union were very formative for me. I only wish that I could have been healthier, then I would have probably consumed more." Further, she says, "I know that I was hired on several church staffs because of my degree at Union. That degree has opened many doors for me."

The other critical experience that provides context for her reflections is her participation in a spiritual renewal program for women pastors: "Twenty women were chosen, and I am one of two black women in the group. Yes, I am among white women again. . . . One of the things that came up in our interviews often was my negative feelings about the white women at Union. I did not realize how closed I was to relating to them. I was so self-focused that I put the blame all on them. . . . Reading the transcripts [of my interviews] made me aware of the parts that I failed to own as my responsibility for not developing relationships."

Being in the renewal program and reading the interviews from the 1970s, she suggests, helped her confront some things about herself: "I had to confess to God that I have been wrong in grouping all white women as the same. I have been racist in my views and closed to any possibility of befriending them. The very things I accused them of, I have been guilty of as well. Once I could admit that, it freed me to risk relationships with them. My husband commented to me on the seventh day of my stay there, 'Do you realize that you are not calling them white women anymore, but they now have names?' This is part of what is changing in me. I don't want to miss another opportunity to connect with people who are different from me." All the struggles she had with feminist, womanist, and liberation theological perspectives have now become "life changing" for her as she embraces what she once pushed away.

When asked whether she would choose a career in ministry again, Anna says, "Yes. Now that I am conscious and more honest, I would follow the call to ministry all over again. This journey has been one of great heights and valleys. But as the Negro spiritual says, 'I wouldn't take nothing for my journey right now.' I have been broken, shaped, and molded by this great call of God upon my life. Would I have done some things differently? Yes. But it is what it is. It is my spiritual journey."

David

David begins his reflections by discussing the relationship between theological education and ministry, and he reasserts, as expressed in earlier interviews, that the education he received at Union was not especially relevant to his ministry, especially his commitment to the needs of Hispanics. Nevertheless, as flawed as the education he received at Union may have been in his eyes, David concludes that it was imperative to his role as "the voice of the people." In fact, even before entering Union, David received encouragement to believe he had a special role to play among Hispanic Christians. As he says, "The late Dr. Richard Kenny at Bethany College during the oral interview for graduation, at the end of it, said to me to remember that I was going to be 'a leader among my people.' I took this to heart and pursued it. Little did I know that the people supporting me were not the Hispanics, but rather it was the white Americans who were always there to support me and to encourage me in all my endeavors."

The unhappy paradox that David has felt more support from Anglo-Americans than from Hispanics is an obvious disappointment in his life. Yet he remains confident in the rightness of the positions he has taken and feels certain that he has fought the good fight for a more compassionate understanding of faith and practice among Hispanics.

"Many of my Hispanic colleagues did and do not agree with me. . . . I knew that the job was cut out for me—fighting against discrimination within my own denomination . . . , confronting for the first time a dualism and religious struggle of liberalism versus fundamentalism, even more so because Hispanics tend to be more conservative. Once more I discovered that my fight was not only with the status quo of the United States but with those people whose political agenda is different from the people of the pews."

As an example of the clashes that he has had with other Hispanics, he speaks of a pastor who was a member of the Independence Party of Puerto Rico, which is dedicated to Puerto Rican separation from the United States. According to David, he had what he believed to be an innocent misunderstanding with the pastor, but the incident snowballed and ended with the pastor criticizing him in front of the congregation and accusing him of being opposed to the ideals of the Independence Party. David tried to explain his views but only found himself in more trouble:

"I responded to the pastor and those of the same persuasion that my concern was not with the independence of Puerto Rico, but rather I was concerned with the treatment and life of those Hispanics living on the mainland. I was of the belief that a person who is interested in fighting for the independence of Puerto Rico should move to the island and live with the people there and stop receiving the benefits of living a good life in the United States, of discrediting the United States while reaping the harvest. What I discovered was that many of the Hispanic religious leaders ... and those in high positions within the denomination held the same belief as the pastor. I became enemy number one. ... The Hispanics believed that I had sold myself to the side of white Americans, defending them against the Hispanics. Discrimination comes at me from both sides."

David then speaks of his practical difficulties as a minister, including his small salary and lack of pension and the lack of growth in his own congregation. He even wonders if he made the right decision to leave the job he held decades earlier in the fiduciary department in the Bank of New York. "Looking back, if I would have stayed with the bank my profit sharing would have been double, my pension would have been greater, and the social security benefits greater. It is possible that the house would have been much bigger and a better car."

However, sensing the futility in such regrets and the reality of his commitment to his ministry, he then rallies himself and says, "The reward in the past thirty-six years outweighs any of the above benefits. The many families receiving counsel, direction, and support in their beliefs fill any voids. ... Would I do it again? The answer to this is a resounding loud voice, screaming from the top of my lungs, Yes! All is well that ends well."

Sarah

The conflict with the Pennsylvania congregation that caused Sarah to leave and reevaluate her life no longer seems to hold her in its emotional grip, and her satisfaction in her new role as a hospice chaplain is evident. She begins her reflections, therefore, by speaking of her joy at now, finally, being in a "place of ministry where I am able to be most fully who I am—using the God-given gifts I had from the beginning and finally being affirmed for those gifts."

When asked about the formative aspects of her theological education, Sarah acknowledges that Union showed her, a farm girl from rural Pennsylvania, a world beyond the Brethren. She then enumerates the good things and the discouraging things that she experienced in the traditions that formed her. She speaks of the denomination's devotion to service, its commitment to peace and justice, and its ritual Love Feast, which, in her early interviews, she found so much more sustaining than the communion offered at Union's services. On the other hand, she continues to rankle at the "forced humility" of the Brethren and the emphasis on community that "has often been oppressive to those who would dare to be different."

Sarah's relationship with her Brethren background is still ambivalent. She values much of the tradition in which she was raised, especially the close-knit family connections and the warmth of relationships in the church. But these same things also feel oppressive to her—an almost smothering sense of control explained as love that can make disagreement almost impossible. The experience with the Pennsylvania congregation made her confront these issues directly, and she left that church feeling like an outsider.

In fact, she began to feel that she did not have to be defined by the Brethren connection—either in accepting or rejecting it—and she has since that time felt free to look at other theological traditions and even considered transferring her ministerial standing to a denomination such as the United Church of Christ. On the other hand, there is a sense in which Sarah wants to place all ecclesial institutional connections on hold as she takes time to explore her religious commitments and newly found pastoral gifts. In this regard, her responsibilities as a hospice chaplain have provided her a setting she recognizes as a place where she is free to roam in fields once off limits to her.

As she ponders these things she connects them with the freedom she felt as a student at Union: "I was encouraged to speak out, to share my views, to rise above the oppression of the community, to take responsibility for the education that I needed, to claim my gifts of intellect and spirit, to stand up and be counted, to be free to be the person God created me to be."

After looking back over the many events of her life, she says, "In college, I had a sense of God calling me into ministry. I was not clear about the where or how, but the call was clear." She acknowledges that circumstances have sometimes caused her to have "doubts about staying in ministry. When those doubts were strong, something always happened to confirm that I was called to ministry. Even in the [Pennsylvania] parish during some middle-of-the-night dark night of the soul times when I cried out to God saying, 'Shall I leave?', something would happen—a parishioner would stop by unannounced to thank me for something I had said or done; a lesbian couple talked to me at an ecumenical gathering saying 'We've heard what you're doing and we want to say thank you;' a youth hugs me and thanks me after that sermon which later created such an uproar; a note of thanks or encouragement arrives—and I knew God was still calling me."

"Now," she says, "I have found a new ministry and a new calling. What tomorrow will bring is unknown, but I have faith I am God's beloved, living among God's beloved, on a journey toward healing and wholeness, and I will follow God's calling wherever that leads me."

Chris

Chris begins by describing his discomfort at revisiting his past, particularly because he anticipates the experience being awkward. Yet he agrees to press on and offers an articulate and extensive overview of his life and career.

Interestingly, the mere mention of his tendency to "move on" and avoid revisiting previous associations raises for him the unpleasant specter of MoveOn.Org, the liberal political interest group. Thus, the first topic Chris raises in his reflection is not faith, ministry, education, or childhood, but politics. It is a topic, in fact, that arises throughout his reflections and seems to color many of his judgments; it is a passionate interest that connects the various strands of ministry for him.

While many of the other participants in the study are committed to social issues that have political implications (usually liberal), they tend to address those issues in nonpolitical language. Chris does not avoid such language and is clearly the most overtly political of all of the participants. Ever since his years at Union, Chris has tended to assert his views and sense of self in a decidedly political fashion. He sees himself as a conservative political anomaly in the liberal milieu of mainstream Christian ministry. Perhaps he is like many Southerners of the 1960s and 1970s who saw themselves as liberals trying to achieve significant reform in the region, particularly regarding civil rights, yet often finding themselves out of step with Northern liberal assumptions. He brought this brand of Southern liberalism to Union only to discover that his views were not taken seriously by East Coast liberals who stereotyped him as a conservative apologist. To Chris and many progressive white Southerners, the Northerners who criticized them so harshly were little more than confrontational radicals out of touch with the realities of U.S. society in general. Even to this day, Chris can still describe himself as a liberal, but he obviously defines the term differently than other liberals would.

Chris next discusses his initial hopes for ministry, which he has largely achieved—of returning to the South after Union and becoming "one of those quiet, wise, thoughtful, intellectually oriented, pastorally sensitive, and politically liberal Presbyterian pastors I had known from tenth grade on."

He then describes the influence on him of "African American narrative preaching" as he experienced it first at Union in New York City and later through other nationally known preachers: "Something about the preaching of all these folks had the power both to stir my soul, warm my spirit, and challenge my mind. The narrative preaching they did so well has served as a major intellectual and homiletical force in my life to this day."

This leads him to speak of the importance of narrative in his life and to tell how, during the summer of 1999 when he was in the midst of his second divorce, he became engrossed in another form of narrative—in this case, fiction, primarily short-story fiction. "I retreated to the bedroom . . . and buried myself in fiction," including the works of Flannery O'Connor, Raymond Carver, Tobias Wolff, and Anton Chekhov. The following summer he enrolled in a summer writing workshop and began writing short stories. He later went on to write poetry as well. "The love of writing, reading, narrative, has shaped and formed my ministry."

Another important aspect of his life and career has been his involvement with a lectionary study group that began in 1983 with a core of four ministerial friends gathered to discuss issues in preaching and recently celebrated its twenty-fifth year in existence. "It is probably the most exhausting and exhilarating group 1 have ever known." It is obviously a group with which he is tightly bonded, and yet he dropped out for nine years, not, as one would think, because of personal issues, but because of political differences. The core group had become too liberal for his comfort, so he withdrew for ideological reasons. But nine years after he withdrew, he was accepted back into the fold: "At the twenty-fifth anniversary dinner this past January, as one of the founders, 1 was asked to give a brief tribute. 1 thanked the group for taking me in, for letting me leave, for letting me come back, for being with me through two divorces and a beautiful, recent remarriage."

He then told the group of some of his faith struggles and how he has learned to cope with them: "1 have been in the ministry all my adult life, and 1 have done so, as an 'un-born again Southerner,' with precious few experiences—direct or indirect—of the presence of God, and with many times of wondering whether or not, in the absence of such experiences, 1 am really a Christian or just a charlatan who has built a rather comfortable and rewarding ministry on just a few grains of sinking sand. But . . . while I've never really seen God, while I've never really heard the voice of Christ speaking, while I've never really had a born again experience, 1 do see in the scriptures and in literature black print on white page, and in whatever it is that happens in the transaction between that black print and my heart and mind is a life-giving experience that 1 have long since come to believe is the presence of Jesus Christ to me."

Chris next goes back to his fascination with politics. He mentions his "quiet, non-pietistic Republican" upbringing. He describes the fallout shelters and the fear of nuclear war with which he grew up. "1 remember my grandparents talking about the John Birch Society. . . . 1 remember the virulent hatred among adults, reflected by their children in my first-grade class, when John F. Kennedy was elected president." Yet by 1968, he "was a devotee of Martin Luther King, Jr.," . . . and "had Humphrey-Muskie bumper stickers on my bulletin board." Four years later, when fifty-five members of his senior high school class chose Richard Nixon in a straw poll, he was one of two members who chose McGovern.

By the time he reached Union, however, he was questioning liberal orthodoxies, and when Iranian radicals took over the American embassy in Tehran on November 4, 1979, he began turning forcefully away from liberalism. In 1985, he began reading *The New Republic*, "a magazine which leans heavily Democratic but which has proven to be, throughout most of the twenty-three years in which I have been a loyal reader, relatively hawkish in foreign policy." In 1991, "I was nearly alone among clergy and academic friends in supporting, usually in private conversations, the first Gulf War." It was at this time that he withdrew from the lectionary study group. "I withdrew not so much over my disagreement with what was the near universal, and, in my opinion, romantically naive views of my fellow feasters but, more importantly, over my unwillingness to speak out and express my disagreement."

After the attack on the World Trade Towers on September 11, 2001, "from the pulpit on September 23, I offered a rare voice from the mainline tradition of affirming that a military response was in order, a position that led me to receive significant criticism from some in the congregation and most on the staff." He also supported the invasion of Iraq. However, he asserts, "my support for the war was always for taking a stand against genocide; it was never about weapons of mass destruction."

He concludes this description of his political views by describing the exhilaration he feels being the minister of a church with a "healthy mix of politically active members who seek to relate their faith to their diverse political views and genuinely enjoy learning from one another."

Chris has recently entered into his third marriage. This is a happy time for him, and he feels that he has reached a point in his life where he can identify some valuable lessons. He has learned, he says, "how fragile and flawed human relationships are, how rare genuine and healthy love is, and how important it is to support people in searching for it and to protect people from the demonic forces that lead us to injure one another physically, sexually, and emotionally. All this has moved me, politically, left and right—left, in seeing human love as such a rare and precious thing the church should affirm the ways in which people find it, even when outside the traditional marriages between one man and one woman that have become the legal norm in my denomination; right, in affirming that use of force so necessary in preventing domestic and sexual violence. . . ."

When asked whether, if given the choice, he would again choose a career in ministry, Chris says, "I have never had significant doubt as to my career choice, which may be a reason that no therapist has really pushed on to explore if it was so tainted by trauma as to need exploring." Furthermore, he says, "I would do it again because, despite its challenges and painful periods, I genuinely feel called to preach, teach, lead a congregation, extend pastoral care." However, "if I would change anything, it would be to have tried to deal with my personal issues sooner. . . . Had my personal life been in better order sooner, I may have contributed more to the church and had a more successful career." Nonetheless, having been through all of the ups and downs that he has experienced and having claimed some sense of being more at peace with himself, Chris can confidently assert that "now would be the least likely time I would ever leave the ministry. I simply feel it is what God has called me to do and that it fits me."

Beth

In reflecting on her life, Beth speaks about the variety of her experiences, about what has changed and what has not, about her ongoing questions regarding the Episcopal church, about the continuing importance in her life of feminism and political realities, and about the importance of Union for her. She says that she is "profoundly grateful for the tools given me at Union. . . . I always tell my [confirmation] class that the purpose of faith is not to give easy answers but to provide a framework for exploring life's tough questions. My education at Union gave me the tools and the confidence to keep wrestling with questions that continue to engage my mind and my spirit. Union combined intellectual rigor with a healthy skepticism as well as an appreciation for honoring life experiences different from my own."

When reflecting on the origin of her sense of call, she admits that that has been a troubling question for her. When she began her ordination process in the late 1970s, she was asked, as were other candidates, to describe her call to ministry. "I noticed," she says, "that generally men would give a very specific answer to this question. They would often describe a moment in time when they heard God calling to them. I was not able to do that and so often questioned whether or not I had a call to ministry." Nevertheless, since "there were very few women in ministry at that point, and I was clued in to Jungian notions of feminine modes of being, I raised this with my committee as an issue in which women may come to describe a call in ways different from the traditional male experience."

Beth then revisits influential moments from her formative years and explains that "throughout my ministry I have struggled to maintain an authentic sense of self. At times my vocation undermined that, but in another way, priesthood has helped me to cultivate a core being that feels lively and genuine." Looking back to her brief time as a social worker helps remind Beth how vital and fulfilling her career in the priesthood has been. She is "aware of how limiting the role of a social worker is compared to a priest when one is dealing with emotional pain and death. Ministry has allowed me to be involved with people's lives from a spiritual depth that rings very true for me and which I think really touches the souls of others. For that I am very grateful."

She speaks of the pride she felt when, at his college graduation, her son "gave a speech as the salutatorian of his class . . . that articulated from his own authentic self ideas that I truly cherish." But when considering whether her son should follow in his parents' career paths, she says, "I would unequivocally discourage it."

"Working in the church," she says, "leaves one in a financially precarious situation in trying to provide an acceptable quality of life." In fact, she says, "at this stage in life, I am where I should have been professionally in my late 30s." Nevertheless, she adds, "I do not think our son would be that negative about his growing up experience. The church provided an extended family network for him that he really enjoyed. He also perceived his parents as having a status position. Also, working in the church did set a context of intellectual stimulation from which he benefited. And he says that he benefited from having moved several times. Nonetheless, I always felt like I was not able to establish a real home, both in terms of having a routine and also having a sense of place."

"It is discouraging," she says, "to work in what I often consider to be a dying institution, where the problems are so difficult and the resources are meager." Further, she says, "the church was and is the only place I have been told I could not do something because of being female. . . . I felt myself at the mercy of an institution that I found consistently to be narrow-minded and unfair."

Although Beth remains critical of the church, she also remains fully committed to its purpose and ministry. While unhesitating in her judgments, she is hopeful in her outlook, and committed to the work of pastoral ministry.

In fact, after listening to the other participants describe their own ministries, Beth finds that she is "feeling invigorated about moving into the next stage of my life and ministry. Having the opportunity to be open and honest helped me to clarify muddled feelings about the past and my future. Hearing other people's stories gave me a rich context from which to reflect upon my own situation. . . . Prior to attending this meeting, I had seen myself as trying to make it to retirement within five to eight years. . . . In reflecting upon my story, I began to recognize that the past four to five years of ministry have been very satisfying. I decided to think of that as the beginning of my real work in the church and to look toward working until close to seventy. Rather than trying to get to retirement, I would like think of it as looking for ways to grow professionally for what could be a fifteen-year career."

Still, lest anyone assume that all is certain in her view of the world, Beth concludes by adding, "At the same time, my history in the church continues in play, as it leaves me with a degree of mistrust and cynicism as I move forward. My hope is that over time these experiences of the past might serve to heighten my awareness of things but that they might lose some of their negativity for me."

Marvin

As Marvin revisits his years at Union, he reflects on his relative na-ivete upon entering seminary. "I sported an idealism that was unreal-istic and myopic. . . . It seems almost paradoxical that I had a childlike innocence coupled with precociousness. I was mature in some ways, yet there was so much room for growth."

He then goes on to talk about Dr. Samuel D. Proctor, who was a mentor and the pastor that he worked for at Abyssinian Baptist Church. Dr. Proctor warned him against "trying to change the world, but just trying to change or touch ten people, because if you change ten, then you will change one hundred." These are precepts he has tried to live by, and he illustrates it by telling several stories, one of which concerns a young convict.

Marvin describes how he was approached by a member of his congregation who asked "if I could hire her grandson, who needed a job so that his parole from prison could be expedited. I had no room in my budget or in my program for an ex-con with no appar-ent skills." However, "I decided to test the waters and see if he was serious about changing his life. I sent word for him to meet me at the church at some ungodly hour in the morning. When I arrived at work, there he was, sitting and waiting for me with a cup of coffee. I interviewed him and asked about his resume, knowing full well that he did not have one. He assured me that he was willing to do any-thing. I asked him; 'What is the one thing that you can do?' Without hesitation he said: 'Clean!' I assigned him to cleaning the church's kitchen. This kitchen had not been thoroughly cleaned in decades; it was a monumental task. However, this young man worked diligently for six weeks; he never missed a day's work; he was never late. He promised me that if I gave him a job, he would not disappoint me or his grandmother. He was faithful to his word."

Sixteen years later that same young man walked into Marvin's church "and told the congregation that I had given him a chance many years ago. I gave him a job. And he wanted to come back and say thank you. He went back to school and was now running his own computer company, and he owed it all to God, his grandmother, and to me."

Marvin is also proud of the community activism he has encouraged his congregation to undertake. On one occasion, a liquor store opened in the same building that housed his church. Marvin complained to his local zoning board, saying that not only was it inappropriate to have a liquor store next door to a church, but the dark history of the effect of alcohol on the black community ought to be taken into account. Marvin's appeal was denied, but when asked what he now intended to do, he replied, "We are going to close that store." For three months the congregation picketed in front of the store, and on the Fourth of July, Independence Day, the liquor store, which had opened on Good Friday, closed its doors for good. To mark the moment emphatically, Marvin had funeral wreaths placed in front of the barred doors. Such stories represent the triumphs that help ministers like Marvin continue in their work.

Marvin next discusses his call to ministry, which he says began with his work with children in the Head Start program in Brooklyn but was also connected to his interest in social work, law enforcement, and the environment. He was told by a local pastor, a graduate of Union, "that all of my concerns, interests, and desires could be fulfilled in ministry. This marked the beginning of my faith journey."

At Union, he says, he was forced to expand his awareness of the world, and that process has continued throughout his life. He feels fortunate that he "adjusted easily, contrary to my sexist, male-dominated church experience. . . . I have come a long way. My experiences in life, with family and congregation, have done its job. I have gays and lesbians in my congregation; they are colleagues, friends, and family members. God increased my compassion, sensitivity, and growth in this area."

Yet for all the successes of his ministry, he admits to a certain weariness at being in the same congregation for more than twenty-nine years. Such weariness leaves him yearning for a sabbatical. "It would be a time to write, take some classes, a time to reflect." Unfortunately, sabbaticals are "not a black church tradition," and Marvin worries that such a request on his part could cause divisions in the congregation.

As he follows this train of thought, he wonders aloud about needing to pace himself and being especially careful "to refrain from placing myself in a situation where I might be tempted to abuse my office." He speaks of his feeling that within African American churches pastors sometimes take on an almost demagogic role and lead autocratically. Even as he acknowledges this difficulty, however, Marvin is also aware that the church expects him to be a strong and assertive leader. The line, of course, between being assertive and being autocratic is not always easy to differentiate and represents the kind of ambiguity of leadership he is acknowledging.

"Few respect a weak leader," he says. "The challenge is to find the balance between abusing power and being weak or ineffective. My mother often taught me that if you let folk push you around, they will." One of Marvin's apparent struggles as a traditional black pastor has been in determining how to be "a strong, effective, compassionate leader and not be mean and insensitive."

When he reflects on his interaction with the other participants in the study, he comments particularly on the positive emotional impact of being given the opportunity in the colloquium when the group of eight gathered to share thoughts and concerns that he and the others seldom allow themselves to share: "We shed tears that flowed from the wounds that we had been carrying for decades. We all had wounds of betrayal, wounds of lack of appreciation, wounds of being taken for granted, wounds of insensitivity, the wounds of being burnt out, and wounds that could only come from a shepherd's heart, a pastor."

He then goes on to say, "We were all intrigued by the candid fact that many of us, if it were our choosing, would not do this again. I was amazed that we did not qualify it by noting that we would do it differently. . . . I was one who said no." He then reflects on what he was saying no to. "I would never say no to God. . . . I was saying no to the rejection of visions given by God."

Marvin identifies himself and the other participants as wounded healers, referring to Henri Nouwen's book *The Wounded Healer*.[2] As a young seminarian, he says he was clueless as to what that phrase actually meant. "But I have found that I am a better pastor now, that I am able to pastor out of those wounds. I find that I can connect not only to those who are broken, ostracized, abused, lost, lonely, . . . but most of all to Jesus."

He arrived at the colloquium, he says, "anxious to hear the journey of others, my classmates. I was yearning for stories of victory, success. I was disheartened that most of us are still swimming upstream and fighting against many meaningless traditions that have nothing to do with the resurrection of Christ."

Then, having given vent to his discouragement, Marvin speaks about his life, his family, and his pastorate, and in this moment he seems to reconfirm what is most important to him. He feels blessed to have been married to the same woman throughout his adult life, to have three children of whom he is quite proud, and to have had a thirty-year commitment to a single church. After such reflection he finds that "my personal no turns into a spiritual yes, and all I can say is, it's been worth it."

Ruth

After reading the old transcripts, Ruth says, "I felt embarrassed about how indecisive I seemed, how wishy-washy I was, and the lack of clarity and depth I showed." Yet she asserts, and this seems substantiated by her reflections, that she is "still in many ways that same person. . . . I was born and raised in the black urban community where the living is sometimes hard, and I have never really lost that as a heritage or left that as a commitment in terms of my life or my work."

When asked what has kept her in pastoral ministry, she speaks of the encouragement she received at Union and, over the years, from family and other lay people, which "seemed to be a cloudy word from God that I should continue the journey." She speaks about the support of her husband of twenty-seven years, with whom she has shared all of her ministries, all three of which have been "urban, primarily African American. . . . Each ministry situation has been Lutheran, and we have always worked together, always shared but one salary, and always worked with common folk who are mostly doing just pretty well or perhaps pretty poorly at making it. . . . When I look back to who I was and what I said during those years at Union, I see that I have perhaps changed little."

She speaks of her passion for "the community of faith in a neighborhood." But she then adds: "Small in height, I have also always thought of myself as small in my skills and abilities and ambitions." Then, almost as an afterthought to correct this expression that seems so lacking in self-worth and confidence, she adds that she is, nevertheless, "seeking to be faithful in my commitment and obedience and effort. God's gift of humility can carry us along the way for a pretty far distance."

While she does not regret becoming an "ordained African American female in the Lutheran Church," she says, ". . . there are days of weariness, burdens, and confusion. . . . I have seen so many urban churches in those struggling neighborhoods closed, so many people abandoned, and virtually little gain in people of any color in the Lutheran denominational membership."

Over the years she and her husband have dealt with various conflicts in their ministries, but as she says, "I have faced those challenges of broken down buildings, limited budgets, missing or overburdened lay leadership, good programs that don't last, and bad practices that ought not survive. . . . Sometimes I have felt like I can't give anymore. Sometimes I have felt like my husband and children get the physical and emotional scraps that are left over at the end of long days." Some days she yearns for retirement, yet she fears that "our thirty-plus years of sharing one salary will leave us a little ragged when we do retire. . . . But I would do it again. I would be a pastor again, in these black urban communities that so much are my past and my heritage and my identity. . . . I absolutely mean it when I say that the salary has never mattered that much to either of us over the years and that both of us have felt financially blessed."

Although she has occasionally considered leaving ministry to return to teaching, she feels that she has had "a great and meaningful lifetime . . . to be a part of persons' lives at key times, to see lives change, blossom, and grow through encounters with Christ and his church, to see strangers arrive, connect, and become part of the family of faith and love and service, to witness the rippling effects that even a small church can have on the surrounding community, to see compassion and mercy and reconciliation and peace and justice and liberation at work here, there, and beyond, to be even a small part of the good news being declared and revealed through the living Christ. O Lord, just the joy you give me singing the songs, praying with the people, worshiping you!"

So here they stand, these eight—students, pastors, husbands, wives, parents, sojourners, writers, leaders—having revealed in their own words the roads they have taken and not taken, the pitfalls they have stumbled through, the stops they have made, whether intended or not. Their years in ministry are almost done, and some of those years have been hard to weather, yet these eight remain dedicated to their work.

For some, there is a feeling they would not choose the work of ordained ministry if given the choice again. As they express these feelings, however, there is at the same time the sense that the work itself has been worth all the difficulties it has caused them. In this regard, the context of a declining church, the unmitigated financial pressures, and the slow erosion of the traditional role of pastors have contributed to their feelings of uncertainty.

Most, however, would again take up this work and calling. For them, despite all the issues they have faced, this has been a vocation that has been the fullest expression of their lives that they could imagine. The fact that they care so much about this work of ordained ministry is one of the reasons the actual work itself sometimes drives them to distraction. In the end, this calling has mostly been work that is meaningful and important. Although what they have done in ministry has remained largely anonymous, seldom acknowledged in ways that provide concrete rewards, it has been the vocation that has claimed them.

About a year after the first colloquium, a second was held during which the manuscript draft of this book was discussed. The participants were asked to read carefully what was written about them, the quotes that were used, and most of all, to consider whether my interpretations and commentary rang true to their own experience and perceptions. In addition, they were asked to identify anything they wanted added, revised, deleted, or made more anonymous. My hope was to have them share a kind of editorial authority with Ken Huggins and me. As it turned out, they were generally in agreement with the content and spirit of the book and requested few changes.

Rather than concealing personal difficulties, they tended to treat kindly the younger versions of themselves that they found here, understanding from the vantage point of time why they said what they said, felt what they felt, or misconstrued what they thought they had understood. They were willing to see their lives without the cloak of piety or self-absorption that many clerical reflections contain, and through that willingness they were able to perceive value in themselves that they may have otherwise overlooked or forgotten. They were reminded of those moments when they had been courageous and faithful even when doing so was neither easy nor recognized. Moreover, by being in each other's presence and learning of each other's experiences as their words were read and discussed, I hope they were able to add to their sense of fellowship and community.

In the following chapter, I will summarize what I have learned over the years in getting to know these men and women and discuss some of the issues that pertain not only to themselves but to others as well.

chapter 8

Summing Up

I have had to disassemble everything I learned in seminary and start all over again, apprenticing myself to Jesus. Little by little I have learned to open my heart, to let go of fear and judgment, and find in return I receive grace upon grace. — TIM

WHEN THIS STUDY BEGAN IN 1976, I HAD LITTLE IDEA OF ITS emerging significance in my life. What started as an inquiry into what could be gleaned from students about theological education developed into a conversation that became the deepest kind of learning. My own life as a teacher and a minister has been touched by the stories I have been told, particularly the eight stories that constitute the center of this book. My aim, foremost, has been to portray as faithfully as possible the self-understanding of these eight men and women whose lives have been shaped by their work in ministry. They lead us into journeys we too can follow and through which we can recognize questions that confront us as well.

One such question is that of the relationship between personal and professional identity, an elusive relationship that each of us must negotiate and attempt to reconcile, as have the eight participants in this study. The person that we are most of the time is certainly expressed in the work we do, but the identity that some kinds of work confer does not always square with our most integral self. Ordained ministry in particular attaches a weighty and sometimes intractable professional identity that can defer as well as fulfill personal identity. Men and women in ministry are confronted with expectations they are seldom likely to fulfill, yet through a combination of faith, naivete, persisting hopes, deflated dreams, and intellectual and moral commitment we have seen in this book how four women and four men have tried to meet the professional expectations placed upon them. At the same time, we have perceived the points at which they have claimed the issues that have confronted them as persons, as well as those moments when they have denied or deferred such issues. Each has heard a call to ministry, each has sought the academic setting of Union Seminary in the late 1970s to help them comprehend and respond to that call, and each has used all of his or her intellect, strength, and humility to survive and succeed in a vocation that is endlessly changing and demanding yet ultimately rewarding.

Discerning the Call to Ministry

The fact that these eight participants have felt themselves called and able to respond to such expectations is itself revealing of the incipient grandiosity contained in any sense of calling to ordained ministry. The tension between a sense of calling and the tugs of ego and ambition requires those who feel sent by God to a task, a place, or a responsibility to differentiate between what is self-serving and what is self-giving, knowing that such distinctions are seldom evident or even separable. It cannot be otherwise, because a call is always a risk.

While the calling of clergy is exceptional in certain ways, it is not unique and shares traits with the calling felt by poets, artists, physicians, and other vocations in which individuals believe themselves to have certain gifts that claim their ambitions and inmost identity. I am not sure, for example, how possible it would be to become a poet if it were not for some basic confidence that what is composed would be worthy of being read. Since not many poets are published and even those that are published are not widely known, there has to be some intrinsic sense of purpose that keeps them writing and keeps them grounded in their work. If they depended on outside recognition, most would be doomed from the beginning. So there is some kind of inner voice, a certainty that takes on a religious-like sense of calling that enables one to take up this work.

The poet Czeslaw Milosz speaks of poems themselves as epiphanies during which "what struck us as so ordinary is revealed as miraculous."[1] In the same vein, Kay Ryan, U.S. Poet Laureate, 2008–2009, acknowledges that her very sense of calling to be a poet came as a kind of epiphany, though she uses the term "reluctantly."[2]

Unlike poets, pastors have their congregations as a built-in audience, and this makes things more complicated. While a minister's calling is felt internally, the expression of that call and its predominating means of affirmation is external. A poet can write a poem, and that poem, whether published or not, can still be claimed by the poet as a creative achievement. It takes a lot of forbearance to write and not be read, but it can certainly be done. One need only think of Emily Dickinson writing in her room every day in Amherst, then collecting her hundreds of poems into little bundles and tying them with ribbon, seldom if ever to be read in her lifetime. I cannot conjure up a comparable image of a minister composing a sermon that is not to be preached. The words can be written, but they remain incomplete without the community where they are heard and responded to in the midst of the church's life and mission.

For clergy the inward and compelling sense of calling that brought them to seminary and led them toward ordination becomes something that is tested and validated outside themselves. But such testing and validation by denominations and congregations is not necessarily what a neophyte minister might have anticipated, at least to the extent to which a congregation may enter and sometimes invade the inner space where creativity and imagination reside. Of course, the ideal version of ministry portrayed in much of the biblical tradition is the mutuality of ministry. In Ephesians 4:11–12, ministers are described as teachers and pastors whose primary calling is to equip the whole church for ministry. But most congregations in practice are voluntary associations that hire clergy—as they might any other professional—to meet religious needs and carry out ecclesiastical duties, so that over time the artistry and imaginative nature of calling may be diminished as the routine aspects of clerical life come to predominate. The easy solution is to fall into cynicism and gradually lose sight of the calling that enlivened and motivated the earlier decision to pursue ordination. How to hold on to their calling and at the same time lead a church that only approximates the faithful company once imagined is the emotional crucible in which pastors live. It is also the theological task that lies at the center of pastoral leadership, essentially the question of how this all too human institution can be in any way a sign and embodiment of the "Word becoming flesh."

Part of the weightiness of a clerical calling is the extent to which pastors are seen as exemplars of a moral and spiritual life. Despite countless stories of clergy who are not such paragons, congregations want and expect their ministers to live according to a standard of conduct befitting the so-called higher calling they have answered. Clergy may resist such expectations, but they know that both inside and outside the culture of the church people carry exceptional expectations of ministers. Other professions also have exemplary expectations. Teachers and physicians certainly come to mind. But clergy are especially caught by the nature of their calling, which they claim is from God. Physicians may be held to the Hippocratic oath, but Hippocrates was a mortal. Not so with Yahweh. This attendant divine connection with ordained ministry shapes expectations, even unrealistic and unfair ones. Clergy struggle with this situation, but they can never completely escape the straitjackets that many church members typically place on them, however inadvertently.

The Christian ideal of vocation is rooted in baptism, whereby the very act of becoming a Christian is the fundamental authorization for ministry. This is the ministry of the laity, literally the "people of God," which is shaped by the gospel and its mandate for service. The devolvement of vocation into something reserved for clergy thus distorts the nature of calling. Nonetheless, the clerical definition of vocation predominates, and the image of a minister is shaped largely by popular expectations of clergy and not by the biblical ideal.

This means that a minister's presentation of a public self has to take into account the images that church members often hold of clergy and the role they are expected to play. For example, when a pastor enters the hospital room of an ill parishioner, that pastor enters as a representative of the church—including all of its systems of belief—and, on mostly unconscious levels, as a reminder of the presence of God. When clergy recognize that they represent all these things without necessarily being them, they can assume a form of servanthood that assists people in their search for the holy and for healing. When they are not aware of the difference between themselves and what they represent, clergy serve only themselves.

On a practical and personal level, clergy are not often in a place where they can be themselves without being aware at the same time of how much their self is bound by the office and role they embody. While clergy struggle with these questions, the families of clergy live each day with a gap between what their spouse or parent is presumed to be in the church and what that person actually is at home. Divorce or ongoing dissatisfaction is sometimes the consequence of clergy marriages that do not wrestle with the problem and find some appropriate way to deal with it. For some of the eight men and women we have followed, issues with partners have been complicated and difficult. The challenges of trying to balance the practice of ministry with the responsibilities of being a spouse or a parent never really go away. Even when both spouses are clergy, stresses seem unavoidable.

The group of eight has recognized these challenges. They have seen the places where their own confidence will not carry them, and they have recognized the distance between what they once expected and what they now experience in ministry. Yet all of them have tried to craft ways of being in ministry that keep them faithful to themselves, to those they love, and to their sense of calling, while still responding to the necessities of pastoral work itself.

We have seen throughout the experiences of these eight men and women how their call to the ordained ministry of the church has raised in them questions about their adequacy to carry out this role. This is, of course, the other side of grandiosity, and both are part of the differing dynamics of a call first felt and a call lived out in ministry. For some more than others, these questions have been primary, and they have struggled profoundly and relentlessly, but all have remained committed to this work that both inspires and disturbs them, perhaps because they have in the end seldom doubted that it is a vocation worth the cost.

With all the twists and turns along the way, with so many confusing choices placed before them, with so many of their fellow students choosing other forms of ministry or dropping out altogether, why did these eight continue to commit themselves to pastoral ministry? The quick answer is that they all seemed to have strengths that came from being formed in the church and supported in their early explorations in ministry before entering seminary. Tim is the exception to this, yet even Tim could claim a family history of clergy, and his deliberate pursuit of an understanding of religion and his fortunate connection with a pastor who mentored him can be perceived as a foundation similar to that of his colleagues.

Another factor is that all eight (though Sarah, as we have seen, moves in a different direction because of congregational conflict) saw the local congregation as the primary community in which their call to ministry was oriented, although at some points they might have assumed leadership in other parts of the church for a while. Each of them occasionally confronted the church's protocols, but they all found ways to make their peace with the limits of its structures. In this regard, there was a concreteness to their understandings of ministry that kept them centered when others might have floundered.

When considering the divergent paths of the women and the men in this study, the women were forced to deal with ordination in ways that the men were not.[3] They were confronted almost daily with objections to women's ordination and the realities of women's place or displacement in the ecclesiastical house. None of the four women was certain that the path ahead led obviously into ordained ministry, but the context at Union would not permit them to avoid this issue. In the face of the roadblocks the four women often met regarding ordination, they drew upon improvisatory skills they may not have known they had. Because they were breaking new ground, few models were available for them to follow. They had to find their own models, make it up as they went along, and stand on their own two feet.

The four men followed a more linear path. They came to Union relatively certain of who they wanted to be and what they wanted to do in ministry. Throughout their childhood, youth, and young adulthood they had observed men as pastors. Such men had provided them with models, and they felt confident in adopting these models for their own ministries. While each of the four men faced different kinds of personal issues in seminary and in ministry, the question of whether they, as men, would be allowed to practice ministry was never an issue. Seldom, therefore, did they think seriously about other forms of ministry or even different experiences in ministry.

The eight participants offer a portrait of individuals pretty much on their own. Their experiences with denominational structures and leadership is mixed at best and more often distrustful, verging on hostile. Even on a congregational level, in the parishes they have served, the participants have sometimes felt ill-used. As one participant remarked: "No other institution has treated me as badly as the church."

Despite such feelings, there is little zeal within this group to reform the church's structure. Denominations appear far removed, something to be encountered when required but not much of an ongoing presence in any positive or enabling way. Cohort groups with other clergy are mentioned, and while such groups occasionally offer the kind of transparency and candor that provides real collegiality, they have just as often proven to be superficial and disappointing.

The stories we have heard point toward how essential it is for all of us to seek some continuing sense of ourselves even as we know the impossibility of such wholeness as a stable state. The paradox is that we are more apt to realize such a quest when we are able to accept the various and often conflicting selves we actually turn out to be. For clergy, who so often expect to be one thing—ever faithful and ever true to their calling—this is an especially difficult task. Sometimes we are caught within the illusion that ordination offers some kind of protection from all the vicissitudes of our own humanity. While not all clergy come to ministry out of their own brokenness or abuse, a great many do, and they often believe that they must bear such wounds in secret, hoping perhaps that if they help in the healing of others, then they might in the process heal themselves. But one of the insights we have gained from these stories is that there is no secondhand healing.

To comprehend their complex understandings of their calling, it may help to look again at the eight participants' experience in seminary and the context in which their vocational questions were so compelling.

The Union Experience: Change and Continuity

As mentioned earlier, the years in which the eight students were at Union was a tumultuous era in the history of the seminary during which it dealt with the aftereffects of the volatile 1960s when Union was swept up in the Columbia student protests on Morningside Heights and took on its own internal issues around racism, governance, and curriculum change. In particular, faculty division over a recently rejected proposed M.Div. curriculum revision and the institution's financial struggles created an often contentious atmosphere. It was not an environment that could easily support the growth and development of students.

Union's involvement in theological and ecclesiastical controversies has been one of its continuing characteristics. It clearly identified with the modernist camp in the early twentieth century and positioned itself as a liberal institution committed to the church and its ministry but not bound by any particular denominational politics or policies. Like many liberal institutions, Union sometimes found itself being for freedom of conscience, individual rights, and equality without a corresponding sense of what it most wanted to conserve and hold on to other than resistance to any ideological or theological platform. Ironically, though, this very resistance can become its own credo, enforced indirectly but nevertheless effectively toward those who departed from such latent orthodoxy. Living within the tensions of its life, Union has had to confront its own ambiguity and self-contradiction. While it has often held onto its privileges as one of the elite institutions of the old Protestant establishment, it has also been an advocate for the poor and the oppressed—those without voice in our society.

The group of eight was, by and large, able to deal with the issues they faced at the seminary and find resources within themselves and support from faculty and friends who were close to them. At the same time, the church itself, in the form of fieldwork placements, helped them maintain some equilibrium when Union's institutional politics and the students' personal dilemmas loomed too large. At the least, the seminary's own struggles forced them to recognize what they did or did not like and pushed them to a clearer sense of themselves. In fact, the difficulties of Union in these years almost certainly helped them anticipate many of the issues they would face later in their lives, because the issues that divided Union in the 1970s and that seemed to some observers to be unique to this liberal institution eventually became widespread within church life across the country. Actually, the questions faced by Union in the 1970s are now present throughout theological education regardless of denominational identity or theological persuasion. Various schools will, of course, have different answers and responses to these questions, but the questions are there without consideration of creed, region, or status.

Homosexuality, racial, ethnic, and theological diversity, the feminist critique of biblical interpretation and ecclesial practices, and other issues that many students first faced at Union eventually have come to define not only theological schools but denominational meetings and congregational politics as well. Fiscal challenges similar to the ones Union confronted are now almost endemic on national and local levels throughout the religious community. Issues about institutional and faculty identity and the emerging questions about the nature of theological teaching and learning in this changing context are primary concerns for every theological seminary and university divinity school.

Another powerful force affecting the seminary in the mid to late 1970s consisted of the profound shifts occurring in the student body. As an expression of its advocacy of social justice, Union began to enroll and actively recruit a more diverse student population—one more inclusive of race, ethnicity, sexual orientation, class, age, education, and church experience. The seminary attempted to embrace what it expected to be a more encompassing future. Yet it was at times inconsistent in the way it adapted to the changes it was trying to make. For example, while women were coming to Union in increasing numbers, only four women were on the 28-member Union full-time faculty in 1976 when the eight students entered the seminary. There were four African American faculty members but no Hispanic or Asian faculty. While the eight students were still at the seminary, several more women, African Americans, and an Asian theologian were appointed. (Throughout this time, however, there were a number of African American and Hispanic administrative and maintenance staff. In fact, the vice president for administration, Georgina Pesante, was from Puerto Rico.) In future years, Union continued its efforts to deal with faculty diversity and sought to fulfill the commitments it had made to address imbalances in academic appointments.

As the students became more diverse, so did their interests and guiding thoughts. Therefore, they often connected themselves to various issues and the caucuses often attached to them. At the same time, whether intending to or not, various faculty members represented for students their own competing aims and ideologies. While in the past, faculty disputes were generally kept within the family, by the 1970s these disputes were public knowledge. Union, then, was a context in which ideas were circulating with competing vigor, faculty personalities were sorting out relationships among themselves, and the school in general was trying to find its way and adapt to the world in which it now found itself.

Most of the eight students entered Union feeling they were mavericks in their own church traditions. They were grounded in these traditions but often disagreed with at least some of the familiar practices of church life. Without necessarily being conscious of the fact, most of them saw Union as a reflection of themselves—an established institution that had its own maverick history. Moreover, each of the students was aware of Union's elite status and the kind of legitimacy that a Union degree would confer upon them, and they perceived—again without necessarily ever making it explicit—that the institution expressed much of their own uncertainty regarding the relationship between tradition, status, and social commitment.

At Union they found an institution willing, though often reluctantly, to accept the rewards of being part of a privileged world but also attempting to fulfill its commitments to social activism. In this way, the seminary provided an institutional expression of how the students' own status and ideologies—while self-contradictory at times—could be maintained. As Pierre Bourdieu, the French sociologist who spent his life studying and interpreting academic

institutions, often pointed out, schools essentially attempt to replicate or reproduce themselves in their students.[4] Despite everything
said to the contrary, education is by inclination a conservative and
conserving activity.

Occasions of individual transformation do occur, but faculties,
intentionally or not, sometimes try to extend themselves through
their students, and the students, in turn, join this effort from the
start by generally choosing schools that are in some fundamental
way expressions of themselves as they are or hope to be.

At the same time, though, that students participate in the life of
a school and try to follow its expectations, they also find ways to
resist and exempt themselves from what is going on. This resistance
takes various forms as students reject institutional values and behaviors that seem to contradict what is most important for them and
the cultures in which they were raised. For those who, by and large,
reflect the dominant culture of the school, this is less true, but for
those who do not, there is an ongoing struggle of acceptance and
rejection of what is expected of them to meet the academic and cultural standards of the institution.[5]

While the eight students in this study—like students every-
where—sometimes criticized the faculty as a whole, they were mostly appreciative of their teaching and scholarship. Each of the eight
was able to identify with at least one faculty member whom they
might want to emulate. All of the African American students—Marvin, Anna, and Ruth—had a sense of connection with Union's black
faculty, who represented an inner corps of teaching and learning
within the institution itself. Full-time faculty, such as James Cone,
James Washington, James Forbes, Cornel West, and Samuel Roberts,
and tutors, such as Jacqueline Grant, were models, if not mentors,
as well as teachers. Although the students often wished for closer
ties to these faculty, they appreciated the relationships they were
able to develop with them. As professor of preaching, James Forbes
was particularly formative in students' lives regardless of their race
or gender.

For Sarah, courses with Beverly Harrison and Mary Pellauer that
introduced her to feminist perspectives were important, but it was a
unique experience in dance with an adjunct professor, Caroline Bil-

derback, that proved to be pivotal to her own self-understanding. In a similar way, Beth found in Ann Belford Ulanov a teacher who influenced her greatly by introducing her to Carl Jung and D. W. Winnicott, whose work and thought have remained lifelong interests. Moreover, Ann Ulanov's approach to the nature of faith was key to Beth's own understanding of ministry.

Although David did not easily find his way with the faculty in general, his year-long participation in ISTEM led by Richard Snyder was important in helping him find a place where some of his practical concerns were addressed. Chris, who valued the classical academic traditions at Union, admired Christopher Morse in Theology and Raymond Brown in New Testament. For Tim, David Lotz and his lectures about Martin Luther and Reformation history were influential, although of all the participants, Tim most keenly seemed to feel that the real curriculum at Union was the one he encountered informally in the life of the community itself.

The faculty member mentioned by almost all of the eight was George Landes, who taught Old Testament. His name often came up as someone whose teaching was admired and whose commitment to individual students was much appreciated. Obviously, the eight students' perceptions about faculty were limited by their own experience. Other students in those years would have had a different list of faculty names and would likely have mentioned the fortuitous accident of being students at the same time that Union's visiting professors included Dietrich Bonhoeffer's friend and biographer, Eberhard Bethge; the Swiss pastor and theologian, Henri Mottu; and such well-known liberation theologians as Gustavo Gutierrez and Dorothee Soelle and the former moderator of the Presbyterian Church (USA), Thelma Adair.

One faculty member during this period seemed to signal the very changes that Union itself was experiencing. Robert McAfee Brown had taught for many years at Union before leaving for Stanford University in 1962. He was widely known and respected as a writer and lecturer. The pre-Stanford incarnation of Robert McAfee Brown personified the ideals of an earlier Union—he was an international theological figure, East Coast in academic style (including the tweed sports jacket and tie), and prophetic as a teacher and activist.

He moved from the seminary as someone associated with mainline theological traditions, but when he returned to Union's faculty in 1976, he came back as an advocate of liberation theology. His East Coast attire had been replaced by a Guayabera shirt, and his second language now was Spanish rather than German or French. Just as Union was attempting to sort through various versions of its future, Robert McAfee Brown seemed already to be living in one vision of that future, having resolved those issues for himself before coming back to the seminary. He was restless to get on to the work and not just the discussion of a more radical understanding of church, school, and world than Union was able to agree to upon. After several years, he concluded that the kind of work he wanted to do was better done in the place he had just left, so he and his wife, Sydney, who had shared leadership of Union's ecumenical program with him and led her own action research project on the nature of work, returned to California.[6]

What many of the eight most sought in their formal theological education at Union, namely education to inform their souls and form them in the practices of ministry, was not really something that Union set out to do directly. Such things could happen along the way, but they were not direct aims of the curriculum. In the words of James Hillman, the students might then have asked, "Where can the heart go to school?"[7]

These eight men and women have given us an answer to that question: The practice of ministry itself has been a school of lifelong learning. They point us to their work in the church and their life in relationships, to the experiences of hope and healing as well as the occasions of grief and pain. While seminary was not without its difficult moments for them, the school was a setting that gave them certain levels of protection. It was an experience of a certain way of being in the world, but it was not the world itself. As much as they engaged current and troubling issues as students, the school provided a relatively safe place in which to do this.

In pastoral ministry, there is no such protection, and the eight found themselves having to learn as they went along, drawing upon what they had been taught but transposing this learning within the congregational contexts in which they found themselves. Learning in this regard is not accumulative; it is episodic. One thing does not necessarily build on what has gone before, and each situation is distinctive in its own way. In fact, what answers we think we have found in one moment often come apart and must be reconceived and put together again, never in exactly the same form, but as something new as emerging situations arise. In this context, the M.Div. Program was a first learning, a place to begin and not an end in itself. A larger learning was ahead for these men and women in pastoral ministry, the work of the church, and the ongoing life of the world.

Issues and Implications

The stories of the eight lives in ministry that have been the subject of this book raise important issues for the church, theological education, and ministry itself.

The first issue is simply the recognition that things are changing. The landscape of American religious life is a varied terrain. We live with the paradoxical reality that while church membership in mainline denominations continues to decline, there is a widespread search for some meaningful spiritual life going on throughout our culture. Yet even as interest in spirituality grows, we know that fewer Americans see any need to connect this spirituality to organized religious institutions. While there are many congregations that are thriving and growing, many face lowered membership, financial strain, and internal dissension. Pastoral leaders, who were not necessarily educated for this new reality, are often caught in a complex web as they try to equip the church for its contemporary mission but meet fantasies of restoration to a more secure past that are powerful and resistant to change.

All of the eight ministers in this study follow their callings in relatively traditional churches. Some of them lead congregations that are large and prosperous, following models that are familiar and fulfilling. Others who are in churches dealing with falling membership numbers have sometimes sought new forms to meet the needs of a changing congregation or appeal to a new constituency, but mostly they have tried to renew rather than replace familiar and longstanding patterns of worship and church life. The difficulty has been to find ways to do this work without feeling overwhelmed or disheartened by the challenges themselves.

A second issue is that few of the eight reported any real experiences of assessment or evaluation as a regular part of their life and work. Most have been involved in episodic occasions of evaluation in the church, though such occasions have sometimes arisen out of political motives aimed at removing them rather than benefitting their ministerial practices. Thus, they have seldom had any kind of regular feedback on their work, nor have they been given much opportunity to reflect on their practices of ministry with congregational members or denominational officials. Evaluation, when it comes, therefore, often arrives as something ominous—a political thing—rather than something constructive as in "speaking the truth in love" (Eph. 4:15). Beth alone among the eight has developed a pattern of annual review led by an outside denominational official in an evaluation process that focuses on the mutual ministries of priest and people.

Third, a pressing concern is how theological faculties can hold on to the best of their traditional strengths while yet recognizing the need to attend to questions of professional growth and formation of their students. Faculty have in the past tended to see practical matters as an afterthought, a kind of application issue that bright students can handle once they are in ministry. Such perceptions are increasingly being set aside for a more engaged relationship between theological teaching, learning, and the practice of ministry. My experience is that most theological faculty, regardless of their discipline, are interested in and committed to their vocation as teachers. They have the church and its ministries in mind as they teach, and they are concerned about how their students will be prepared for pastoral leadership. The challenge is how to take these intentions and find collaborative ways for the faculty as a whole to deal with them. What many faculties have found is that the first step in engaging this issue is to look at the relationships between academic disciplines and the practice of ministry and move beyond the assumed theory–application mode to a more accurate understanding of how clergy actually function in ministry.

In this regard, a question that theological faculties regularly discuss is how to help students think theologically, that is, whether

students are able to reflect on and act within situations in the practice of ministry out of a theological and biblical framework, rather
than turning to a grab bag of technical fixes that have little to do
with the gospel.

The eight men and women we have followed have expressed ways
of thinking about and acting out of a biblical–theological angle of
vision. However, they do not think like academics; they think like
pastors because their context is congregational life and not the acad-
emy. While their thinking is shaped by what they know from formal
study and personal reflection, it is most of all thinking that is formed
and reformulated in the actual practices of ministry. It is not systematic, and it is seldom elegant in its expression or design, though it is
sometimes. Such thinking aims at faithfulness. It is more a matter
of "reflecting-in-practice" than it is an issue of applying a set core
of knowledge to a pastoral situation. In fact, the situation itself requires its own interpretation apart from what is projected on it from
previous experience. In effect, a dialogue is established in which the
pastor is required to respond to the immediate situation not only
out of what has been learned before but out of what is now being
revealed in the current moment, and that makes everything new.[8]

The ability to do this kind of theological thinking while engaged
in pastoral ministry comes from many sources, especially the minister's own calling and formation in faith, but the faculty's role in
encouraging students in classrooms and ministry settings to develop
such habits of mind and heart is crucial in sustaining those habits
through a lifetime. This work is significant and too often under-
appreciated. Some of the eight felt that the seminary did not provide enough of this kind of learning, and they are probably right, but
what I have heard in their stories indicates that what they did learn
made it possible for them to take these first learnings and transpose
them within the actuality of their experience and understanding in
the practice of ministry.

Fourth, these stories make clear that congregations are key to the
calling and formation of pastoral leaders. The formation in faith and
practice provided in the life of local congregations is a crucial setting
in which youth and adults as well first feel some sense of calling.
The fundamental Christian education they experience in worship,
mission, and the activities of congregational life is something that

continues to inform their understanding of ministry and something they can call on in later years. Nascent ministers are nurtured in congregations. Here, then, we are met once again with the importance of reconnecting theological schools and congregations in partnerships that shape the education of youth and adults in churches and inform the objectives of theological teaching for the church's ministries in seminaries. All of the eight, although some later than others, were formed in the Christian life by congregations before coming to seminary. They were often given leadership roles and opportunities to explore the nature of ministry. Most importantly, in this context, they were touched by others who saw in them the stirrings of a call to ordained ministry.

Fifth, in *Young Man Luther*, Erik Erikson made the observation that for certain types of religious leaders, who, from an early age, have become responsible for other people and for tasks usually reserved for persons far older than themselves, the issue of integrity arrives prematurely.[9] In Erikson's developmental scheme, integrity is the final season of life when we try to come to some acceptance of the person we have been and the things we have done. It is a time for caring for others and taking care of last things that may have been postponed from earlier years. For many religious leaders, though, this season comes at a youthful age when, by circumstance and sometimes by choice, they are pulled into ways of being more appropriate for men and women far older than themselves. As Ruth says, "I learned to be responsible a little too soon and also learned back then to not take too much time for myself. That shapes me even today in my life and ministry."

Here Ruth expresses what is true for other clergy as well—focusing so much on doing the work of ministry that they cease to take care of themselves. Recent studies point to the reality that a number of clergy are overweight, illness prone, and tending toward depression.[10] Many seldom if ever take vacations, much less reserve time for themselves and their families during the week. When confronted with the needs and demands of congregational life, they too easily sacrifice what is important personally for them.

Congregations think little about these matters, and though seminaries often try to assist students in anticipating what clerical life will be like, the pace of seminary life itself tends to contradict these admonitions for managing time and caring for one's self and family. The fact is that clergy have few advocates who can help them represent their interests. Garrison Keillor on the *Prairie Home Companion* once dealt directly with this in a story about a Minnesota pastor and his wife who are all set to go to a conference in Florida for both study and recreation. It is their first such trip in many years. During the course of a committee meeting at the church, however, it becomes clear that one way of handling a budget shortfall is for the minister to give up the trip. There's not much debate and no explicit decision by the committee, but the minister knows acutely which way the wind is blowing and volunteers to give up the trip.

Part of the difficulty clergy face in such situations, besides their own personal issues, is the ambiguity about ministry as a profession. Clergy are certainly included within professional ranks, but they hardly have the same kind of benefits and authority as lawyers or physicians. Their authority is based on the office of pastor, but much of this authority is essentially informal, not formal. Gone are the days when clergy made independent decisions out of the authority of their office. Other professionals are compensated in ways commensurate with the importance of their work for their clients and the rest of society, but this is not so with clergy. In fact, there is often a begrudging attitude within congregations that the minister is paid at all. Sometimes there is a low level resentment that the pastors might claim anything for themselves. This often places ministers in a beholding relationship with church members upon which depends their livelihood and sometimes even their own sense of personal worth.

Denominations can help alleviate this situation by striving harder to deal with clergy compensation and educating congregations on the most fruitful and appropriate relationship with their pastors. To an extent clergy add to the confusion around these questions by not being able to recognize that their vocation is to equip the ministries of the church and not to be the vicarious minister for everyone else. Standards of compensation can be developed in recognition of the activities of ordained ministry—such as teaching, leading worship, and institutional leadership—but it is impossible to develop such standards if the minister is essentially being defined as the resident saint of God. For all of this to occur, clergy have to gain a better understanding of both the theological and practical aspects of their work.

These kinds of issues are difficult to handle in theological education, partly because students themselves often have little interest in addressing such questions, which they assume they already know enough about. Moreover, many theological schools are reticent to touch upon questions that they consider nontheological and which complicate ecclesiologies that do not include the all too human face of the church as the body of Christ. But we do students a disservice when we do not prepare them for issues that will affect much of their life and ministry.

Sixth, the spaces that we inhabit are not neutral. Sometimes we are aware of how the habitats in which we live affect us, but most of the time we are not conscious of what we so take for granted that we no longer perceive it. Schools, and churches for that matter, seem to run to the extremes of acute awareness of space or dismissal of its importance. The architect Christopher Alexander has pointed out, "The specific patterns out of which a building or a town is made may be alive or dead. To the extent they are alive, they let our inner forces loose, and set us free; but when they are dead they keep us locked in inner conflict."[11]

Alexander's use of the word "pattern" to describe the nature of spaces assumes that space is essentially defined by what happens there. Designs arise out of the purposes they serve, and they are modified and transformed by changing purposes and new usages. This is why old buildings and towns that are collections of various styles built up over time and for diverse usages often create a more hospitable and lively space than newer buildings without such history.

Don Shriver was conscious of the symbolic nature of space, and, in the midst of the seminary's renovation of the chapel, requested that a door be created in the wall that separated the chapel and the school refectory. For generations the community had left worship and walked down one flight of stairs and up another in order to enter the dining room. Union's President felt that this was an architectural anomaly for a theological school where worship and common life should be closely related. So the wall was broken through and a doorway created, becoming both a practical and a symbolic passageway.

Walking through the rooms and hallways of Union seminary constitutes a journey through significant eras in the history of theology
and the church. Images of Paul Tillich, Reinhold Niebuhr, and many
other theological teachers may come to mind, reminding us of their
significance as influential intellectual and political figures. Within
this space, for example, Dietrich Bonhoeffer, while at the seminary
in 1939 to teach a class in the summer term, made the momentous
decision to return to Germany and take an even more active part in
the resistance to the Nazis, eventually leading to his arrest, impris-
onment, and execution.

I once asked an older member of the maintenance staff, someone who had collected years of institutional memories, to show me
around Union's buildings. Along one of the ground floor corridors,
we came upon the faculty robing room, a space that no longer exists. The room's walls were lined with tall oak lockers. Imprinted in
gold on the doors of those lockers were names that evoked literally
what was often referred to as a "golden age of theological professors."
The most recent name, however, was that of Samuel Terrien, the Old
Testament scholar who had joined the faculty in the 1950s. When I
asked my guide why the names had never been updated, he answered
simply, "We can't afford the gold paint anymore."

This room expressed for me some of the institutional issues that
Union faced in the 1970s. The Union faculty were the inheritors of a
remarkable theological tradition, yet for some the school seemed no
longer a place where such distinction was recognized and rewarded.
Moreover, I sensed an underlying sadness, or at least regret, among
a few faculty who wanted to engage current issues but who also felt
the pull of the past that had formed them and which they had assumed would be their future as well. They felt that part of what they
had hoped for had been put on hold and that, perhaps, the kind of
recognition they had expected when named to this historic faculty
had been taken away.

Other faculty, however, were more concerned with creating
a different kind of future, one that was less constrained by established traditions and more open to new priorities and theological
tasks. They felt that Union should be involved in ethical issues not
just intellectually but existentially as well. The seminary needed to

confront issues of racism, feminism, and sexual orientation within its own life and not as issues to be studied and written about as if they were far removed.

Thus, the eight students entered not just a set of buildings but a culture made up of past events and current experiences—subtexts and undercurrents permeating the environment of the school.

Seventh, it is obvious that the narrative mode is a powerful means of expressing who we are and what is important to us. Stories allow us to craft the elements of our life in a narrative thread that takes us to places and realizations we cannot manage in more prosaic forms. Stories have a way of unfolding in unpredictable ways that do not avoid the contradictions we so often try to hide or defer; in fact, a story told one day may change direction on another. The stories we tell about ourselves and others may be inventions, but the stuff out of which they are told is the real stuff.

Telling a story with others is a means of mutual learning, as long as judgment is withheld and we become companions on the road the story itself is traveling. Within the dynamics of institutional life, finding a way to listen to the stories of students, faculty, and staff tells us much about its actual reality. No survey, questionnaire, or planning process will reveal as much about an organization as the narratives that inhabit the nooks and crannies of the institution itself.

The Lexington Seminar: Theological Teaching for the Church's Ministries, which involved forty-four faculties from 1998 to 2008, encouraged seminaries to engage in this very sort of constructive storytelling. Among other activities, participating seminaries invited faculty to tell the stories of their vocation, what it was that evoked within them a sense that they wanted to be theological teachers and how their academic disciplines related to and were informed by the practice of ministry. The schools often used retreat settings for this work and frequently shared their efforts by publishing the faculty stories in booklets to be circulated with the rest of the seminary community. One school decided that it did not know how students experienced their first year of theological study because, frankly, nobody had ever asked them. In light of this, the faculty appointed several of its members to lead a listening project throughout the entire first year of an entering class. Regular, structured times were scheduled when students could relate their experiences and their perspectives on their entry into theological education. On the basis of this kind of listening, the faculty had a better understanding of how the curriculum actually functioned and some idea of the various things that were actually important to students within the life of the school.[12]

Eighth, since ministers are often put on a pedestal of moral and emotional strength, either by others or themselves, it is often difficult for them to seek the help they need. This does not seem to be an issue for the eight women and men we have followed, but it is for others in ministry. Such reticence in seeking help is sometimes a matter of limited finances to pay for therapy or analysis. At other times it arises from the fear that someone will find out that they are seeking help and will judge them negatively. For a few, the insulation they have built around emotional difficulties has become so thick and confining they cannot hear the sounds of their own pain.

In some settings, clergy are free to deal with these issues without fear of reprisal from church members or denominational officials. But this is not true in many congregations or denominations where, if it is known that a minister is seeing a therapist, then that is viewed as a mark against them, a sign of weakness or emotional instability that raises questions about their ability to lead a congregation. Our society, unfortunately, seems to be offering fewer rather than more places where concerns about professional and personal life can be shared with the assurance that they will be held in confidence. In a *Facebook* culture everything seems to be fair game.

With few props and even fewer tangible rewards, the eight have held on to their calling. And, in the end, what is most important about the eight is their faithfulness. They have been able to bring together what has called them to life and ministry and expressed this in their work. All of this urges a new realism in characterizing and encouraging the ordained ministry of the church. We too often focus on a few clergy who are privileged to serve congregations that have a relative abundance of fiscal and material resources. The actual life of most clergy is very different from their more affluent colleagues who do not confront daily the hard grind of leading a congregation struggling with its own survival. Seldom are the ministries of such churches lauded; instead, they are more often criticized as being neither large nor successful. The fact is that our usual notions of what constitutes success in ministry seldom correspond with biblical measurements of faithfulness. Most of the eight men and women we have followed have served churches that express, perhaps, a more typical portrayal of congregational life than what we usually see.

Stirring the Muddy Water

Throughout their similar yet diverging journeys, the ministers in this study have sought a clear understanding of themselves, their calling, and their life in ministry, but they have not easily found such clarity. Perhaps that is not so great a loss as one might think. As another student—who died far too young—once said to me by way of summarizing his experience, "It's amazing, the means by which this seminary as a whole with all its talented individuals . . . moved into my psyche and consciousness and, not disrupted, but stirred the muddy water a bit and allowed things to settle."[13]

Something in the nature of stirred water provided insights for this student that a more pristine view might not have. Many times during the following years I thought about his words. Then one day I happened across another voice, that of Carl Jung, and his words seemed remarkably to echo and interpret the student's observation.

"Life itself," says Jung, "flows from springs both clear and muddy. Hence all excessive 'purity' lacks vitality. A constant striving for clarity and differentiation means a proportional loss of vital intensity, precisely because the muddy elements are excluded. Every renewal of life needs the muddy as well as the clear."[14]

For many of us, that which is muddy is often seen as an obstacle to the truth. We want to get things cleaned up as quickly as possible so that in the clear light of day we may see what is going on. However, if I have learned anything from these years of overhearing the evolving lives of these eight persons who have devoted themselves to the vital and intense vocation of pastoral ministry, it is the reminder that rational understanding is only one sort of insight and that other, perhaps richer and more subtle, truth may be found in the muddy and unsettled lives we all lead. The sediment that gets stirred up is full of nutrients necessary for life, and we deny the truth it offers at our peril.

This is an issue for all human beings, but for clergy, whose lives are often monitored by those whom someone once termed "God's assistants," the pretense of a sanitized life is a sham that prevents them from knowing the sediment of their lives and makes them even more liable to behavior that is the opposite of what is expected.

All eight of these ministers have known the muddy elements in their lives. When confronted with questions they could not solve alone, most of the eight have had the wisdom to seek help for themselves. They have worked with therapists and psychiatrists to address personal issues that seem to get in the way of the work that claimed them. More than that, they have sought out therapy or analysis for their own education and a more profound understanding of themselves as human beings. However, this search for psychological understanding, which often has spiritual significance as well, should not be seen as a detour from the passion for social justice that has been central to all of them. The eight have been very aware of the times in which they have lived and the necessity of engaging the political and social crises that have defined the larger context of their lives. In this regard, they have often quoted Frederick Buechner's familiar words about vocation as "the place where your deep gladness and the world's deep hunger meet."[15]

This place where the theological and the psychological, the social and the personal, the spiritual and the ordinary meet is often a place prepared by prayer, by the practices of awareness, silence, study, and intercession that allow the voice of the Other we call God to be heard. While the actual forms and occasions of prayer differ widely among the eight, they have all found and reclaimed ways in which to pray and meditate as a fundamental and continuing part of their life and work.

As varied as their notions and practice of prayer are, their understandings of God are just as diverse. For Ruth, God is felt in grace and mercy, the One who has given her life each new day. Chris finds God in practices of study, preaching, and teaching in which piety and intellect come together in moments when personal and public life meet the biblical story. For Sarah, God is a "dancing spirit" leading her to places she had not imagined and to gifts she had never before been able to find. For Marvin, God is a mystical presence who, nevertheless, has definite things in mind for the faithful to carry out.

For Beth, God is known in otherness—in spaces where in creating our own selves we may find a sense of this otherness and a sense of oneness with other people. Tim seems to know God most in the moments of healing and hope where he has found what could be called a second birth and an invitation to live in trust. For David, God is a divine Being who speaks clearly, directly, and authoritatively. In God, Anna has found liberation from the pain and suffering that she carried for so long, and her ministry now especially reaches out to others who share her story.

All eight are more concerned with what they will do with this varying sense of God than in nailing down exactly what they mean by God, though they share an essential faith in Christ as the one in whom they see God most of all and in whom they see the pattern of servanthood they feel called to emulate as leaders. They are less interested in abstract definitions than they are in the work they feel called to pursue. This work sometimes aggravates them, bores them, and at times threatens to overwhelm them, but these things do not have the last word in defining what the work of ministry means to them. This work that they do is, in significant moments, creative, and in this creativity they have often found the person they want to be. This continuing crafting of the self is interwoven into the fabric of all that makes them feel alive, and this sense of coming to life is what brings them close to an understanding of God.

The men and women we have followed have been willing to speak truthfully and to share their lives with us, and for this we can be grateful not only for what we have learned about them but for what they have taught us about ourselves.

Afterword

My first visit to Union Theological Seminary's James Chapel was in February of 2008. On campus for a presidential search committee interview, I was taken to a worship service that occurs daily at noon, so I could "get a feel for the place."

It felt . . . unusual. Gazing about, I saw that the gabled ceiling and stained glass windows were in stark contrast to the modern pew-chairs sitting on the hard stone floor. Swaths of richly-colored fabric hung between the pillars, but so did swags of heavy black electrical cords in what seemed a distressingly tenuous form of connectivity. That James Chapel's parts did not fit together perfectly, however, did not stop worship from happening. For here was the Union community, in all its unresolved diversity, having a seamlessly good time.

We sat together in the round as the service started with jazz piano and women dancing down the aisles, blessing us with waving hands. A student led a pastoral prayer that included a four-page list of community concerns. A faculty member preached on "listening to your call." To conclude, we sang an old-style hymn, the name of which I no longer recall—maybe it was "Draw Us in the Spirit's Tether"? After the benediction, we lingered in Quaker silence, listening to each other breathe.

We did, that is, until a loud noise outside the sanctuary sent everyone scurrying to see what had happened. A spire from James Chapel Tower had broken off in the high winds and there, in the middle of the quadrangle, laid huge pieces of shattered masonry. Mercifully, no one was underneath when it fell, or it would have been a tragedy. Even so, I could not help but wonder if this was a divine sign. Would things at Union continue to crumble and fall if I assumed leadership? In my mind, it was a portentous event.

Imagine my surprise, then, when nearly everyone quickly drifted away and went about their business as if nothing had happened. Sure, a couple of administrators scratched their heads about the cost of fixing the damage, but soon enough lunch was served, classes resumed, and students gathered as always in the Pit. So a steeple crashed? At Union, apparently, you learned to expect the unexpected.

This, I thought, was an unusual place.

It is now 2011, and I still think this. What struck me initially as odd is now reassuringly natural, because I realize I have gone through the Union educational process that Mac Warford so carefully and lovingly maps in these pages.

What I and the scores of seminarians who have lived in these rooms and halls have discovered here is that nothing lasts forever. No understanding about the past or present is unshakable (not even steeples!), and nothing about Christianity or Jesus or even the Trinity can be considered "hands off" or beyond hard questioning and scrutiny. Indeed, the only thing that we hope never changes about Union is an ever-sturdy zeal to see justice done and a willingness to discover new ways to do God's work in the world.

As it is today, so it was among the students Mac Warford describes. I found myself nodding in recognition throughout this remarkable book as Ruth, Chris, David, Tim, Sarah, Marvin, Beth, and Anna are all still students here. Meaning they each have a spiritual twin in today's classrooms, albeit twins that are likely to sport nose rings and to be fiddling constantly with their laptops and iPhones. Like the students of yore, contemporary seminarians arrive with a large sense of adventure but not much clarity about what lies ahead. They are willing, even eager, to be changed by the education—in all its dimensions—they will receive here, even if they do not yet know what that involves.

What is it about this place that facilitates such life-altering experiences to occur? Perhaps, as suggested in chapter 1, it has something to do with Union's architecture.

Just recently I learned more about the seminary's original design. The campus was created as a neo-Gothic quadrangle with a road from the outside leading into it through what is now the front entrance. There was an open-air cloister walk around the quadrangle's interior, and along these pathways were doors that connected various parts of campus to the courtyard. To move from James Chapel to the Social Hall, for instance, one would have to step outside into the center space and then go back in. To enter Burke Library next or a Hastings dormitory room, one could either cross through the garden or take the longer way along the cloisters.

There was a theological purpose to this layout, as it was then believed seminary buildings should encourage spontaneous interaction between ideas and people. At an intellectual level, this echoes the interconnected disciplines students attempt to master in their study of the Bible, theology, and oratory; it also mirrors the emotional and spiritual skills pastors need to develop. In ministry, we are called to look at the world in all its parts and to help people see that the grace of God runs though everything. If Union's stones could talk, they would tell us that God is present to us not in hermetically sealed (or hermeneutically sealed) rooms but in the messy buzz and hum of the communal life we share.

Understanding the theological intent of the original architecture has helped me understand Union better. Ministry is fundamentally built upon our being open not only to the word of God but also to the world we serve.

Although the road into our quadrangle is now enclosed, Mac Warford shows us with these stories that what remains unchanged is Union's commitment to an open, integrated, and ever-circulating model of learning.

SERENE JONES
President, Union Theological Seminary, New York

Notes

Preface: Stories of Work and Calling

1. William G. Perry, Jr., *Forms of Intellectual and Ethical Development in the College Years: A Scheme* (New York: Holt, Rinehart & Winston, 1970).

2. Roy Pascal's *Design and Truth in Autobiography* (New York: Garland Publishing Inc., 1985) has been a book I have returned to many times. For example, in discussing the nature of autobiographies on page 95, he makes the observation: "Interesting and perhaps moving as it might be to see the man behind the work, the private individual behind the public facade, this is not the primary purpose of good autobiography. What we want to see is the man within the work."

Though I came late to Elliot G. Mishler's *Storylines: Craftartists' Narratives of Identity*, I have found it very helpful in terms of his approaches to the craftartists who were part of his study. Again, as in the case of William Perry, I have not tried to replicate his research model, but it has been a point of reference as I have thought about and written this final manuscript. His discussion of "narrative praxis" has been a source for clarifying what I have found in this study of eight women and men whose work and calling is ordained ministry. See Elliot G. Mishler, *Storylines: Craftartists' Narratives of Identity* (Cambridge: Harvard University Press, 1999).

Over the years, Robert Coles' documentary research that resulted in the *Children of Crisis* series of books has been important for me. His empathetic relationships and observations of the children and adults he has interviewed have provided an image of research conducted with the highest regard for study participants. See Robert Coles' edited collection of excerpts from his five volume series: *Children of Crisis: Selections* (New York: Little Brown & Company, 2003).

While there are a number of well-known longitudinal studies (such as Michael Apted's *7-Up*, the ongoing study of several British children and how they have grown up), perhaps the most influential has been the study of a group of Harvard students, begun in 1938 and continuing for over seventy years, whose long-term researcher has been George Vaillant. See *Adaptation to Life* (Boston: Little Brown & Company, 1977) and more recently *Aging Well* (New York: Time Warner Books, 2002).

Chapter 1: Setting the Context

1. Tom Wolfe, "The Me Decade," *New York Magazine*, August 24, 1976, and Christopher Lasch, *The Culture of Narcissism: American Life in an Age of Diminishing Expectations* (New York: W. W. Norton & Company, 1979).

2. The most recent history of the seminary is Robert T. Handy's *A History of Union Theological Seminary in New York* (New York: Columbia University Press, 1987). For a personal reflection on the years we are discussing, see Donald W. Shriver, Jr., "Serving the Future by Unsettling the Present: Leadership," *On Second Thought* (New York: Seabury Books, 2010), 131–160.

3. This is now a common observation, but William McKinney, president of Pacific School of Religion and well-known sociologist of religion, is the person I first heard make the comment.

4. Thanks to Glenn T. Miller, Waldo Professor of Ecclesiastical History at Bangor Theological Seminary, for pointing out to me Union's connection to *The Poseidon Adventure,* which was first published in 1969 and issued as a paperback by MacMillan in 1970.

Chapter 2: Childhood and Formative Events

1. Saint Augustine, *Confessions,* Translated with an Introduction and Notes by Henry Chadwick (Oxford: Oxford University Press, 1991), 179–201.

2. Ibid. 186.

Chapter 3: Beginning Theological Education

1. During the recession of 1975, the government of New York City went bankrupt. When President Gerald Ford refused to support a financial bailout for the city, the *New York Daily News* featured the famous headline, "Ford to City: Drop Dead."

Chapter 4: The Middle Years of Theological Study

1. William Sloane Coffin was senior minister at Riverside Church and a well known civil rights and peace activist. He was the long-time chaplain at Yale University before becoming pastor at Riverside. His uncle, Henry Sloane Coffin, was Union's president in the pivotal era of 1926 to 1945.

2. Eugen Rosenstock-Huessy was a remarkable figure. A refugee from Hitler's Germany, he taught at Dartmouth for many years. Though never well known, he has been a persisting and important influence in theological writing, referred to, unfortunately most often in footnotes. I knew of him when I served as a pastor in Vermont. A friend of mine, Yorke Peeler, was his minister at the church in Norwich, and through Yorke I became acquainted with Rosenstock-Huessy's life and work. His book *The Christian Future: Or the Modern Mind Outrun* (New York: Harper, 1946) is still a relevant and significant commentary on our times.

Chapter 6: Years in Ministry

1. Robert K. Greenleaf, *Servant Leadership: A Journey into the Nature of Legitimate Power and Greatness* (New York: Paulist Press, 1977).

2. Eugene H. Peterson, *Under the Unpredictable Plant: An Exploration in Vocational Holiness* (Grand Rapids: William B. Eerdmans, 1992), 97–99.

Chapter 7: Looking Back and Going Forward

1. Karl Rahner, S.J., "The Man with the Pierced Heart," *Servants of the Lord*, trans. Richard Strachan (New York: Herder and Herder, 1968), 107–119.

2. Henry J. M. Nouwen, *The Wounded Healer* (New York: Doubleday, 1972).

Chapter 8: Summing Up

1. Czeslaw Milosz, *To Begin Where I Am* (New York: Farrar, Strauss & Giroux, 2001), 383.

2. Kay Ryan, quoted in Louisa Thomas, "The Reluctant Poet Laureate," *Newsweek* (July 13, 2009), 63.

3. See Susie C. Stanley's extensive bibliography on women in ministry, which was funded by Lilly Endowment Inc. and developed for the "Women in Ministry Initiative" at Messiah College (2005). Susie C. Stanley, "Women in Ministry," http://www.messiah.edu/christian_vocation/women_in_ministry/ (September 9, 2010).

4. Pierre Bourdieu and Jean-Claude Passeron, *Reproduction in Education, Society and Culture*, trans. Richard Nice (London: Sage, 1990).

5. The work of Henry Giroux, in particular, has dealt with this dynamic of resistance. His work builds on Paulo Freire's critical pedagogy. See Henry A. Giroux, *Theory and Resistance in Education: Towards a Pedagogy for the Opposition*, foreword by Paulo Freire, preface by Stanley Aronowitz (Westport, CT: Bergin & Garvey, 2001).

6. See Robert McAfee Brown's and Sydney Brown's interpretation of these years in Robert McAfee Brown, *Reflections over the Long Haul: A Memoir* (Louisville: Westminster John Knox Press, 2005), 183–195.

7. James Hillman, "The Feeling Function," in Maria Louisa von Franz and James Hillman, *Lectures on Jung's Typology* (Zurich: Spring Publications, 1971), 130.

8. Donald A. Schon's work is fundamental to the way I think about the practice of ministry and it has stood the test of time since his theories were first published in *The Reflective Practitioner: How Professionals Think in America* (New York: Harper Basic Books, 1983). Schon's perspective is helpful in understanding how inadequate the assumed theory-application model of professional practice is for interpreting how clergy actually think about and practice ministry. His use of the language of "reflection-in-practice" (59–69) and his description of how a situation "talks back" to the practitioner (135) are especially important. It is not a matter of finding the correct theory to apply to a problem because the situation itself demands a redefinition of what constitutes the problem itself. This involves rethinking and reframing what actually is going on and what is needed to respond creatively. This action–reflection is dialectical and dialogical, requiring practitioners to draw upon what they know as well as what they discover through reflecting within action.

9. Erik Erikson, *Young Man Luther* (New York: W.W. Norton, 1958), 261. Erikson writes, "The integrity crisis, last in the lives of ordinary men, is a lifelong and chronic crisis in a *homo religiosus*. He is always older, or in early years suddenly becomes older, than his playmates or even his parents and teachers, and focuses in a precocious way on what it takes others a lifetime to gain a mere inkling of: the questions of how to escape corruption in living and how in death to give meaning to life." Erikson goes on to point out that such persons will probably have to deal with the other parts of emotional growth that were, perhaps, delayed by this early precocity. What might at first, earlier in life, have looked like a "shortcut," is not in the long run. Ibid.

10. Paul Vitello, "Taking a Break from the Lord's Work," *New York Times*, August 1, 2010.

11. Christopher Alexander, *The Timeless Way of Building* (New York: Oxford University Press, 1979), 101.

12. See the website of The Lexington Seminar, www.lexingtonseminar. org, for the projects and final reports of the participating theological seminaries and university divinity schools. This initiative in theological educa-

tion was supported by Lilly Endowment Inc., and sponsored by Lexington Theological Seminary. As director, I served with continuing consultants Victor Klimoski, Garth Rosell, Gretchen Ziegenhals, Diamond Cephus, and Mary Ann Winkelmes.

13. Malcolm L. Warford and Virginia Brereton, "Stirring Muddy Water," unpublished report by the Office of Educational Research, Union Theological Seminary, 1981.

14. C. G. Jung, *Psychological Types*, vol. 6, *The Collected Works of Carl Jung*, trans. R. F. C. Hull based on a translation by H. G. Baynes, Bollingen Series XX, ed. Herbert Read et al. (Princeton: Princeton University Press, 1971) 244–245; quoted in Francoise O'Kane, *Sacred Chaos: Reflections on God's Shadow and the Dark Self* (Toronto: Inner City Books, 1994), 132.

15. Frederick Buechner, *Wishful Thinking: A Seeker's ABC* (San Francisco: Harper San Francisco, 1993), 119. Frederick Buechner graduated from Union in 1958.